EVERYDAY COOKING
WITH
GOOD HOUSEKEEPING

D0586589

EVERYDAY COOKING WITH

GOOD HOUSEKEEPING

Contents

Introduction 7

Basic recipes and techniques

Information

This edition first published exclusively
for Marks and Spencer p.l.c. in 1982 by
Octopus Books Limited
59 Grosvenor Street, London W1

© 1973 National Magazine Company Limited

ISBN 0 86273 056 2

Printed in Hong Kong

This edition is an extract from
Good Housekeeping Cooking for Today
which was published previously by
Octopus Books Limited in 1973
as a hardback edition

Introduction

Cooking should be a pleasure rather than a chore and Everyday Cooking sets out to help you enjoy catering for the family or midweek guests.

All the essential cookery methods are given as well as a comprehensive collection of recipes from soups to desserts, sauces to cakes. There are also illustrated step-by-step recipes for 13 classic dishes.

In 'Information', a selection of helpful advice is given on basic equipment, herbs and spices, freezing and storing food and what to do when things go wrong. There is also an extensive glossary of cooking terms, and the blank 'Notes' pages are useful for recording your own recipes and ideas.

Good Housekeeping Institute Principal
Margaret Coombes

Left: Vacherin (page 115)

Previous pages: Lobster thermidor (page 95)

SOUPS

Soups may be thin and clear, thick and creamy, hot, cold, or so full of meat and vegetables that they make a nourishing meal in themselves. Whatever kind of soup you are planning to make, the basis will always be a tasty stock. Nowadays there are many ready-made stock preparations available, the most popular being bouillon cubes, which make an acceptable stock and save an enormous amount of time and trouble. Beware of the strength of the seasoning if using a bouillon cube and don't add more until you have tasted the finished soup; remember, too, that cubes do not give 'body' to a soup in the same way as bone stock. There is nothing to beat a rich home-made stock – a pressure cooker cuts time and if you own a freezer it is easy to keep stock by freezing it in pint or ½-pint quantities.

White stock – which can be made from veal or mutton bones, or poultry carcasses – is used for the pale, delicately flavoured soups. It can also be used for one of the darker soups with the addition of a few drops of gravy browning. However, a brown stock – made from bones and beef first browned in the oven – is really more satisfactory for a dark soup. It is essential for consommé to use a really tasty brown stock. Turn to the end of the section for stocks.

This is a French classic and can almost make a meal in itself

Use up your surplus garden lettuce in this tasty soup

SOUPE A LA PAYSANNE
serves 6

2 oz. carrots
1 oz. turnip
1 oz. celery
2 oz. leeks
1 oz. butter
salt and pepper
2 pints (5 cups) brown stock
bouquet garni, consisting of:
    2–3 parsley stalks, bay leaf,
    sprig of thyme
croûtons

Cut the carrot and turnip into rough squares; thinly slice the celery and leeks. Bring a pan of water to the boil, add the vegetables and blanch for 3 minutes. Refresh under cold running water. Drain. Melt butter in a pan, add the vegetables and cook without colouring until tender.

Pour the stock over them, bring to the boil, skim and add the bouquet garni. Cover and simmer for 20–30 minutes. Remove bouquet garni and skim well, using absorbent kitchen paper to remove any remaining fat. Adjust the seasoning if necessary. Pour into a pre-heated bowl and serve the croûtons separately.

SUSAN'S GERMAN SOUP
serves 4; this soup is a meal in itself

2 pints (5 cups) household
    stock
½ lb. potatoes, peeled
2 leeks, cleaned and sliced
½ lb. turnips, peeled and cubed
¼ lb. carrots, peeled and sliced
1 red or green pepper, sliced
2 sticks of celery, sliced
½ lb. piece streaky bacon,
    rinded
½ lb. Mettwurst

Place the stock in a large pan with the potatoes cut in small pieces. Simmer until the potatoes are tender. Sieve potatoes and stock together or purée in a blender and return to the pan. Add leeks, turnips, carrots, pepper, celery and bacon and simmer gently, covered, for 1½–1¾ hours.

Meanwhile remove the skin from the Mettwurst and cut into oblique slices. Add to the soup and simmer for a further 15 minutes. Adjust seasoning if necessary and cut the bacon into bite-size pieces before serving.

FRENCH ONION SOUP
serves 4

2 oz. butter
sugar
1 lb. onions, skinned and
    sliced
1½ pints (3¾ cups) brown stock
salt and pepper
2–3 oz. (½–¾ cup) Gruyère or
    Emmenthal cheese, grated
4 thin slices French bread,
    toasted
white wine (optional)

Melt the butter, add a few grains of sugar and fry the onions slowly until well browned and soft. Stir in the stock, bring to the boil and simmer, with the lid on, for 30 minutes. Season to taste.
Pour into flameproof soup bowls. Sprinkle the grated cheese on the slices of French bread and float one on each bowl of soup. Place the bowls under a hot grill or in the oven at 450°F. (mark 8) until the cheese melts and bubbles, then serve immediately, with more grated cheese if required. A dash of dry white wine may be added to the soup just before turning into the bowls, if wished.

MINESTRONE
serves 4–6

½ a leek, cleaned and
    shredded
1 onion, skinned and finely
    chopped
1 clove of garlic, skinned and
    crushed
1 oz. butter
2 pints (5 cups) white stock,
    preferably home-made
1 carrot, peeled and cut into
    thin strips
1 turnip, peeled and cut into
    thin strips
1 stick celery, scrubbed and
    thinly sliced
1 oz. macaroni
¼ cabbage, washed and finely
    shredded
3 runner beans, thinly sliced
1 oz. peas, shelled
1 level tsp. tomato paste or 4
    tomatoes, skinned and
    diced
1–2 rashers of bacon,
    chopped and fried
salt and pepper
Parmesan cheese, grated

Lightly sauté the leek, onion and garlic in the melted butter for 5–10 minutes, until soft but not coloured. Add the stock, bring to the boil, add the carrot, turnip, celery and macaroni and simmer for 20–30 minutes. Add the cabbage, beans and peas and simmer for a further 20 minutes. Stir in the tomato paste or tomatoes, bacon and seasoning to taste. Serve the Parmesan cheese in a separate dish.

MAMA'S LEEK SOUP
serves 3–4

½ lb. leeks
2 oz. butter or margarine
½-pint (1-oz.) pkt. white sauce
    mix
1 pint (2½ cups) milk
1 oz. (¼ cup) Cheddar cheese,
    grated
salt and pepper
croûtons

Thinly slice the leeks, wash thoroughly and drain well. Melt the butter, add the leeks, cover and cook gently for about 10 minutes, until tender. Off the heat, shower in the contents of the sauce mix packet and gradually add the milk, stirring briskly. Bring to the boil, stirring, and cook for about 3 minutes. Purée in a blender or work through a wire sieve. Add the cheese, reheat and adjust seasoning – add a little more milk if necessary. Serve with toast croûtons.

BROAD BEAN SOUP

serves 3–4

4 oz. (1 cup) chopped onion
1 clove of garlic, skinned and
    crushed
2 oz. butter
1 oz. (¼ cup) flour
1 pint (2½ cups) chicken or
    ham stock
½ lb. shelled broad beans,
    fresh or frozen
1 level tsp. dried thyme
lemon juice
salt and pepper
flaked almonds (optional) for
    garnish

Fry the onion and garlic in the butter until soft but not coloured. Stir in the flour, cook for 2 minutes and then add the stock. Bring to the boil and add the broad beans and thyme; simmer, covered, until the beans are tender. Blend or sieve the contents of the pan, adding more stock if necessary to give a thin creamy consistency.

Adjust the seasoning with lemon juice, salt and pepper. If wished, sauté a few flaked almonds in butter and add to the soup just before reheating.

LETTUCE AND ONION SOUP

serves 6

2 oz. butter
1 large onion, skinned and
    finely chopped
1 large lettuce, washed and
    finely shredded
2 pints (5 cups) chicken stock
salt and pepper
2¾ fl.oz. (⅓ cup) double cream

Heat the butter in a saucepan, add the onion and fry gently until soft, being careful not to allow it to colour. Add the lettuce and cook in the butter for a few minutes, then add the stock and seasoning. Bring to the boil, cover and simmer for 5–7 minutes. Place half the mixture in a blender and purée. Turn into a bowl and repeat with the remaining mixture.

Return to the saucepan. Bring to the boil, remove from the heat and gradually add the cream, stirring all the time. Serve with cheese straws.

VEGETABLE SOUP

serves 6

1 lb. vegetables
2 oz. butter
½ pint (1¼ cups) white stock
salt and pepper
1 oz. (¼ cup) flour
1 pint (2½ cups) milk

An oxtail makes a rich, meaty soup for a cold day

Consommé princesse, the clearest of soups garnished with asparagus

Wash, trim and roughly slice vegetables (e.g. carrots, leeks). Melt 1 oz. butter in a pan, add vegetables and fry gently for 5 minutes without browning. Add stock and simmer, covered, for 10–15 minutes, until tender. Season to taste. Make a white sauce with 1 oz. butter, the flour and milk. Blend vegetables, stock and sauce in a blender on low speed for a few seconds, then on high until smooth and creamy. Check seasoning, return to the pan and reheat without boiling.

CREAM OF CELERY SOUP

serves 4

1 oz. butter
1 head of celery, scrubbed
    and chopped
1 oz. (¼ cup) flour
1 pint (2½ cups) chicken stock
1 blade of mace
1 tsp. lemon juice
salt and freshly ground
    pepper
2 oz. carrots, peeled and
    finely diced
½ pint (1¼ cups) milk

Melt the butter, add the celery and fry gently for 5 minutes. Stir in the flour, cook for a few minutes, then gradually add the stock, stirring.

Add the mace and lemon juice, season with salt and pepper; bring to the boil, cover and simmer for 20 minutes. Discard the mace. Purée the soup in a blender or work through a sieve, return it to the pan, add the diced carrot and simmer until the garnish is tender –about 15 minutes. Remove from the heat, add the milk and adjust the seasoning if necessary.

POTATO AND ONION SOUP

serves 4

2 oz. butter
½ lb. onions, skinned and
    thinly sliced
1 lb. potatoes, peeled and
    diced
1 pint (2½ cups) chicken stock
½ pint (1¼ cups) milk
salt and pepper
½ lb. tomatoes, skinned and
    seeded
1 oz. cheese, grated
1 tbsp. chopped parsley

Melt the butter and fry the onions for 10 minutes. Add the potatoes, cover and continue to cook over a low heat for a further 10 minutes. Add the stock and cook until the potatoes are soft and mushy. Add the milk and sieve or purée in a

blender. Adjust the seasoning. Slice the tomato flesh in strips and add to the soup, together with the cheese and parsley. Reheat before serving.

OXTAIL SOUP

serves 6–8

1 oxtail, jointed
1 oz. butter or margarine
2 onions, skinned and
    chopped
1 carrot, peeled and sliced
2 sticks of celery, scrubbed
    and sliced
3–4 pints (7½–10 cups) brown
    stock
1 oz. lean ham or bacon,
    chopped
bouquet garni
salt and pepper
3 level tbsps. flour
a little port wine (optional)
squeeze of lemon juice

Wash and dry the oxtail and trim off any excess fat. Fry the pieces of oxtail in the butter with the vegetables for 5 minutes, until evenly browned. Just cover with the stock and bring to the boil. Add the chopped ham or bacon, bouquet garni and seasoning, cover the saucepan and simmer for 3–4 hours, until the tail meat is tender. As oxtail is very fatty, it is necessary to skim the soup occasionally with a metal spoon.

Strain the soup, remove the meat from the bones and cut it up neatly. Return the meat and strained liquor to the pan and reheat. Blend the flour and a little water (or port wine, if used) to a smooth cream. Stir in a little of the hot liquid and return the mixture to the pan. Bring to the boil, stirring until it thickens, and cook for about 5 minutes. Add a squeeze of lemon juice and seasoning to taste before serving.

CONSOMME PRINCESSE

serves 4

2 pints (5 cups) home-made
    brown stock (bouillon
    cubes will not do for this
    soup)
¼ lb. lean beef
¼ pint (⅝ cup) cold water
1 carrot, peeled and
    quartered
1 small onion, skinned and
    quartered
bouquet garni
1 egg white
small tin of asparagus tips
salt
2 tsps. sherry (optional)

Remove any fat from the stock.

Gazpacho, modern-style

Shred the meat finely and soak it in the water for 15 minutes. Put the meat and water, vegetables, stock and bouquet garni into a deep saucepan; lastly add the egg white. Heat gently and whisk continuously until a thick froth starts to form. Stop whisking and bring to the boil. Reduce the heat immediately and simmer *gently* for 2 hours. (If the liquid boils too rapidly, the froth will break and cloud the consommé.)

Scald a clean cloth or jelly bag, wring it out, tie it to the four legs of an upturned stool and place a bowl underneath. Pour the soup through, keeping the froth back at first with a spoon, then let it slide out onto the cloth. Again pour the soup through the cloth and through the filter of egg white. The consommé should now be clear and sparkling. Meanwhile heat the asparagus tips according to directions. Drain, rinse well. Reheat the consommé, adding salt if liked and a little sherry. Add the hot asparagus tips and serve.

SHRIMP CHOWDER
serves 4

- 1 large onion, skinned and sliced
- ½ oz. butter
- ¼ pint (⅝ cup) boiling water
- 3 medium potatoes, peeled and diced
- 1 pint shrimps, shelled
- 1 pint (2½ cups) milk
- 1–2 oz. (¼–½ cup) cheese, grated
- chopped parsley to garnish

Lightly fry the onion in the butter for about 5 minutes, until soft but not coloured. Add the boiling water, potatoes and seasoning. Cover and simmer gently for 15–20 minutes, or until the potatoes are just cooked. Add the shrimps and the milk and reheat. Stir in the grated cheese and parsley and serve with crusty bread or toast.

GAZPACHO, MODERN-STYLE
serves 4

- 1 lb. ripe, juicy tomatoes, skinned and sliced
- 1 small onion, skinned and finely chopped
- 1 small green pepper (capsicum), seeded and chopped
- 1 clove of garlic, skinned and crushed
- 1 tbsp. wine vinegar
- 1 tbsp. olive oil
- 1–2 tbsps. lemon juice
- salt and pepper
- small can tomato juice, optional
- ¼ cucumber, peeled and diced
- 1 thick slice of toast, diced

Purée the tomatoes, onion, green pepper, garlic, vinegar and olive oil in a blender. Turn into a basin, add the lemon juice and season to taste and chill thoroughly in a refrigerator. If necessary, dilute with canned tomato juice before serving. Serve sprinkled with the diced cucumber and toast.

STOCKS

BROWN STOCK
makes 2½ pints (6¼ cups)

- 1 lb. marrow bone
- 2 lb. shin of beef
- 3 pints (7½ cups) water
- 2 sprigs parsley
- a pinch of thyme
- a pinch of marjoram
- a small bay leaf, crumbled
- 1 carrot, peeled and sliced
- 1 medium onion, skinned and coarsely chopped
- 1 stick celery, scrubbed and sliced
- 5 peppercorns
- ½ level tbsp. salt

Chop the marrow bone and cut the beef into pieces. Put into a large (approx. 7-pint) saucepan with the rest of the ingredients. Bring to the boil and skim. Simmer for 4–5 hours with the lid on the pan. Strain, cool and leave overnight in the refrigerator to jelly. Skim off any fat from the cold stock. Keep in a cool place for not longer than 2–3 days, boiling up each day.

WHITE STOCK
makes 3½ pints

- 2½ lb. knuckle of veal or meaty veal bones
- 1 glass white wine
- a little lemon juice
- 5 pints (12½ cups) cold water
- 4 oz. sliced onion
- 4 oz. sliced carrot
- bouquet garni
- 1 level tsp. salt
- 4 peppercorns

Wipe the knuckle with a damp cloth and put into a large (approx. 8-pint) saucepan. Cover with cold water and bring to the boil, removing any scum. Drain and rinse. Return to the pan, pour the wine over and allow to reduce to about 2 tablespoons. Add the lemon juice and 5 pints water and bring to the boil. Skim.

Add the vegetables and bouquet garni, salt and peppercorns. Reboil, partially cover with the lid and simmer for 4 hours. Strain, cool and leave overnight in the refrigerator. Remove the fat from the cold stock before using. Store as for brown stock.

HOUSEHOLD STOCK
makes 4 pints

- 2 lb. selection of roast meat bones, chicken or turkey carcass, giblets, bacon rinds etc.
- 1 lb. sliced vegetables, including onion, carrot, leek, celery, mushrooms, celeriac
- 1½ oz. fat
- bouquet garni
- salt
- peppercorns
- water

Chop the bones and carcass. Put in the oven and brown lightly to add flavour. Sauté the prepared vegetables in fat in a large (approx. 10-pint) pan for 10 minutes, add the bones and remaining ingredients and just cover with water. Bring to the boil and skim.

Cover and simmer for 3–4 hours. Strain, cool and treat as for brown or white stock.

Shrimp chowder – a party soup

Minestrone, an Italian soup

PATES & TERRINES

A pâté is essentially a blend of different meats—principally liver and pork—which has been minced finely, well seasoned and cooked slowly. Because of the high proportion of liver used they tend to be very rich and only small portions should be allowed per person—particularly as pâté is generally served as an appetizer accompanied by toast.

The most famous (and the most expensive) of these mixtures is, of course, pâté de foie gras, made from the livers of specially fattened geese, but you can follow our recipes and make your own pâté maison quite simply and inexpensively. Apart from the delicate fish ones, most pâtés will keep quite happily for a week in the refrigerator—in fact, this can even improve the flavour.

Anything that can be prepared and cooked ahead of time is a boon for a busy hostess, so this makes pâté an ideal choice for a formal dinner party.

Terrines are generally more robust than pâtés and of a coarser texture. They are not really suitable—except in minute quantities—as appetisers, because of their richness. However, terrines make a wonderful main course for a lunch or supper, served accompanied by salad. They are also particularly suitable to serve at an informal party when you have been out of doors for most of the day. Serve hot soup first and follow it with a selection of 2–3 rich terrines, accompanied by lashings of crusty French bread and even the heartiest appetite will be satisfied. The essential difference in the cooking of terrines and pâtés is that terrines are cooked in the dish from which they will be served—properly a terrine, but a suitably shaped casserole or loaf tin will do just as well. They are wrapped in fatty bacon and after cooking should be pressed with a heavy weight to compress the layers of meat really tightly together. Pâtés are usually at least partially cooked before moulding and are served either turned out and sliced, or in individual dishes.

COUNTRY PATE
serves 12

2 oz. butter
8 oz. onion, skinned and roughly chopped
8 oz. lean bacon, rinded and chopped
8 oz. belly of pork, rinded and cut into strips
12 oz. pig's liver, diced
12 oz. stewing steak, finely diced
8 oz. pie veal, diced
3 cloves of garlic, skinned and crushed
¼ pint (⅝ cup) red wine
4 tbsps. brandy or port
2 bay leaves
salt and black pepper
dash of Worcestershire sauce
bacon fat
1 egg, beaten

Melt the butter in a large saucepan and fry the onion and bacon until they are light golden brown. Add the rest of the ingredients, except the egg, and bring to the boil. Cover the pan and simmer for 30 minutes.

Strain off the liquor and put the remainder through the mincer twice, using the finest blade. Mix thoroughly with the strained liquor and the beaten egg. Season

again well. Place the mixture in a foil lined, lightly buttered 1-lb. loaf tin. Place in a roasting tin with water half way up and cook in the oven at 350°F. (mark 4) for 1½ hours.

Remove from the oven and cool. Chill for at least 12 hours before turning out and serving.

HOME-MADE PATE DE FOIE
serves 6

1 lb. calf's or chicken liver
4 oz. pork fat
1 small clove of garlic, skinned
pinch of mixed herbs
salt and freshly ground pepper
a little water
2 oz. cooked tongue
a little truffle, if available
aspic jelly
truffle or green leek for garnish

Mince the liver and pork fat with the garlic and mixed herbs; season lightly. Heat a thick frying pan; when hot, add the liver mixture and stir well. When the liver has changed colour add a very little water and allow to simmer for 5 minutes. Press through a fine sieve or purée in a blender. Add the tongue, chopped in diamonds, and the truffle, finely chopped. Adjust the seasoning if necessary.

Line the bases of tiny soufflé dishes or ramekins with a layer of aspic and some decoration cut from thin slices of truffle or blanched leek. When the decoration has set, fill each dish with pâté, spread evenly, and chill until firm. To serve, unmould.

THRIFTY PATE
serves 6

1¼ lb. lean belly pork
½ lb. pig's or ox liver
¼ lb. lean streaky bacon, rinded
4 oz. onion, skinned and chopped
1 small clove of garlic, skinned
1 level tsp. salt
freshly ground black pepper
1 oz. butter

Remove the rind and any bones from the belly pork and dice. Rinse the liver under cold running water and dry on absorbent paper. Cut into largish pieces. Mince the pork, liver, bacon, onion and garlic together three times. Work in the salt and pepper.

Turn into a 2-pint terrine or small casserole, cover and place in a small roasting tin with water half way up. Cook at 300°F. (mark 2) for about 1½ hours. Remove the lid. Lay a double sheet of foil over the top, add weights and weight down until quite cold, preferably in a refrigerator. Remove weights and covering. Melt butter over a low heat, pour over pâté and chill.

HUNTER'S PATE
serves 16

1 lb. rabbit or hare flesh
1 lb. belly of pork, trimmed
½ lb. pig's liver
1 lb. pork sausage meat
½ lb. garlic sausage
4 oz. (1 cup) onion, skinned and chopped
3 tbsps. sherry
2 tbsps. chopped parsley
2 level tbsps. dried sage
salt and black pepper
1 lb. fat streaky bacon rashers, rinded

Cut the rabbit or hare into small pieces. Put the pork, liver, sausage meat, garlic sausage and onion through the mincer. Mix in the rabbit pieces, sherry, parsley and sage, and season well.

Take a loaf tin or terrine measuring about 9½ in. by 5½ in. by 3 in. deep,

Chicken liver pâté is a rich starter for a dinner party

and line it with the bacon rashers. Turn the pâté mixture into the prepared tin and fold the bacon edges over the top. Cover with kitchen foil, place in a roasting tin with water to come half way up and cook in the oven at 325°F. (mark 3) for about 3 hours. Allow to cool in the tin.

Turn out and serve in thick slices. If you wish to store the pâté, turn out when cold and wrap in foil.

POTTED BEEF
serves 6

1 lb. stewing steak, cut into ½-in. cubes
¼ pint (⅝ cup) stock
1 clove
1 blade of mace
salt and pepper
2 oz. butter, melted
fresh bay leaves for garnish

Put the meat in a casserole with the stock and seasonings. Cover and cook in the centre of the oven at 350°F. (mark 4) for 2½–3 hours, until tender. Remove the clove and mace and drain off the stock, setting it aside.

Mince the meat twice or place it in a blender and blend for several minutes until smooth. Add 1 oz. melted butter and sufficient of the reserved stock to moisten. Press into ramekins or soufflé dishes, cover with the remainder of the melted butter and chill. Serve garnished with a fresh bay leaf on each portion.

CHICKEN LIVER PATE
serves 10

1½ lb. chicken livers
3 oz. butter
1 medium onion, skinned and finely chopped
1 large clove of garlic, skinned and crushed
1 tbsp. double cream
2 level tbsps. tomato paste
3 tbsps. sherry or brandy

Rinse the chicken livers and dry thoroughly on kitchen paper. Fry them in the butter until they change colour. Reduce heat, add the onion and garlic, cover and cook for 5 minutes. Remove from heat and cool. Add the cream, tomato paste and sherry or brandy. Purée in blender or pass through a sieve. Turn into individual dishes and flood the tops with melted butter if desired. Chill.

SMOKED TROUT PATE
serves 6

8 oz. smoked trout
2 oz. butter
3 oz. (1½ cups) fresh white breadcrumbs
finely grated rind and juice of 1 lemon
salt and freshly ground black pepper
pinch of ground nutmeg
¼ pint (⅝ cup) single cream
¼–½ pint (⅝–1¼ cups) aspic jelly, made from aspic jelly powder

Remove the skin and bones from the trout and finely chop the flesh. Melt the butter in a small pan and pour on to the breadcrumbs with the lemon rind and juice. Season well with salt, pepper and nutmeg. Add the fish to the breadcrumbs and fold in the cream. Spoon into 6 ramekins or small soufflé dishes. Make up the aspic jelly and when on the point of setting, spoon over the pâté. Chill.

FRESH SALMON PATE
serves 8

2 oz. butter
2 oz. (½ cup) flour
¾ pint (2 cups) milk
1 bay leaf
salt and pepper
¼ level tsp. ground nutmeg
½ lb. fresh haddock or cod fillet, skinned
1 lb. fresh salmon, skinned and boned, or 2 7½-oz. cans tuna
grated rind and juice of 1 lemon
1 tbsp. chopped parsley
2 eggs, beaten
melted butter
parsley sprigs and lemon for garnish

Melt the butter in a pan and stir in the flour. Cook for 2–3 minutes, then slowly add the milk, beating between each addition. Add the bay leaf, salt, pepper and nutmeg and boil gently for 2–3 minutes; discard the bay leaf.

Finely chop or mince the haddock and three-quarters of the salmon. Add to the sauce together with the lemon rind and juice, parsley and eggs. Divide between buttered ramekins. Brush the tops with melted butter and decorate with slices of the remaining salmon. Place the dishes in a large roasting tin with water to come half way up the dishes and cook in the oven at 300°F. (mark 2) for about 40 minutes. Chill. Garnish with parsley and lemon.

LIVER PATE DIP
serves 8–12

12 oz. soft liver sausage
dash of brandy or dry sherry
1–2 oz. softened butter
black pepper
large pinch of mixed spice
double cream

Put all the ingredients except the cream into a bowl and beat until smooth and creamy. Add enough cream to make the pâté soft but not sloppy. Serve with savoury biscuits and raw vegetables.

SMOKED FISH PATE
serves 6–8

7-oz. can smoked codling
    fillets
6 oz. butter
⅛ level tsp. cayenne pepper
2 tbsps chopped capers
2 tbsps. chopped parsley
1 tbsp. medium dry sherry
1 tbsp. lemon juice
salt and freshly ground black
    pepper
pinch of ground nutmeg
1 oz. butter, melted
cucumber slices to garnish

Cook the codling fillets as directed. Drain, remove any dark skin and flake the flesh. Cream the butter well, adding the cayenne by degrees to taste. Beat in the fish, capers, parsley, sherry and lemon juice. Season to taste. Spoon the pâté mixture either into one 6-in. soufflé dish or into small individual dishes. Top with a little melted butter and chill. Garnish with cucumber slices.

TERRINE OF VEAL AND CHICKEN
serves 6–8

¾ lb. chicken meat
1 lb. veal
¼ lb. chicken livers
4 tbsps. dry white wine
1 clove of garlic, skinned and
    crushed
pinch of mixed spice
2 oz. (1 cup) fresh white
    breadcrumbs
salt and freshly ground
    pepper
6 oz. streaky bacon rashers,
    rinded
2 bay leaves
sprig of thyme

Mince together (with the medium cutter) the chicken meat, veal and chicken livers. Stir the white wine into the mixed meats with the garlic, mixed spice and breadcrumbs. Season well.
Stretch the streaky bacon with the back of a knife. Line a 2-pint terrine or oval casserole with overlapping rashers, making sure they are long enough to envelop the meat completely later. Spoon in the meat mixture and cover with the bacon. Lay a bay leaf or two and a sprig of thyme on top. Cover. Place in a roasting tin with water half way up. Cook in the oven at 325°F. (mark 3) for about 2¼ hours. Allow to cool. When cool, pour off the juices. Chill the terrine and juices separately. When jelly is on the point of setting, spoon over the terrine.

TERRINE OF DUCK, LIVER AND PORK
serves 10–12

1 lb. duck meat (approx.
    yield from a 3½-lb.
    oven-ready duck)
3 level tbsps. Marsala
1½ lb. belly pork, boned and
    skinned
1 lb. calf's liver
1 medium onion, skinned
1–2 cloves of garlic, skinned
1 medium orange
1 level tsp. salt
freshly ground black pepper
½ level tsp. dried thyme
½ lb. streaky bacon rashers,
    rinded
4 bay leaves

Cut the duck meat into long strips and marinate in the Marsala for 6 hours in a cool place. Keep any small pieces to one side. Dice the pork and liver and mince together with the duck trimmings, onion and garlic. Into the minced ingredients blend the juice from half the orange, salt, pepper, thyme and Marsala drained from the duck.
Stretch the bacon by drawing the blade of a knife along each rasher two or three times. Line the terrine with rashers, leaving the ends long enough to envelop the terrine mixture completely later. Spoon one-third of the minced meat into the terrine; then lay half the strips of duck meat along the length of the terrine. Repeat the layers, finishing with minced meat. Wrap the bacon over the top of the meat.
Slice the remaining half of the orange and lay over the terrine with the bay leaves. Cover and place in a roasting tin with water half way up the dish. Cook in the oven at 325°F. (mark 3) for about 2½ hours.
When cooked, remove the lid and place a piece of foil over the pâté (leaving the orange slices and bay leaves in place). Press down firmly with a small plate. Add a 2-lb. weight and allow to cool.

LIVER TERRINE
serves 4–6

1 lb. pig's liver
¼ lb. fat bacon
3–4 anchovy fillets
4 eggs, beaten
1 clove of garlic, skinned and
    crushed
½ pint (1¼ cups) thick white
    sauce
salt and pepper
12 rashers of streaky bacon,
    rinded

Many terrines are encased in rashers of streaky bacon

Mince the liver, fat bacon and anchovy fillets finely, three times – or mince the mixture twice and finally purée in the blender. Mix in the beaten eggs, garlic, sauce and seasonings to taste.
Line a shallow ovenproof dish with the bacon rashers, fill up with the liver mixture and place in a roasting tin with water half way up the dish. Cook at 325°F. (mark 3) for 2 hours. Cover the top of the liver mixture with greaseproof paper or foil, put a weight on top and chill.

TERRINE OF DUCK
serves 6

1¾ lb. frozen duck breast
    portions, thawed
2 level tsps. salt
1 lb. belly pork
1 lb. pie veal
¼ lb. pork back fat
¼ pint (⅝ cup) dry white wine
1 clove of garlic, skinned and
    crushed
freshly ground black pepper
1 small orange, washed and
    thinly sliced
aspic jelly to glaze

Place the duck portions in a roasting tin, sprinkle with the salt and cook in the centre of the oven at 325°F. (mark 3) for 40 minutes. Meanwhile, trim the surplus fat from the belly of pork and trim the pie veal into neat pieces. Cut 4–6 thin strips from the pork fat and reserve for a garnish.
Put the belly of pork, the veal and the rest of the pork fat through the mincer twice. Add the wine, garlic, salt and pepper and mix thoroughly. Take the duck from the oven, remove the skin, cut the flesh from the bones and dice it. Moisten the minced ingredients with some of the cooking juice.
Put half this mixture in a 2- or 2½-pint terrine or casserole, add the duck meat and cover with the rest of the minced ingredients. Arrange the strips of pork fat in a lattice on top and cover the dish with foil. Stand the terrine in a roasting tin with water half way up the dish and cook in the centre of the oven at 325°F. (mark 3) for 1½–2 hours.
Remove the terrine from the oven, take off the foil and leave for 15 minutes. Then cover the meat with folded foil, place some weights on top and chill thoroughly. When chilled, arrange the orange slices in a pattern on top, glaze with nearly-set aspic and chill again.

Kipper pâté is the simplest to make

GARNISHES

Suitable decorations add good looks as well as flavour to food and drinks—but they must be very fresh, and preferably quite simple and comparatively small. The garnish for any particular dish should be decided on beforehand. Colours should be chosen to tone with both the food and the serving dish—two, or at most three, colours are sufficient. Sometimes ingredients which are an integral part of the recipe can also add decorative value.

VEGETABLE AND SALAD GARNISHES

Turned mushrooms have a nicely tailored look. You need to use large button mushrooms and 'turn' them with a small, sharp-pointed knife, by making a series of cuts from the top of the cap to the base at intervals. Then repeat in the opposite direction to remove each narrow 'fillet'. Sauté the mushrooms in butter.

Baby turnips can be 'turned' prettily in the same way.

Carrot curls look crisp on open sandwiches, and in salads (or served as cocktail nibblers). Scrape raw carrots and slice them lengthwise and paper thin, using a vegetable peeler. Roll up, fasten with a toothpick and put them in iced water until they curl. Serve on or off the picks.

Another simple way to cut carrots raw is with a fondant cutter or tiny pastry cutter—simply scrape and slice the carrot then flute the edges by stamping out with a cutter.

Pickle fans always stay fresh, and suit hot or cold dishes. Make lengthwise cuts almost to the end of each gherkin, from the 'flower' end. Spread carefully to form an open fan.

Radish roses to garnish open sandwiches or cold meat platters are always popular. Cut off a narrow slice from the root end of each radish, then cut thin 'petals' from stem to root. Put into iced water until the cuts open to form petals.

To make radish water lillies, make 4–8 small deep cuts, crossing in the centre of the radish at the root end, and leave in iced water to open out.

Celery curls are made by cutting the celery into strips about ½ in. wide and 2 in. long and then slitting one or both ends in narrow strips almost to the centre. Leave the pieces in iced water for an hour or so until the fringed ends curl.

Spring onions split down the stem and left in cold water will open out in the same way.

ORANGE OR LEMON GARNISHES

Citrus twists look cool on an iced drink or on top of a chiffon dessert. Using a sharp-edged potato peeler, start to remove a strip of peel from the narrow end of a lemon, orange or grapefruit. Work in a continuous spiral, removing only the coloured part of the peel. Let the peel twist naturally as a garnish.

Orange and lemon slices, deftly twisted, suit fish and chicken dishes and may be used wherever these flavours are present in a recipe. Slit the slice through the rind to the centre, then twist in opposite directions. A double twist with 2 slices gives more emphasis.

SAVOURY GARNISHES

Croûtons are small, fancy-shaped pieces of bread which are fried or toasted. Cut the slices of white bread ¼–½ in. thick, remove the crusts and then either cut the bread into ¼–½ in. cubes and fry them, or leave the slices whole and grill them before cutting up. Use as a garnish for soups.

Croûtons cut into larger triangles and crescents are used as a garnish for minced meat or au gratin dishes.

Cheese triangles are good with soups and savouries. Well butter 6 slices of crustless bread and arrange close together on a baking sheet. Sprinkle 1 oz. finely grated cheese over. Bake in the oven at 350°F. (mark 4) for about 40 minutes. Overlap round the edge of a savoury dish or float on puréed soups.

Fleurons Roll out some puff, flaky or rough puff pastry to ¼ in. thickness, then stamp it into shapes with small fancy cutters, or cut with a sharp knife into squares, triangles or diamonds. To make crescents, which are a traditional shape, use a small round cutter; place it about ½ in. on to the edge of the pastry for the first cut, then move the cutter a further ½ in. inwards and cut again, making a crescent. Continue the length of the pastry, moving the cutter ½ in. each time. Place the fleurons on a baking sheet, brush the tops lightly with beaten egg and bake in the oven at 450°F. (mark 8) until well risen, golden brown and crisp—7–10 minutes.

Buttered crumbs Melt 1 oz. butter and add 1 pint fine white breadcrumbs. Let them absorb the fat, forking the mixture several times. Spread out on baking sheets and dry in the oven on its lowest setting. When ready, they are cream-coloured and dry. Stored in a screw-top jar or polythene bag in a cool place, these will keep fresh for 2 months. Use dry for coating rissoles; toss with butter or grated cheese for topping other dishes.

Crunchy topper Fry 2 oz. fresh white breadcrumbs in 1½ oz. butter until golden brown. Sift together 8 oz. self-raising flour, 1 level teaspoon salt, pepper and ½ level teaspoon dried onion powder. Stir in 3 tablespoons cooking oil and enough milk to give a soft dough. Drop tablespoons of the dough into buttered crumbs and roll into balls in the crumbs. Arrange on top of a casserole about 50 minutes before serving. Bake uncovered in the oven at 375°F. (mark 5).

SAVOURY SOUFFLES AND MOUSSES

A traditional soufflé dish is round and straight sided; it is smooth inside and fluted outside. Plain white china is the most common colour, but brown earthenware, coloured china and ovenproof glass are also available. In some classic soufflé recipes it is recommended that a paper band be tied round the outside of the dish to come about 3 in. above the rim. After cooking the paper is peeled away and the soufflé still stands well above the edge of the dish. This is not strictly necessary, though, as a good soufflé will rise well without and looks just as attractive. Simply butter the dish and dust with breadcrumbs or Parmesan cheese. The paper is necessary to give a 'risen' appearance to a cold soufflé.

A hot soufflé is made on a base of a thick white sauce, or panada, flavoured with meat, fish, cheese or vegetables. Egg yolks are beaten in to make it rich and the egg whites are whisked separately until really stiff and then folded gently in with a metal spoon. The amount the soufflé rises depends on the air whipped into the egg whites, the air expands in the oven heat and raises a hot soufflé, and gives bulk to a cold one. Don't beat or stir the egg whites in rapidly.

To cook a soufflé place in the oven at 350–375°F. (mark 4–5) for 30–45 minutes, until well risen and brown on top. Be careful not to open the door of the oven too early in the cooking or your soufflé will collapse! To test when a hot soufflé is ready, open the oven door after 30 minutes and give the dish a slight movement without taking it out. If the crust moves considerably in the centre, leave it a little longer. Serve a hot soufflé straight from the oven – it will spoil if kept for more than a few moments. This unfortunately makes a soufflé an unsuitable choice for a dinner party, when you cannot rely on the guests being precisely on time – but give the family a treat from time to time. Cold soufflés and mousses are less temperamental and ideal party dishes. They are set with gelatine and a mousse may be served in the dish or turned out of a mould on to a flat serving plate – a ring mould is often used. To turn out a moulded mousse, dip the mould quickly into hot water and invert it on to a wet plate; the mousse will then slip easily out of the mould and will slide into place on the plate if it is not quite central.

CHEESE SOUFFLE
serves 4

4 large eggs
1½ oz. butter
1 oz. (¼ cup) plain flour
½ pint (1¼ cups) milk
6 oz. dry Cheddar cheese, finely grated
salt and pepper

Butter a 2-pint capacity soufflé dish. Separate the eggs. Melt the butter, stir in the flour and cook for 2–3 minutes. Gradually stir in the milk, beating the mixture until smooth. Cook for a few minutes longer. Add the egg yolks one at a

time, beating well, stir in the cheese and season. Stiffly whisk the egg whites, fold these quickly and evenly into the cheese mixture with a metal spoon and turn into the soufflé dish.

Bake in the centre of the oven at 350°F. (mark 4) for about 45 minutes until well risen and brown. Serve immediately.

RED HOUSE SOUFFLE
serves 6

2 oz. butter
8 oz. onions, skinned and
    thinly sliced
1 small pkt. frozen sweet corn
8 oz. tomatoes, skinned and
    thickly sliced
2 tbsps. chopped parsley

For the sauce :

4 oz. butter
4 oz. (1 cup) plain flour
1 pint (2½ cups) milk
salt and freshly ground black
    pepper
6 oz. strong Cheddar cheese,
    grated
6 eggs, separated

Butter a 3½-pint soufflé dish or casserole. Heat 2 oz. butter in a frying pan, add the onion and sauté until soft but not coloured. Add the corn and continue cooking for 5 minutes. Remove from the heat and add the tomatoes and parsley.

For the sauce, melt 4 oz. butter in a saucepan, stir in the flour and cook for a few minutes. Gradually add the milk, stirring all the time, bring to the boil and simmer for a few minutes. Add half the sauce to the vegetables and check the seasoning. Turn the mixture into the soufflé dish or casserole.

Add the cheese to the remaining sauce in the pan, beat in the egg yolks and adjust the seasoning again. Stiffly whisk the egg whites and fold into the sauce with a metal spoon.

Spoon the mixture over the vegetables and bake in the centre of oven for about 1 hour at 350°F. (mark 4), until well risen and golden.
Serve at once.

BACON AND ONION SOUFFLE
serves 4

1 oz. butter
6 oz. lean bacon, rinded and
    chopped
8 oz. onion, skinned and
    chopped
1 tbsp. chopped parsley
salt and pepper

Cold ham soufflé will satisfy the heartiest appetite

For the sauce :

2 oz. butter
1½ oz. (⅜ cup) plain flour
½ pint (1¼ cups) milk
3 egg yolks
4 egg whites

Butter a 2½-pint capacity soufflé dish. Melt 1 oz. butter in a medium pan, add the bacon and fry for 2–3 minutes. Add the onion and continue cooking until the onion is tender. Remove from the heat. Add the parsley and season to taste.

Melt the 2 oz. butter in a saucepan, add the flour and stir well with a wooden spoon. Cook for 2–3 minutes. Add the milk gradually and bring to the boil, stirring continuously. Mix half the sauce with half the bacon and onion mixture and spoon into the soufflé dish.

Beat the egg yolks one at a time into the remaining sauce. Whisk the egg whites until stiff and gently fold, with a metal spoon, into the sauce. Add the remaining bacon mixture.

Turn into the soufflé dish, bake near the top of the oven at 375°F. (mark 5) for about 45 minutes until well risen and golden.
Serve at once.

MARROW SOUFFLE
serves 4

1 lb. marrow, peeled
2 oz. butter
1 oz. plain flour
½ pint (1¼ cups) milk
salt and pepper
2 level tsps. dried summer
    savory
3 eggs, separated
4 oz. cheese, grated

Butter a 2-pint capacity soufflé dish. Cut the marrow into thick slices and discard the seeds. Cook in boiling, salted water until tender but still firm. Drain well and roughly chop.

Melt the butter and stir in the flour. Gradually stir in the milk and seasoning. Pour half this sauce over the marrow, add the herbs and spoon into the soufflé dish.

Beat the egg yolks and add to the remaining sauce, with the cheese. Adjust seasoning. Stiffly whisk the egg whites and fold in. Spoon over the marrow.

Bake in the oven at 375°F. (mark 5) for about 30 minutes, until well risen.
Serve at once.

SPINACH SOUFFLE
serves 4

4 oz. onion, skinned and
    sliced
3½ oz. butter
6-oz. pkt. frozen leaf spinach,
    or 1 lb. fresh spinach, part
    cooked and roughly
    chopped
salt and freshly ground black
    pepper
¼ level tsp. grated nutmeg
1 oz. plain flour
½ pint (1¼ cups) milk
3 large eggs, separated
1½ oz. Parmesan cheese,
    grated

Butter a 1½-pint capacity soufflé dish. Gently sauté the onion in 1½ oz. butter until tender, add the spinach and cook a little longer. Season lightly with salt, pepper and nutmeg.

Melt the remaining butter in another pan, stir in the flour and cook for 1 minute. Add the milk all at once, stir well and bring to the boil. Season and add half the sauce to the spinach and onion. Turn into the soufflé dish and place on a baking sheet.

Beat the egg yolks and most of the cheese into the remaining sauce, reserving a little cheese to sprinkle over the soufflé. Stiffly whisk the egg whites and fold carefully through the sauce with a metal spoon. Pour on to the spinach base and sprinkle the remaining cheese over the top. Cook in the centre of the oven at 375°F. (mark 5) for about 40 minutes.
Serve immediately.

COLD HAM SOUFFLE
serves 4

1 oz. butter
1 oz. plain flour
½ pint (1¼ cups) milk
4 large eggs, separated
4 level tsps. powdered
    gelatine
4 tbsps. water
8 oz. cooked ham, finely
    minced
½ level tsp. chopped tarragon
¼ pint (⅝ cup) single cream
salt and pepper
cress and slices of ham for
    garnish

Prepare a 1-pint capacity soufflé dish by tying a double band of greaseproof or non-stick paper round the outside, to stand about 3 in. above the rim of the dish.

Melt the butter in a pan, stir in the flour and cook over gentle heat for 2 minutes. Add the milk and bring to the boil, stirring constantly until the sauce thickens. Remove from the heat and beat in the egg yolks 1 at a time.

Dissolve the gelatine in the water in a basin over a pan of hot water; add to the sauce and leave in a cool place, stirring occasionally until it begins to set.

Stir in the minced ham, tarragon and cream. Adjust seasoning according to taste; beware of adding too much salt, as the ham may already be salty.

Whisk the egg whites until stiff. Fold into the ham mixture, turn into the prepared soufflé dish and leave to set.

To remove the paper collar, wet a palette knife under the hot tap and run it carefully between the 2 layers of paper; gently peel the paper away.

Serve garnished with cress and rolled slices of ham round the dish.

Smoked haddock is the basis for this appetizing savoury mousse

SHRIMP RICE MOUSSE
serves 4

3 oz. long grain rice
½ oz. powdered gelatine
½ pint (1¼ cups) warm water
6–8 oz. shelled shrimps (fresh, canned or frozen, thawed) or prawns, roughly chopped
¼ pint (⅝ cup) mayonnaise
4-oz. pkt. frozen peas, cooked
2 sticks of celery, chopped
salt and freshly ground black pepper
¼ pint (⅝ cup) double cream, lightly whipped
sliced cucumber

Cook the rice in boiling salted water for about 12 minutes until tender; drain. Dissolve the gelatine in the water in a bowl over a pan of hot water; allow to cool, stirring from time to time.
Mix most of the shrimps (or prawns) with the mayonnaise, peas, celery, salt, pepper and dissolved gelatine. Fold in the lightly whipped cream and the rice. Allow to cool.
When nearly set, turn the mousse into a wetted mould and chill thoroughly. When set, turn out on to a wetted serving dish and garnish with reserved shrimps and sliced cucumber.

SMOKED HADDOCK MOUSSE
serves 6

1 small carrot, peeled and halved
1 small onion, skinned and halved
½ pint (1¼ cups) milk
1 bay leaf
3 parsley stalks
6 peppercorns
1½ oz. butter
1 oz. plain flour
½ pint (1¼ cups) aspic jelly made with aspic jelly powder
½ lb. smoked haddock
3 eggs, hard-boiled
1 tbsp. chopped parsley
¼ pint (⅝ cup) double cream, whipped
juice and finely grated rind of 1 small lemon
salt and freshly ground black pepper
parsley sprigs
watercress

Put the carrot, onion and milk in a pan with the bay leaf, parsley and peppercorns, bring to the boil and allow to infuse off the heat for 10 minutes.
Melt the butter, stir in the flour and cook for 1–2 minutes without colouring. Off the heat, stir in strained milk. Return to the heat bring to the boil and cook, stirring, for 30 seconds. Stir all but 3 tablespoons of the aspic into the sauce. Meanwhile, poach the fish in water to cover for 10 minutes. Drain the fish, discard the bones and skin and flake the flesh. Shell 2 of the eggs and chop. Add to the flaked fish with the parsley. Fold the whipped cream into the aspic sauce when it is on the point of setting. Finally fold in the lemon rind and juice, the fish, eggs and parsley. Adjust seasoning. Turn into a 2½-pint soufflé dish and leave in a cool place to set.
Slice the remaining egg and arrange over the surface of the mousse with sprigs of parsley. Dilute the remaining aspic with a further 3 tablespoons water and spoon over the decoration. When set, garnish with watercress.

PRAWN MOUSSE
serves 4

¼ pint (⅝ cup) aspic jelly, made from aspic jelly powder
8 oz. shelled prawns
1 pint (2½ cups) milk
1 small onion, skinned and quartered
1 carrot, peeled and quartered
1–2 cloves
1 bay leaf
3–4 peppercorns
1½ oz. butter
1½ oz. (⅜ cup) plain flour
2 eggs, separated
salt and pepper
½ oz. powdered gelatine
¼ pint (⅝ cup) dry white wine or stock

Make up the aspic jelly, pour a thin layer into a 2-pint mould, add a few prawns for decoration and leave to set. Put the milk, onion, carrot, cloves, bay leaf and peppercorns into a covered pan, bring to the boil, turn out the heat and leave to cool for about 15 minutes, until the milk is well flavoured. Melt the butter, stir in the flour and cook for 2–3 minutes. Gradually stir in the strained milk. Bring to the boil and continue to stir until the sauce thickens. Remove from the heat, cool slightly and beat in the egg yolks and seasoning to taste. Dissolve the gelatine in the wine or stock in a basin over a pan of hot water and stir it into the sauce. Add the remaining prawns, roughly chopped, and leave in a cool place until the mixture begins to set.
Whisk the egg whites stiffly, fold them in and turn the mousse into the prepared mould and leave to set.
Unmould and serve with salad.

SALMON AND ASPARAGUS MOUSSE
Do not attempt this recipe unless you have an electric blender; serves 8

2 level tbsps. aspic jelly powder
1 pint (2½ cups) water
1 oz. butter
1 oz. (¼ cup) plain flour
½ pint (1¼ cups) milk
¼ level tsp. dry mustard
pinch of cayenne pepper
salt and pepper
1 tbsp. cider vinegar
3 eggs, separated
2 7½-oz. cans salmon, drained
1½ level tbsps. powdered gelatine
¼ pint (⅝ cup) double cream, lightly whipped
8-oz. pkt. frozen asparagus, cooked and cooled

Make up the aspic jelly with the water as directed on the packet. Leave until beginning to set, then pour a little into an 8¼-in. spring-release cake tin fitted with a plain base or a 3-pint fluted mould. Use the jelly to coat the sides of the tin and place in refrigerator to set.
When this lining is set, pour more aspic jelly into the tin until it is ¼ in. deep. Leave to set.
Meanwhile put the butter, flour, milk and seasonings into the blender and blend for 15 seconds. Turn into a pan, bring to the boil and cook for 3 minutes. Beat in the vinegar, then the egg yolks. Return the mixture to the heat and cook without boiling for a few more minutes. Add the drained salmon to the sauce and check the seasoning. Put 6 tablespoons liquid aspic in a small basin or cup, sprinkle in the gelatine and stand the cup in a little hot water until the gelatine is dissolved. Add to the salmon mixture. Pour half into blender and blend for about 30 seconds, until smooth. Turn out and repeat with remainder. Leave until just setting. Fold in the cream, followed by whisked egg whites. Spoon into the tin.
When set arrange the asparagus spears on top. Spoon the remaining aspic jelly over and leave for about 1 hour to set.
To unmould, hold a warm cloth round the sides of the tin, release the clip and remove the ring. Warm the base and slide the mousse on to a serving plate.

Salmon and asparagus mousse

CHEESE AND CHEESE DISHES

When cheese is made, the best and richest part of the milk, the curd, is separated from the whey, the watery part, pressed and allowed to mature. The quality of the milk and the animal from which it came (whether cow, goat or ewe, or even camel or buffalo), give rise to a wide range of different types of cheese. Local conditions of climate and vegetation, different methods of making it and varying storage conditions during ripening affect the cheese so that almost no cheeses taste the same.

Cheese is an important source of protein, fat and minerals in the diet and is one of the tastiest savoury foods, whether eaten in its natural state or cooked and combined with other foods. Remember never to cook cheese for longer than it takes to heat through and melt – over heating makes it tough and indigestible.

BRITISH CHEESES

HARD CHEESES

Blue Vinney (Blue Dorset) Hard cheese made from skimmed cows' milk; white with a blue vein; rather strong flavour.

Caerphilly A soft, crumbly, whole milk cheese, eaten when about 10 days old; white; creamy, mild flavour; best uncooked.

Cheddar Hard, yellow, whole milk cheese; slightly salty and varying in flavour from mild to quite strong; good cooked or uncooked. The cheddaring process is easily mechanized and carried out under factory conditions and the cheese is therefore produced in many parts of the world, notably New Zealand, Australia and Canada. "Farmhouse" Cheddar is still usually considered the best.

Derby Hard, close-textured, white cheese; mild when young but developing a full flavour as it matures; sage leaves sometimes added to give a green cheese known as **Sage Derby**.

Double Gloucester Hard, orange-yellow cheese; close, crumbly texture; rich flavour similar to mature Cheddar.

Dunlop Scottish cheese similar to Cheddar, but more moist and with a closer texture.

Lancashire A fairly hard cheese but crumbly when cut; mild, tangy flavour when new, developing as the cheese matures; excellent for cooking.

Leicester Hard cheese; orange-

Reading clockwise from bottom left : Camembert, Sage Derby, Leicester, Lancashire, Emmenthal, Danish Blue, Edam, Boursin and Brie

red colour; mild, slightly sweet flavour.

Stilton Semi-hard, double cream cheese (i.e. made from rich milk to which extra cream is added); white with evenly distributed blue veining caused by a mould inoculated into the cheese; the rind should be a dull, drab colour, well crinkled, regular and free from cracks; best after 6–9 months. Made only during May–September. A milder, white Stilton is also available. Not suitable for cooking.

Wensleydale Double cream cheese originally matured until blue; now usually sold white and unripe, when it is mild and flaky.

SOFT CHEESE

These are no longer given regional names in Britain.

Cream cheese Made from cream only; may be double cream cheese (from cream with a 45–50 per cent fat content) or single cream cheese (made from cream with a 25–30 per cent fat content); made in small quantities as it keeps for only 6–7 days; soft and rich. Available plain or flavoured with herbs, fruit, nuts etc.

Curd cheese Made by the same method as cream cheese, but from milk; soft, but slightly firmer than cream cheese and not so rich.

Cottage cheese Made from the same method again, but using skimmed milk; very soft, loose-textured, rather flavourless cheese. Mixes well with salads and used for making cheesecake. Available plain or flavoured with herbs or fruit.

CONTINENTAL CHEESES

Bel Paese Italian; rich, creamy cheese; mild flavour; made usually from October to June.

Brie French; soft farm cheese made from whole milk and mould-inoculated; creamy-white, with a brownish, slightly mouldy crust; mild, rich flavour; made in flat rounds 1–1½ in. thick and about 14 in. across, but also available, boxed, in wedges; does not keep well. Not good for cooking.

Camembert French; made from creamy cows' milk inoculated with a white mould; creamy-white, with a light crust similar to Brie; delicious at its best, when starting to soften, but if allowed to over-ripen it becomes too soft and generates unpleasant gases. Made in rounds 4–5 in. across and sold boxed; also sold in individually wrapped portions.

Reading clockwise from top left: Cheddar, Jarlsberg, Stilton, Bleu de Bresse, Port-Salut, Windsor Red and Raybier

Danish Blue White, crumbly cheese with blue veining produced by mould; sharp, salty taste.

Demi-sel French; soft cream cheese; sold in small, square, foil-wrapped packs.

Dolcelatte Italian; a milder, creamier form of Gorgonzola.

Edam Dutch; firm, smooth cheese; ball shaped, bright red outside, deep yellow inside; mild flavour. Good for cooking; low in calories. Also made in other countries but only the Dutch has the true flavour.

Emmenthal Swiss (also French, Italian and Austrian); similar to Gruyère but slightly softer in texture, with larger 'eyes'. Excellent for fondues, quiches, etc.

Fontainebleau French; soft, fresh cream cheese.

Fromage à la crème Soft cheese made from soured milk; served softened with a little milk and with caster sugar and cream.

Gorgonzola Italian; semi-hard, blue veined cheese; sharp flavour.

Gouda Dutch; similar to Edam in texture but creamier and with a better flavour, and a yellow skin. Usually made as large rounds but also exported as small cheeses.

Gruyère Swiss (also French and Italian); hard cheese honeycombed with 'eyes' or holes caused by rapid fermentation of the curd; pale yellow; distinctive, fairly sweet taste; good uncooked but also cooked in many classic European dishes.

Havarti Danish; smooth, light yellow cheese with numerous holes, large and small. Full flavoured, with a piquant after-taste. Foil wrapped.

Limburger Belgian (also German and French); semi-hard whole milk cheese; full flavoured and strong smelling.

Mycella Danish; has the golden yellow colour of rich cream, with green veining.

Mysöst (Gietöst) Norwegian; whey cheese, made principally from goats' milk; hard and dark brown; sweetish flavour.

Parmesan Italian; the hardest of all cheeses; pale straw colour and full of tiny holes, like pin pricks; used finely grated in cooked dishes or sprinkled on top of hot dishes such as pasta, rice and soups.

Petit Suisse (Petit Gervais) French; unsalted cream cheese; very mild; sold in small, cylindrical, foil-wrapped packs.

Pommel French; unsalted double cream cheese; not unlike Petit Suisse.

Pont l'Evêque French; semi-hard cheese, salted repeatedly while maturing; yellow; made in small squares. Somewhat similar to Camembert and should be eaten soft and not too ripe.

Port-Salut French; semi-hard, round cheese; creamy yellow; mild flavour; should be eaten while still slightly soft.

Roquefort French; ewes' milk cheese layered with a culture of moulded breadcrumbs (the same mould as that inoculated into Stilton); made only during the lambing season and only in the Roquefort district; white, curd-like cheese, mottled with blue veins; sharp, peppery taste.

Samsoe Danish; firm in texture with regular holes, and a mild, sweet nut-like flavour. Cuts well into thin slices or cubes.

STORING CHEESE

The drier, harder cheeses will keep well when stored correctly, but softer cheeses deteriorate quickly, so should be bought only as required. To store cheese, wrap it loosely in polythene, aluminium foil or greaseproof paper – trap some air in the package otherwise the cheese will sweat and mould

will grow quickly – then place it in a cool larder or refrigerator. If you keep it in the refrigerator, make sure that it is brought to room temperature for serving. Wrap different types of cheese separately, so that one does not take on the flavour of another. Pre-packaged cheese keeps well in the refrigerator, but once opened it should be re-wrapped and stored as for fresh cheese. Soft cheeses, including Brie, Camembert and cream cheese, freeze well.

Cottage cheese and cream cheeses have a comparatively short life and must be kept covered in the refrigerator.

PRESENTING THE CHEESE BOARD

A cheese board or platter is one of the best ways of finishing a meal; many people prefer the sharp flavour to a sweet, and others will return to cheese after the sweet, to finish off the last of a dry wine or to enjoy a glass of port.

A good cheese board does not have to offer the number of cheeses that might be available in a restaurant, but there should be a good variety. A balance of hard and soft cheeses, mild and full flavoured ones is the most important consideration and the colours and shapes of the pieces make it more interesting visually. A fairly modest but well-balanced board would offer, say, English Cheddar and Caerphilly, Stilton or Roquefort, Brie and Gouda. Many people will be delighted if you offer something new or unusual for them to try; others will be disappointed if their favourite, good, English cheese is not there.

The board itself may be any attractive platter large enough to hold your chosen selection without looking crowded. For a small selection, an old-fashioned china dish with its own cover is ideal – these are usually a pretty shape and they are perfectly designed for keeping the cheese in good condition, covered but airy. For more pieces, a well-scrubbed bread board or a meat dish serves the purpose, and may also be large enough to accommodate a garnish such as celery, or a small bunch of grapes. For a big party use a tray or the top of a trolley; the first has handles, the latter wheels and either will overcome the problem of lifting a very heavy board carrying a large selection of cheeses. Provide 2 or 3 knives so that the person taking Cheddar does not get unwelcome traces of Stilton

Spaghetti con formaggio is covered in melted cheese

with it.

To go with the cheese, offer a selection of plain and sweet biscuits, and a few salty crackers, or a basket of chunky breads or rolls. Several small dishes of fresh, unsalted butter, in small chunks or individual pats, saves endless passing of a single dish.

Nothing looks more attractive or goes better with cheese than a big bowl of fresh fruit. Polished apples and pears, freshly washed peaches and nuts are probably the most popular at this stage of the meal. Again, make sure there are enough small, dessert knives to go round – it is difficult to skin a peach with an ordinary table knife.

For a change, try serving a selection of crisp salad vegetables with the cheese. Quartered lettuce hearts, chunks of celery, chicory leaves, tomato wedges, small whole radishes and carrot sticks all go down well, with the addition of a little salt.

SPAGHETTI CON FORMAGGIO
serves 2

5 oz. spaghetti
½ lb. lean streaky bacon, rinded and chopped
2 oz. onion, skinned and coarsely grated
1 oz. butter
¼ lb. button mushrooms, sliced
salt and freshly ground black pepper
1 tbsp. salad oil
6 oz. mature Cheddar cheese, grated
chopped parsley

A quick and appetizing supper – asparagus au gratin

Cook the spaghetti in boiling salted water for 10 minutes. Put the chopped bacon in a frying pan and fry gently for 3 minutes, stirring occasionally with a wooden spoon. Add the onion and cook for a further 1 minute. Add the butter and sliced mushrooms, season lightly and cook for 4 minutes, stirring occasionally. Drain the pasta and return it to the pan with the salad oil. Using 2 forks, coat the spaghetti in the oil until it glistens. Light the grill.

Turn the spaghetti into a flameproof dish and spoon the bacon and mushroom mixture on top. Sprinkle with grated cheese and grill under a fierce heat for about 30 seconds. Sprinkle with chopped parsley before serving.

ASPARAGUS AU GRATIN
serves 6

1 lb. asparagus, fresh or frozen
2 oz. butter
4 level tbsps. flour
1 pint (2½ cups) creamy milk
3 tbsps. port
1 oz. Parmesan cheese, grated
3 oz. Cheddar cheese, finely grated
salt and pepper

Trim fresh asparagus to even lengths. Plunge fresh or frozen asparagus into boiling salted water, bring to the boil again and blanch for 5 minutes. Drain.

Butter a shallow au gratin dish and arrange the asparagus in the base. Melt the butter, stir in the flour and cook for 1–2 minutes. Remove from the heat and whisk in the milk. Bring to the boil, stirring. Stir in the port, Parmesan and 1 oz. of the Cheddar. Adjust seasoning.

Use this sauce to coat the asparagus. Sprinkle remaining Cheddar over the top and bake towards the top of the oven at 400°F. (mark 6) for about 20 minutes.

CAULIFLOWER AU GRATIN
serves 4

2 lb. potatoes
2 eggs, beaten separately
salt and pepper
margarine
2 lb. cauliflower
10½-oz. can condensed cream of celery soup
2 tbsps. milk
4 oz. well-flavoured Cheddar cheese
2 oz. buttered crumbs

Peel potatoes and cook in boiling

salted water. Drain and sieve back into the pan, then beat in 2 tablespoons beaten egg. Season. Using a large star vegetable nozzle, pipe the potato round the edge of a shallow au gratin dish, brush with the remainder of the first egg. Brown in the oven at 400°F. (mark 6) for about 20 minutes, or under the grill.

Meanwhile, break the cauliflower into sprigs and cook in boiling salted water until tender but not mushy. Drain well and arrange in the centre of the potato.

In a saucepan, whisk together the soup, the second egg, milk and cheese. Bring to the boil, stirring, adjust seasoning and pour over the cauliflower. Top with the buttered crumbs and return to the oven or grill to reheat.

MUSHROOMS WITH GRUYERE
serves 4–6

1½ lb. firm button mushrooms
2 oz. butter
¼ pint (⅝ cup) water
2 tbsps. lemon juice
1 clove of garlic, skinned
salt and pepper
2 oz. Gruyère cheese, grated
2½ lb. potatoes, freshly boiled
2 tbsps. warm milk
1 oz. butter
pinch of grated nutmeg
1 egg yolk (optional)

Wipe the mushrooms with a damp cloth. In a large saucepan, melt the butter in the water, add the lemon juice, garlic, salt and pepper. Add the mushrooms and cook without covering over a fairly high heat until the moisture has evaporated (about 25 minutes). Remove the clove of garlic.

Sieve the potatoes and cream with the milk, butter, seasonings and egg yolk if used. Use to pipe a border round a flameproof dish. Place in a hot oven or under the grill to brown. Spoon the mushrooms into the centre of the potato border and sprinkle with grated cheese. Return to the heat to melt the cheese. Serve at once.

CORN AND CHEESE OMELETTE
serves 2

4 eggs
2 tbsps. water
salt and freshly ground black pepper
1 oz. butter
7-oz. can sweetcorn with peppers
2 oz. Lancashire cheese, grated

To make an omelette for 1 person, beat 2 eggs lightly with 1 tablespoon water. Season to taste. Heat ½ oz. butter in a heavy-bottomed frying pan, tilting the pan to grease the whole surface, and pour in the egg mixture. Stir gently with the back of a fork, from the sides towards the centre, until no liquid egg remains. Stop stirring and cook a little longer to lightly brown the omelette underneath. Meanwhile, heat the sweetcorn in a separate pan.

When the egg mixture has almost set, spread half the corn down the centre and towards one side. Sprinkle with 1 oz. grated cheese. Tilt the pan and let the omelette fold over.

Repeat for the second omelette. Serve at once.

CHEESE WHEEZIES
serves 2

½ lb. pork sausage meat
3 oz. Cheddar cheese
dried breadcrumbs
oil for deep frying
15-oz. can sweetcorn kernels
4 tomatoes, halved
black pepper
watercress, to garnish

Divide the sausage meat into 6 equal-size pieces. Cut the cheese into 6 equal-size cubes and wrap the sausage meat round each one. Roll into balls. Dip them into the breadcrumbs until well coated and then re-shape with your hands. Heat the oil to 350°F. and fry the sausage balls for about 5 minutes, until golden brown. Turn the wheezies once or twice during cooking so that they cook evenly. Meanwhile put the corn in a saucepan and warm over a low heat. Sprinkle the tomatoes with pepper and grill.
Arrange the wheezies on the corn, on individual plates, and garnish with the grilled tomatoes and watercress.

CHEESE FRITTERS
serves 2

2 oz. butter
1½ oz. (⅜ cup) flour
½ pint (1¼ cups) milk
salt and freshly ground black pepper
½ level tsp. dry mustard
6 oz. Edam cheese, rinded and diced
7½-oz. can button mushrooms, drained
1 egg, beaten with a little salt
2 oz. dried breadcrumbs
oil for deep frying

Melt the butter in a small pan. Remove from the heat and stir in the flour, return to the heat and cook gently for 30 seconds. Pour in the milk, stir thoroughly and bring to the boil. Season well with salt, pepper and mustard, remove from heat.
Add the diced cheese and the mushrooms to the sauce and blend well together. When cool shape the mixture into fritters with a spoon, coat with the beaten egg and roll in breadcrumbs. Pat the crumbs on firmly with a palette knife and carefully shake off any excess.
Heat the oil to 350°F. and deep fry the fritters for 5 minutes. Drain thoroughly on absorbent kitchen paper.
Serve at once, with salad and potato crisps.

Orange cheesecake is a delicious dessert for a special occasion

ORANGE CHEESECAKE
serves 6–8

3 oranges
juice of 1 lemon
2 level tbsps. powdered gelatine
2 eggs, separated
½ pint (1¼ cups) milk
3 oz. (⅜ cup) caster sugar
1 lb. 4 oz. plain cottage cheese
¼ pint (⅝ cup) double cream, whipped
extra whipped cream for decoration

For crumb base :
4 oz. digestive biscuits
2 oz. (¼ cup) caster sugar
2 oz. butter, melted
3 oranges, peeled and segmented

Finely grate the rind of 2 oranges, squeeze the juice from 3 and add the lemon juice. Put 4 tablespoons of the mixed juices in a small bowl and sprinkle the gelatine over.
Whisk together the egg yolks, milk and 2 oz. sugar; turn into a pan and cook without boiling for a few minutes. Add the soaked gelatine and stir continuously until dissolved.
Leave to cool until just starting to set; then add the grated orange rind and 6 more tablespoons mixed juices.
Sieve the cheese and beat it into the jelly mixture, or blend them together in an electric blender. Whisk the egg whites stiffly, add 1 oz. sugar and whisk again until stiff. Fold quickly into the almost set cheese mixture, followed by the whipped cream.
Turn into a 3-pint (9½-in.), deep, sloping-sided cake tin, its base lined with non-stick paper. Crush the biscuits and stir in the sugar and butter. Spread this over the cheese mixture and press lightly with a round-bladed knife. Chill thoroughly.
To serve, turn out and decorate with overlapping segments of orange and a whirl of double cream.

BLUE CHEESE DRESSING

3 tbsps. French dressing
½ oz. blue cheese
1 spring onion, skinned and snipped

Whisk the French dressing to emulsify it thoroughly. Chop the blue cheese as finely as possible and snip the onion with scissors. Mix thoroughly. Serve spooned over lettuce wedges.

STUFFED EGGS AU GRATIN
serves 4

15-oz. can celery hearts, drained
4 rashers streaky bacon, rinded
4 eggs, hard-boiled
4 oz. Cheddar cheese, grated
¾ pint (1⅞ cups) white sauce made mustard
4 slices white bread, crusts removed
butter, melted

Cut the celery hearts in thick slices and place in the base of a 2-pint casserole. Grill the bacon until crisp and crumble or chop it finely. Halve the eggs lengthwise and remove the yolks.
Cream the bacon and egg yolks together, fill the mixture into the egg whites and pair up the halves again. Place them on the bed of celery.
Mix most of the cheese into the white sauce, adding a little mustard to taste. Pour over the eggs. Dice the bread, dip in a little melted butter and spoon in a ring round the outer edge of the dish. Sprinkle the remaining cheese in the centre.
Place the dish under a low grill until the bread cubes are brown and the sauce bubbling.

VEAL CORDON BLEU
serves 4

4 veal escalopes, unbeaten (6–7 oz. each)
4 slices of lean cooked ham
4 slices Gruyère cheese
2 oz. butter
3 tbsps. cooking oil
½ pint (1¼ cups) rich brown stock
¼ pint (⅝ cup) Madeira
freshly ground black pepper

Bat out escalopes until of even thickness – about ¼ in. Top each with a slice of ham cut to fit. Cover half with a slice of cheese and fold escalopes in 2. Secure with 2 cocktail sticks.
Melt the butter and oil in a large frying pan. Fry the escalopes quickly on each side. Reduce heat and cook for about 6 minutes on each side until tender and golden brown. Add stock and Madeira and simmer on top of the stove for 5 minutes.
Remove the meat and keep hot on a serving dish. Season the juices with black pepper and boil rapidly to reduce. Take the cocktail sticks from the escalopes, cover with the juices and serve.

CHOOSING YOUR MEAT

All meat needs to be hung in a suitable temperature and for the correct length of time before it is sold, otherwise it is tough and tasteless. Any reputable butcher will see that this is done.

A shoulder of lamb has more fat but also more flavour than the leg

BEEF

What to look for

1. The lean should be bright red, the fat a creamy yellow.
2. There should be small flecks of fat through the lean; this fat (called marbling) helps to keep the lean moist and tender when the meat is cooking.
3. There should be no line of gristle between lean and fat–this usually suggests the meat has come from an old animal and it may be tough.

Chuck and blade

Fairly lean with no bone, suitable for stewing and casseroles. Allow 6–8 oz. per person.

Rib

A large joint, sold on the bone or boned and rolled. Usually roasted. With bone, allow 8–12 oz. per person; without bone, allow 6–8 oz. per person. (Wing rib is sirloin without the fillet.)

Sirloin

A large joint including the under-cut which is particularly tender. Usually sold on the bone, but also boned and rolled. Almost always roasted. With bone, allow 8–12 oz. per person; without bone, allow 6–8 oz. per person.

Rump

Cut into steaks for grilling and frying; no bone.

Aitchbone

A big joint with a large bone, often boned or partially boned for convenience when carving. Usually roasted, but also boiled and braised. Sometimes salted and boiled. Allow 12 oz. per person.

Topside

A lean joint with no bone; good flavour. Usually slow roasted, but also braised and pot roasted. Allow 6–8 oz. per person.

Silverside

A boneless joint needing long, slow cooking such as braising. Often salted, for boiling. Allow 8–12 oz. per person.

Flank *(the belly–may be thick or thin)*

A boneless cut, rather coarse. Needs slow, moist cooking such as stewing, braising or pot roasting. Allow 6–8 oz. per person.

Brisket

A fatty joint but with a good flavour; sold on and off the bone. Slow roast, braise or stew; often salted for boiling. With bone, allow 8–12 oz. per person; without bone, allow 6–8 oz. per person.

LAMB, MUTTON

What to look for

1. The younger the animal the paler the flesh; in a young lamb it is light pink, while in a mature animal it is light red.
2. A slight blue tinge to the bones suggests that the animal is young.
3. The fat is firm and white, or creamy coloured.

Scrag and middle neck

A high proportion of bone and fat but a good flavour. Suitable for stews and casseroles. Allow 8–12 oz. per person, on the bone.

Best end of neck

A series of tiny cutlets that may be divided up and fried or grilled, or left as a whole joint and roasted. 2 joints, back to back, form a crown of lamb. Allow 12 oz. per person.

Loin

A prime cut sold on the bone or boned, stuffed and rolled for roasting, or divided into chops for grilling or frying. When roasting with the bone, allow 12 oz. per person; without bone, allow 4–6 oz. per person.

Chump

Cut into chops for grilling, frying and casseroles. Allow 1–2 chops per person.

Leg

A good cut for roasting. With bone, allow 12 oz. per person. Cut the meat off the bone for kebabs etc.

Breast

A rather fatty cut, usually boned, stuffed and rolled. Roasted, braised, stewed. With bone, allow 8–12 oz. per person.

Shoulder

A large joint with more fat, but often with more flavour, than the leg. Usually roasted. Allow 12 oz. per person on the bone.

VEAL

What to look for

1. The flesh should be light in colour, fine textured, pale pink, soft and moist; avoid flabby, wet meat.
2. If the flesh looks bluish or mottled it generally means it comes from an older animal or is rather stale.
3. The fat–of which there is very little–should be firm and pinkish or creamy white.

Best end of neck

Sold on the bone, or boned, stuffed and rolled. Suitable for roasting, braising and stewing; if divided into cutlets, suitable for sautéing or frying. With bone, allow about 1 lb. per person.

Loin

A prime cut for roasting, either on the bone or boned, stuffed and rolled. Also used for sautés and braised or divided into chops for grilling or frying. With bone, allow 8 oz. per person.

Fillet

Sold in the piece for roasting (usually boned and stuffed before cooking), or cut into thin slices or escalopes for frying. Without bone, allow 4–6 oz. per person.

Breast

Good flavour; usually boned, stuffed and roasted, best cooked slowly. With bone, allow 1 lb. per person.

Shoulder

An awkward shape but suitable for roasting if boned, stuffed and rolled. Portions of shoulder meat are often sold for pies and stews. With bone, allow 1 lb. per person.

PORK

What to look for

1. The lean should be pale pink, moist and slightly marbled with fat.
2. There should be a good outer layer of firm, white fat, with a thin, elastic skin; if the joint is to be roasted, get the butcher to score the rind.
3. The bones should be small and pinkish (which denotes a young animal).

Spare rib

A fairly lean cut, good for roasting, but can be cut up for braising and stewing. Also divided into chops for grilling and frying. With bone, allow 8–12 oz. per person.

Loin

A prime cut which often includes the kidney. Best roasted, it can be cooked on the bone or boned and stuffed; also divided into chops for grilling. With bone, allow 8–12 oz. per person; without bone, allow 4 oz. per person.

Leg

A prime cut, but rather large, so it is often cut into 2. Roasted on the bone or boned and stuffed. Sometimes pickled for boiling. With bone, allow 8–12 oz. per person; without bone, allow 4 oz. per person.

Belly

A fatty cut, usually sold salted for boiling. May be roasted or braised, cut into strips for frying or minced for pâtés. Allow 4–6 oz. per person.

Hand and spring

The foreleg, a little on the fatty side. Suitable for roasting, boiling and stewing. Hand is good salted and boiled. Allow 12 oz. per person.

CARVING A JOINT

When a joint is well carved, the meat looks nice on the plate and goes further. Carving is an art most people can master, given a good knife. If you tell the butcher how you want to serve the meat, he will prepare the joint the easiest way for carving.

In order to carve successfully, the 1 essential tool is a long-bladed, sharp knife. To maintain the sharpness, use a steel or a patent sharpener every time you carve. (To use a steel, draw each side of the blade in turn smoothly down and across with rapid strokes, holding the blade at an angle of 45° to the steel.) Careless sharpening can inflict permanent damage on the knife or your finger!

Also essential is a sharp 2-pronged fork to hold the meat, with a guard to protect your hand should the knife slip. The final accessory is a meat dish with sharp prongs to hold the meat in place – this is by no means necessary, but it is extremely helpful.

Meat is usually best cut against the grain, except when it is very tender (undercut, for instance is cut with the grain). The grain of the meat runs lengthwise along the carcass, hence joints are carved from the outside to the centre of the animal.

Before you start to carve, examine the structure of the joint, and notice the exact distribution of bone, lean meat and fat. Carve standing up and use long, even strokes, keeping the blade at the same angle throughout, to give neat, uniform slices. As you carve, move the knife to and fro, cutting cleanly without bearing down on the meat, which presses out the juices. Serve the carved slices on to really hot plates.

Beef and veal (except fillet) are carved very thinly, but pork and lamb are cut in slices about $\frac{1}{4}$ in. thick. If the joint has a bone, take the knife right up to it, so that eventually the bone is left quite clean.

BEEF

Sirloin of beef on the bone
Stand the joint on its back with the fillet uppermost. First carve out the flank, then remove the fillet from the bone and carve both these into thin slices. Then turn the joint so that the upper-cut is on top, making a long slice against the back bone. Further slices will then separate easily.

Rib
Stand the joint on edge on the bone. Slice downwards along the full length of the joint, cutting each slice down to the bone (if necessary, cutting behind the ribs to free the meat) and slanting a little away from the cut edge, so that the bone is left clean. Support the slices with the fork to prevent them breaking.

Boneless joints
Carve against the grain, usually horizontally. In the case of a long piece of roast fillet, carve downwards.

VEAL

Stuffed breast
Cut downwards in fairly thick slices, right through the joint. Remove the string from each part of the joint as it is carved.

Chump end leg
The bone is sometimes removed and replaced by stuffing. Cut across the grain (i.e. horizontally) into medium-thick slices, right across the joint.
If the bone has been left in, cut the meat in long slices following the shape of the bone. When the bone is reached and cleared, turn the joint over and continue carving vertically on the other side of the bone.

Loin
One of the few joints carved with the grain of the meat. Carve long slices down the length of the back, turning the knife to follow the bone and release the slices. Then turn joint round to complete the cut. Take smaller slices from the chump end and turn the joint over and remove smaller slices.

LAMB

Leg
Begin by cutting a wedge-shaped slice from the centre of the meatier side of the joint. Carve slices from each side of the cut, gradually turning the knife to get larger slices and ending parallel to the bone. Turn the joint over, remove the fat, and carve in long flat slices along the leg.

Shoulder
Cut a long thick slice down to the bone from the centre of the meatier side of the joint. Carve small slices from each side of the hump on the blade bone down to the shank until the whole surface is clean.
Turn the joint over, remove the fat and carve in horizontal slices.

Best end of neck
Remove the chine bone then cut down between the ribs, dividing the joint into cutlets.

Saddle
First carve the meat from the top of the joint in long slices, cutting downwards, to and parallel with the backbone. Do this at each side of the bone, taking about 4 slices from either side of the saddle.

Stuffed breast
Cut downwards in fairly thick slices, right through the joint.

PORK

Loin of pork
Sever the chine bone from the chop bones and put to one side. Divide into chops by cutting between the bones.

Boned and rolled
Remove the string from each part of the joint as it is carved. Cut through the crackling where it was scored half-way along the joint. Lift off the crackling and cut into pieces. Carve the meat into slices.

Leg
Use the point of the knife to cut through the crackling; it is usually easier to remove it and then divide it into portions. Carve as for leg of lamb, but medium-thick.

Spring
Remove the rib bones underneath, then turn the crackling back on top. Remove some of the crackling before carving. Distribute fat and lean evenly by cutting alternate slices from either end until the bone is reached. Turn joint over and carve the meat from the other side of the bone.

GAMMON

Joints for boiling are usually boned and rolled. Carve as for boned and rolled beef, but in slightly thicker slices.

HAM

Cold cooked ham is best carved on a ham stand as this supports the awkwardly shaped joint. A specially long thin knife is used. Carve in the thinnest possible slices, as for leg of lamb.

ROASTING

There is no method of cooking that can give a tastier result than roasting, with so little trouble. Plainly roasted meat, served with fresh vegetables and rich gravy is considered one of the best possible meals.

Meat to be roasted must be prime quality, tender and juicy. Roasting is a quick method of cooking, and will not break down tough, sinewy fibres; joints that are likely to be at all tough should be pot roasted, braised or casseroled instead. Guidance as to which cuts are suitable is given in the section 'Choosing your meat', but be guided by your butcher as well—only roast those joints which he recommends and you will not have cause for complaint.

TRADITIONAL ROASTING

It is traditional to roast in the oven at a high temperature—425°F. (mark 7). This sears the joint quickly on the outside, giving a good meaty flavour, and is the ideal way when you know the meat is of prime quality—well hung and tender. Many people prefer to roast at 375°F. (mark 5). This is the best way if in doubt about quality and for small joints, as it keeps the joint more moist than the higher temperature, there is less shrinkage and the meat is likely to be more tender, though the flavour may not be quite as good. Before starting to cook, arrange the shelves in the oven so that there is room for the joint and so that the meat will be in the centre. Pre-heat the oven; if the meat is placed in a cold oven and heated too slowly, the juices will run too freely, leaving the joint dry and tasteless.

Put the joint in the roasting tin so that the cut surfaces are exposed and the fattest part is on top; this automatically bastes the joint. If the natural fat is meagre, top the meat with some dripping or lard. During the cooking time, spoon the hot fat and juices over the meat from time to time, to keep it moist and juicy. Never pierce the meat with a fork or knife as this will allow the juices to escape, leaving the joint dry.

For those who like less fatty meat, it is a good idea to place the joint on a rack or grid in the roasting tin, so that it is kept free of the dripping. This is particularly convenient if roast potatoes or Yorkshire pudding are being cooked, as they can be placed under the grid and will absorb all the juices and the flavour of the meat.

COVERED ROASTING

Roasting in a covered tin, in aluminium foil or in a transparent roasting bag helps to keep the oven clean. It also keeps the meat moist; because this method is also partly steaming, it breaks down the fibres more thoroughly than conventional roasting, making the meat more tender and rendering the fat almost to nothing. To brown and crisp the outside of the joint, remove the lid or open the foil 30 minutes before the end of the cooking time; transparent roasting bags allow the joint to brown without this.

This is a good method for a joint that you suspect may be slightly tough, or if your family doesn't like any fat at all on meat. It does however tend to destroy some of the true open-roasted flavour. Potatoes cooked with a covered joint will not brown.

FROTHING

If you like a particularly brown, crisp outside to the meat, sprinkle with flour and salt 15 minutes before the end of the cooking time and leave uncovered.

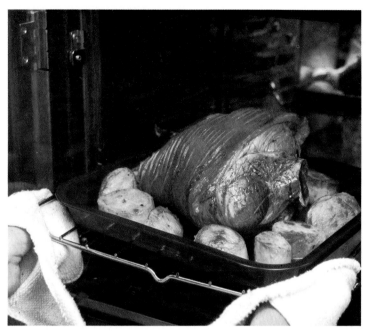

Score the skin of pork to allow the crackling to cook crisply through

Use an evenly shaped joint for successful spit roasting

CRACKLING

The outside skin of pork is left on to form 'crackling'. Make sure this is scored deeply and evenly at ¼-in. intervals all over the joint, or it will be extremely difficult to carve. To make the crackling extra crisp and golden brown, rub cooking oil and salt into the skin before cooking.

MEAT THERMOMETERS

A meat thermometer is an infallible guide to when the joint is cooked. Insert it into the thickest part of the joint (but not against the bone) before you start cooking. The thermometer then registers the temperature at the innermost part of the joint and when it shows the correct internal temperature (see chart), the meat is correctly cooked. This is particularly useful with beef, ensuring that you can have it rare, medium or well done, just as you wish. (It is of course necessary to work out the approximate cooking time, so that you know roughly what time to start cooking.)

SPIT ROASTING (OR ROTISSERIE COOKING)

Spit roasting is a development of the original method of cooking meat, in front of an open fire. (The closed-oven method now commonly used should more properly be called baking.) The flavour of spit roasted meat is as different from oven roasted as the latter is from that of meat roasted in a covered tin. Gas and electric cookers are available fitted with a spit, or you can buy a separate, electrically operated model. On a cooker, the spit is best if fitted to the grill unit—spit roasting in the

oven shows very little difference from ordinary oven roasting. But either way the joint browns more evenly than oven roasted meat and needs even less attention, since it is completely self basting.

Any joint, with bone or boneless, that is suitable for quick roasting may be roasted on a spit. It must, however, be shaped as evenly as possible, so that it will revolve steadily (e.g. a shoulder of lamb on the bone is not really satisfactory). If it is not a compact shape, remove the bone, stuff the joint if you wish, roll it and tie with string. Frozen meat must be completely thawed before cooking starts.

First turn on the heat and allow the grill or oven to become very hot. Push the shaft through the meat, push the holding forks into place on either side and secure them, to hold the meat firmly in place. Place the loaded shaft in position and start the motor. Allow the shaft to revolve several times before you leave it, to make sure that there is no obstruction and it is turning evenly. Cook the meat on full heat for 5 minutes or according to the manufacturer's instructions, to sear the surface, then reduce the heat and cook for the appropriate time. Individual manufacturers recommend different cooking times, so follow the instructions given with your model. If you wish, the joint may be basted from time to time with the juices and fat from the drip tray, though this is not strictly necessary. To vary the flavour, try adding fruit juice or cider to the juices, or more conventionally a sliced onion or a clove of garlic.

COOKING TIMES AND OVEN TEMPERATURES

Beef	on the bone	425°F. (mark 7)	15 min. per lb. plus 15 min. (rare)
		425°F. (mark 7)	20 min. per lb. plus 20 min. (medium)
		375°F. (mark 5)	25 min. per lb. (medium-well done)
	boned and rolled	425°F. (mark 7)	20 min. per lb. plus 20 min. (rare)
		425°F. (mark 7)	25 min. per lb. plus 25 min. (medium)
		375°F. (mark 5)	30 min. per lb. (medium-well done)
Lamb	on the bone	425°F. (mark 7)	20 min. per lb. plus 20 min.
		350°F. (mark 4)	27 min. per lb. plus 27 min.
	boned and rolled	425°F. (mark 7)	25 min. per lb. plus 25 min.
		350°F. (mark 4)	35 min. per lb. plus 35 min.
Veal	on the bone	425°F. (mark 7)	25 min. per lb. plus 25 min.
	boned and rolled	425°F. (mark 7)	30 min. per lb. plus 30 min.
Pork	on the bone	425°F. (mark 7)	25 min. per lb. plus 25 min.
	boned and rolled	375°F. (mark 5)	30–35 min. per lb. plus 35 min.

USING A MEAT THERMOMETER

Meat		Temperature of meat	Results
Beef	Rare	140°F.	Very rare when hot, but idea when cold.
	Medium	160°F.	Brown meat, but with blood running from it; pale pinkish tinge when cold.
	Well done	170°F.	Well cooked. Tends to be d when cold.
	Very well done	180°F.	Fibres breaking up; fat rendered down.
Lamb		180°F.	Moist, brown meat.
Veal		180°F.	Moist, pale meat.
Pork		190°F.	Moist, pale meat.

YORKSHIRE PUDDING
for beef

4 oz. (1 cup) plain flour
a pinch of salt
1 egg
½ pint (1¼ cups) milk or milk and water
1 oz. lard or dripping

Sift together the flour and salt, make a well in the centre and break in the egg. Stir in half the liquid and beat the mixture until it is smooth. Add the remaining liquid gradually and beat until well mixed.

Put the butter in a tin measuring about 7 in. square and heat it in the oven. Pour in the batter and bake at 425°F. (mark 7) for about 30 minutes, until well risen. Cut into squares and serve at once.

HORSERADISH CREAM
for beef

2 tbsps. grated horseradish
2 tsps. lemon juice
2 level tsps. sugar
pinch of dry mustard (optional)
¼ pint (⅝ cup) double cream

Mix the horseradish, lemon juice, sugar and mustard. Whip the cream until it just leaves a trail, then fold in the horseradish mixture.

HORSERADISH SAUCE
for beef

¼ pint (⅝ cup) white sauce
1–2 tbsps. grated horseradish
1 tbsp. vinegar

Mix the ingredients thoroughly and serve warm.

MINT SAUCE
for lamb

small bunch of mint, washed
2 level tsps. sugar
1 tbsp. boiling water
1–2 tbsps. vinegar

Strip the mint leaves from the stalks and put with the sugar on a board. Chop finely. Put in a sauce boat, add the boiling water and stir until the sugar is dissolved. Stir in the vinegar to taste. Leave the sauce to stand for 1 hour before serving.

Most people like roast beef slightly rare

MINT JELLY
for lamb

6 lb. cooking apples
2¼ pints (5⅝ cups) water
a bunch of fresh mint
2¼ pints (5⅝ cups) vinegar
6–8 tbsps. chopped mint
green colouring (optional)

Wash and roughly chop the apples, do not peel or core. Put in a large pan with the water and bunch of mint and simmer until really soft and pulpy. Add the vinegar and boil for 5 minutes. Strain through a jelly cloth. Measure the extract and return it to the pan with 1 lb. sugar to every pint of extract. Stir until the sugar has dissolved and boil rapidly until a 'jell' is obtained on testing a few drops on a cold saucer.

Stir in the chopped mint and a few drops of colouring, if required. Skim and turn into warm, dry jars and seal.

RED-CURRANT JELLY
for lamb

3 lb. red-currants
1 pint (2½ cups) water
sugar

Wash the fruit but don't remove the stalks. Put into a pan with the water and simmer gently until the red-currants are really soft and pulpy. Strain through a jelly cloth, measure the extract and return it to the pan with 1 lb. sugar to each pint of extract. Stir until the sugar has dissolved and then boil rapidly until a 'jell' is obtained on testing a few drops on a cold saucer. Skim, turn into warm, dry jars and seal. Cranberry jelly is made in the same way.

APPLE SAUCE
for pork

1 lb. cooking apples, peeled and cored
1 oz. butter
a little sugar (optional)

Slice the apples into a pan, add 2–3 tablespoons water and simmer, covered, until soft – about 10 minutes. Beat to a pulp with a wooden spoon, then sieve or purée in an electric blender if wished. Stir in the butter and add a little sugar if the apples are very tart.

GOOSEBERRY SAUCE
for pork

½ lb. gooseberries, topped and tailed
1 oz. butter
1–2 oz. sugar (optional)

Stew the fruit in as little water as possible, until soft and pulped. Beat well then sieve the fruit or puree in a blender. Add the butter and a little sugar if the fruit is very sour.

CUMBERLAND SAUCE
for ham and mutton

1 orange
1 lemon
4 level tbsps. red-currant jelly
4 tbsps. port
2 level tsps. cornflour
2 tsps. water

Pare the rind thinly from the orange and lemon, cut in strips, cover with water and simmer for 5 minutes. Squeeze the juice from both fruits. Put the red-currant jelly, orange juice and lemon juice in a pan, stir until the jelly dissolves, simmer for 5 minutes and add the port. Blend the corn-flour and water to a smooth cream and stir in the red-currant mixture. Return the sauce to the pan and re-heat, stirring until it thickens and clears. Drain the strips of rind and add to the sauce.

SAGE AND ONION STUFFING
for pork

2 large onions, skinned and chopped
1 oz. butter
4 oz. fresh breadcrumbs
2 level tsps. dried sage
salt and pepper

Put the onions in a pan of cold water, bring to the boil and cook until tender – about 10 minutes. Drain well, add the other in-gredients and mix well.

PRUNE AND APPLE STUFFING
for pork

4 oz. prunes, soaked and stoned
8 oz. cooking apples, peeled and cored
4 oz. cooked long grain rice
2 oz. shredded suet
2 oz. almonds, blanched and shredded
salt and pepper
juice and grated rind of ½ a lemon
1 egg, beaten

Cut the prunes into quarters and roughly chop the apples. Mix the fruit, rice, suet and nuts. Season to taste, add the lemon rind and juice and bind with beaten egg.

CELERY STUFFING
for pork and lamb

4 sticks celery, scrubbed and finely sliced
1 onion, skinned and finely chopped
2 tbsps. cooking oil
juice and grated rind of 1 orange
salt and pepper
4 oz. fresh white breadcrumbs

Place the celery in a pan, cover with boiling water and simmer for 15–20 minutes, until tender. Heat the oil and sauté the onion until golden.

Drain the celery and put it in a basin; mix with the onion, orange juice and rind. Season well and add the crumbs. Mix carefully with a fork.

GRILLING

Grilling is a primitive method of cooking in which the food is cooked by direct heat from an open flame. One of the best ways of grilling is over charcoal, but this is obviously an outdoor party method now—we normally settle for the more conventional gas and electric grills.

The principle remains the same though. The grill should be turned on well before it is needed, to allow it to get really hot. The meat or fish is brushed with oil or melted butter if it is very lean and placed on the heated grid, in a grill pan. Cooking is then started with the grill on full heat, and if the food starts to burn, the heat is lowered.

GRILLING MEAT

Since grilling is a quick method of cooking, it is suitable only for the best cuts of meat; fresh, under-hung meat and the poorer cuts will remain tough. Many meats benefit from marinading first; for the marinade, mix 2 parts salad oil with 1 part vinegar or lemon juice, add a little chopped onion and some salt and pepper. Keep turning the meat in this marinade for about 2 hours. The remaining marinade may then be used in a sauce to serve with the meat. If you are not marinading, simply sprinkle the meat with salt and pepper (for beef use pepper only), and brush with a little oil or melted butter.

Steak, chops, kidneys, tender liver, sausages, bacon and fish are the foods usually grilled; the only vegetables suitable for this method of cooking are tomatoes and mushrooms.

Steak: Marinade the meat for 2 hours, or brush with melted butter or oil. Cook under fierce heat for 1 minute on each side, then reduce the heat to moderate and cook for the required time, turning the meat from time to time.

Grilling times in minutes:

Thick-ness	Rare	Medium	Well done
¾ in.	5	9–10	14–15
1 in.	6–7	10–12	15
1½ in.	10	12–14	18–20

Chops, lamb and pork: Remove any skin and central bone, and trim neatly. If the chops are unshapely, tie with string or fasten with a skewer; alternatively, remove all the bone, roll neatly and tie or skewer into place. Grilling times: 10–15 minutes (lamb), 15–20 minutes (pork).

Liver: Wash, wipe and cut into slices ¼–½ in. thick. Grilling time: 5–10 minutes.

Kidneys: Wash, skin and cut in half. Remove the core and, if liked, thread on to a skewer to make handling easy. Grilling time: 10 minutes.

Bacon and ham: Lean rashers, such as gammon, require brushing with oil or melted butter. For thinly cut rashers, cook for 2–3 minutes, until the fat is transparent on the one side; turn and cook the other side. Thick rashers may take 10–15 minutes.

Sausages: Prick the sausages and grill slowly, under a medium heat, turning frequently until well browned all over. Grilling time: 15–20 minutes.

MIXED GRILL
serves 4

4 best end of neck lamb chops
½ lb. chipolata sausages
2 lamb's kidneys
4 rashers of bacon
4 tomatoes
4 mushrooms, washed
salt and pepper
melted butter or oil

Trim the chops, separate the sausages, skin, halve and core the kidneys, trim the rind from the bacon, halve the tomatoes and trim the ends of the mushroom stalks. Brush the chops, kidneys, tomatoes and mushrooms with fat or oil and season. Heat the grill and place the tomatoes (cut side up) and the mushrooms (stalks up) in the grill pan, where they will be basted by the juices from the other food and will cook without further attention.

Put the grill grid in place and put on the chops, sausages and kidneys. Cook them under a medium heat, allowing 14–16 minutes altogether and turning the food on the grid frequently to ensure even cooking. The kidneys will probably be cooked first, so remove these and keep them warm. Replace them by the bacon rashers and cook for a further 3–5 minutes. If the grill is small and all the food has to be cooked separately, heat the oven to a low temperature to keep the food warm as it cooks.

Serve the mixed grill on a large plate, with a simple garnish of watercress and lemon. Traditional accompaniments are chipped or matchstick potatoes, and for more formal occasions maître d'hôtel butter.

Note: Small pieces of fillet or rump steak may be substituted for the lamb chop; a small portion of calf's or lamb's liver is sometimes included.

NOISETTES OF LAMB

These are prepared from a whole best end of neck. Ask the butcher to chine the meat, but not to cut through the rib bones.

Remove the chine bones, skin the meat and remove all the rib bones. Season the inside of the meat with salt, freshly ground pepper and herbs and roll it up tightly, starting from the thick end, rolling towards the flap and wrapping it round. Tie securely at 1½-in. intervals.

Using a sharp knife, cut up in portions, with the string coming in the centre of each one.

Brown quickly on both sides under a hot grill, then reduce the

heat and cook for a further 10–15 minutes turning once, until the meat is cooked right through. Top with pats of savoury butter.

GRILLING FISH

Most fish can be grilled, though the drier types are better cooked in other ways. The fish should be seasoned, sprinkled with lemon juice and (except for oily fish such as herrings) brushed liberally with melted butter. Cutlets should be tied neatly into shape.

Fillets and large fish should be cooked in the grill pan rather than on the grid.

Cutlets and fillets: Grill first on one side for 3–10 minutes, depending on thickness, then turn with a flat, metal draining slice. Brush with fat and grill the second side. Serve very hot with a garnish

of grilled tomato halves or parsley sprigs and a sauce.

Whole fish: Wash and scale the fish. Score it with a sharp knife in 3–4 places on each side (this allows the heat to penetrate the thick flesh more quickly), season and brush with melted butter if required. Line the pan with foil if you wish, to catch the juices, place the fish on the grid or in the pan and grill rather slowly, so that the flesh cooks thoroughly without the outside burning.

Turn the fish once or twice, handling it carefully to prevent breaking. To test whether the fish is done, insert the back of a knife next to the bone to see if the flesh comes away easily. Serve with maître d'hôtel butter or melted butter, lemon wedges and chopped parsley.

GRILLED MULLET
serves 4

4 mullet, cleaned
3–4 tbsps. olive oil
3–4 tbsps. vinegar
piece of onion, skinned and finely chopped
few peppercorns
bay leaf or a few parsley stalks

Wash the fish and wipe them well. Put them in a dish with the oil, vinegar, onion, peppercorns and herbs; and leave to marinade for about 1 hour, turning them several times.

Drain the fish and put them on a greased grill grid. Cook under a medium heat for about 10 minutes, basting with some of the marinade and turning them once.

Serve with tomato sauce.

Noisettes of lamb topped with maître d'hôtel butter

GRILLED HERRINGS WITH MUSTARD SAUCE
serves 4

4 herrings, cleaned
½ pint (1¼ cups) white sauce
1 level tbsp. dry mustard
2 level tsps. sugar
1 tbsp. vinegar

Have the heads cut off and the fish cleaned but left whole. Wash and wipe them and make 2–3 diagonal cuts in the flesh on both sides of the fish and sprinkle with salt and pepper. Brush with oil or melted butter and cook on a greased grill grid for 10–15 minutes under a moderate heat, turning the fish once, until thoroughly cooked on both sides.

Make up the white sauce by using all milk or half milk and half fish stock. Blend the mustard, sugar

and vinegar to a smooth cream and stir into the sauce.

Serve the herrings hot, with the mustard sauce either poured over the fish or served separately in a gravy boat.

ACCOMPANIMENTS FOR GRILLS

SAVOURY BUTTERS
Serve these savoury butters chilled and cut into pats, 1 pat on each portion of meat or fish.

Anchovy butter: Beat 1 part of anchovies (pounded to a paste) with 2 parts butter. A little spice or flavouring may be added, but take care with salt – anchovies are very salty themselves.

Maître d'hôtel butter: Beat 4

oz. butter, mix in 2 tablespoons finely chopped parsley and a squeeze of lemon juice, with salt and cayenne pepper.

Chutney butter: Beat 2oz. butter with 2 oz. chutney and ¼ teaspoon lemon juice, until well blended.

Black butter (for meat): Melt 2 oz. butter in a pan and heat until dark brown. Add 1 tablespoon wine vinegar, a little salt and freshly ground black pepper and 1 teaspoon chopped parsley. Pour over the meat while still hot.

Black butter (for fish): Heat 2 oz. butter until lightly browned. Add 1 tablespoon vinegar, 2 teaspoons capers, cook for a further 2–3 minutes and pour over the fish. Sprinkle with chopped parsley and serve at once.

Garlic butter: Skin and crush a

Whole fish should be scored 2 or 3 times before grilling

large clove of garlic. Beat it well into the butter, to taste, and season lightly with salt and pepper.

Horseradish butter: Soften 4 oz. butter and add 2 tablespoons creamed horseradish. Beat them well together.

Green butter: Wash a small bunch of watercress and dry thoroughly. Chop finely. Beat 2 oz. of the watercress into 4 oz. softened butter until well blended.

MATCHSTICK POTATOES

Peel the potatoes and cut them into very small chips of matchstick size. Leave them to soak in cold water for at least 30 minutes. Drain and dry well on absorbent kitchen paper. Fry in hot deep fat for 3 minutes; drain on absorbent paper. Before serving, re-heat the fat and fry for a further 3 minutes.

SAUTE POTATOES

Peel the potatoes as thinly as possible. Cook in boiling salted water until just tender. Drain thoroughly and cut the hot potatoes into slices $\frac{1}{4}$ in. thick. Fry slowly in a little hot butter, turning them once so that they are crisp and golden on both sides. Drain well on absorbent kitchen paper and serve sprinkled with a little chopped parsley or chives.

GAME CHIPS

Scrub and peel the potatoes and slice very thinly into rounds using a mandoline slicer. Soak them in cold water and dry.

Fry in hot deep fat for 3 minutes. Remove from the fat and drain on absorbent paper. Before serving, reheat the fat and fry the chips for a further 3 minutes.

MAITRE D'HOTEL POTATOES

1 lb. potatoes
1 tbsp. olive oil
salt and freshly ground black pepper
chopped parsley
1 tbsp. vinegar

Boil the potatoes in their skins and peel the potatoes while still warm. Cut into $\frac{1}{4}$-in. slices. Heat the oil in a frying pan, add the rest of the ingredients and toss the sliced potatoes in the mixture until well heated. Serve at once.

CRISP FRIED ONION RINGS

4 large onions, skinned and cut into $\frac{1}{4}$ in. slices
a little milk
a little flour
salt and pepper
fat for deep frying

Separate the onion slices into rings and dip in the milk and then the seasoned flour. Heat the fat so that when one ring is dropped in, it rises to the surface surrounded by bubbles. Gradually add the rest of the rings to the fat and fry for 2–3 minutes until golden brown. Drain on crumpled absorbent kitchen paper, season and serve at once.

MARINADED MUSHROOMS

1$\frac{1}{2}$ lb. button mushrooms
juice of 1 large lemon
12 fl. oz. (1$\frac{1}{2}$ cups) wine vinegar
1 small clove of garlic, skinned and crushed
2 medium onions, skinned and chopped
1 bouquet garni
1 level tsp. salt
freshly ground black pepper
$\frac{1}{2}$ pint (1$\frac{1}{4}$ cups) olive oil
1$\frac{1}{2}$ level tbsps. tomato ketchup
chopped parsley, to garnish

Wipe the mushrooms. Put them in a pan with the lemon juice and enough water to cover and bring to the boil. Boil for 5 minutes then leave until cold.

Put the wine vinegar into a pan and add the garlic, chopped onion, bouquet garni, salt and pepper. Bring to the boil. Boil, uncovered, for 5 minutes. Remove the garlic and cool the liquor. Add the olive oil and tomato ketchup.

Drain the mushrooms well and put into a deep bowl. Pour the dressing over and leave to mar-

inade for several hours, or overnight, in the refrigerator.

To serve, lift out the mushrooms, place in a shallow dish, sprinkle with the chopped parsley, and pour over them the dressing, strained through a sieve.

SAUTE CUCUMBER

Peel the cucumber and cut in half lengthwise. Cut into dice and cook very gently in butter in a covered pan for 10–15 minutes.

Serve with a white sauce or melted butter.

CREAMED SPINACH

Allow $\frac{1}{2}$ lb. uncooked spinach per person. Wash well in several waters to remove all grit, and strip off any coarse stalks. Chop roughly. Pack into a saucepan with only the water that clings to the leaves after washing. Heat gently, turning the spinach occasionally, then bring to the boil and cook gently until soft – about 10–15 minutes. Drain thoroughly. Push through a nylon sieve or purée in a blender. Add 1–2 tablespoons of cream and some salt and pepper. Reheat before serving.

SAVOURY LEMON SAUCE

rind and juice of 1 lemon
$\frac{1}{2}$ pint (1$\frac{1}{4}$ cups) white sauce, (using half milk and half fish or chicken stock)
1–2 level tsps. sugar
salt and pepper
1–2 tbsps. single cream (optional)

Simmer the lemon rind in the milk and stock for 5 minutes, strain, and use the liquid to make a white sauce. When it has thickened, stir in the lemon juice and sugar and season to taste.

If the sauce is too sharp, stir in a little single cream just before serving.

Serve with grilled fish or chicken.

BLACK BUTTER SAUCE

2 oz. unsalted butter
1$\frac{1}{2}$ tbsps. tarragon vinegar
salt and pepper
2 tsps. finely chopped parsley

Cut the butter into small pieces and put in a small strong pan. Heat until it is a golden brown colour, then remove from the heat and cool. Meanwhile put the vinegar in another small pan and reduce to about half the original quantity. Stir in the butter and re-heat. Season and add the parsley.

Serve with plaice, sole and skate.

Grilled gammon is delicious with a fruit garnish

FRYING

Frying is a quick method of cooking, giving a tasty, succulent result. Natural fat makes an important contribution to the flavour of many foods, and frying in fat can add extra flavour where this is lacking in the original. Fry tender cuts of meat–steaks, chops, lambs' or calves' liver and kidney, gammon and bacon rashers. Do not fry the poorer cuts of meat as these need long, slow cooking to break down the tough fibres and if fried will remain hard and tough. Most fish can be fried, and it is a particularly good method of cooking for those with little natural flavour or colour. Fried eggs and egg dishes such as pancakes and omelettes are traditional favourites and a large selection of vegetables can be fried. Certain sweet foods–doughnuts, fruit fritters–are also fried.

Frying may be done in shallow fat, or by completely submerging the food in deep fat; either way there are certain basic rules for success.

1. Never add the food to the pan until the fat reaches the correct frying temperature (see chart and individual recipes). If the fat is not hot enough it will soak into the food, instead of sealing the outside crisply, and the result will be soggy and unpleasant.

2. Do not add too much food to the pan at once, as this lowers the temperature of the fat. Add a small piece at a time. Maintain the temperature by carefully controlling the heat.

3. Never overload the pan, or foods will start to stew rather than fry.

4. After frying, drain foods thoroughly on absorbent kitchen paper.

Shallow fat frying

For shallow frying, use a small quantity of fat in a shallow frying pan. This method is suitable for steaks, chops, liver, young chicken, sausages, fish steaks, white fish such as sole, and pancakes–all these need only sufficient fat to prevent them sticking to the pan. Made-up dishes such as fish cakes and rissoles can also be shallow fried, but need enough fat to half-cover them. In this case, most of the foods require a coating of batter or egg and breadcrumbs. Cooking oils, lard, dripping and butter are all suitable for shallow frying. When frying with butter, put a little oil in the pan first to

Dip in beaten egg, then press the breadcrumbs on well

Deep fat frying guide

Food	Size	Temperature	Time
Chipped potatoes Fry for 5 minutes at 360°F., remove from pan and raise temperature to 380°F. Fry for a further 3 minutes	$\frac{1}{4}$ in. thick	360°F. 380°F.	5 minutes 3 minutes
Potato croquettes (egg and breadcrumb coating)	$3\frac{1}{2}$ in. long	375°F.	3–4 minutes
Scotch eggs (egg and breadcrumb coating)	$3\frac{1}{2}$ in. by $3\frac{1}{2}$ in.	325°F.	10 minutes
Chicken Kiev (egg and breadcrumb coating)	4 in. by $2\frac{1}{2}$ in. (approx.)	325°F.	15 minutes
Fritters (using fritter batter) pineapple rings apple rings banana	$\frac{1}{4}$ in. thick $\frac{1}{4}$ in. thick 1 banana cut in half lengthwise	350°F. 350°F. 375°F.	5 minutes 4 minutes 2–3 minutes
Rechauffé dishes		360–380°F.	as recipe
Fish fillets (egg and breadcrumb or batter coating)	approx. $\frac{1}{2}$ in. thick	350–360°F.	5–10 minutes
Doughnuts		350–360°F.	5–10 minutes

keep the butter from browning; when the oil is hot add an equal quantity of butter, then add more butter as the food starts to colour.

Deep fat frying

The food is cooked in sufficient fat to cover it completely. This method is used for batter coated fish, whitebait, chipped potatoes, doughnuts and made-up dishes such as croquettes and fritters. A deep pan and a wire basket are needed, with enough fat to come about three-quarters of the way up the pan; clarified beef fat (for less delicate foods), lard and oil are all suitable. The fat must be pure and free from moisture to prevent spitting or boiling over. After frying, cool the fat and strain it into a basin or wide-necked jar and cover; store it in a cool place for future use.

COATING BATTER – 1

4 oz. (1 cup) flour
pinch of salt
1 egg
$\frac{1}{4}$ pint ($\frac{5}{8}$ cup) milk or milk and water (approx.)

Mix together the flour, salt, egg, and sufficient liquid to give a stiff batter which will coat the back of a spoon; beat well until smooth. Dip the food into the batter, holding the pieces on a skewer or fork, and drain slightly before putting into the hot fat.

COATING BATTER – 2

4 oz. (1 cup) flour
pinch of salt
1 tbsp. oil
1 egg, separated
2–3 tbsps. water or milk and water

Mix together the flour, salt, oil and egg yolk with sufficient water to give a stiff batter which will coat the back of a spoon; beat until smooth. Just before using, whisk the egg white stiffly and fold it into the batter. Dip the food pieces into seasoned flour before coating them with the batter.

This method gives a lighter, crisper batter than the first recipe.

EGG-AND-CRUMBING

Have a beaten egg on a plate and some fresh white or dry breadcrumbs on a piece of kitchen paper or in a shallow dish. Dip the food in the egg and lift it out, letting it drain for a second or two. Transfer it to the crumbs and tip the paper backwards and forwards until the food is well covered.

Press in the crumbs with a small palette knife, then shake the food to remove any surplus.

Alternatively, have the crumbs in a polythene bag and shake the food pieces inside the bag until they are covered.

Do not use this method if the food is likely to break up.

CHICKEN MARYLAND
serves 4

a 3-lb. oven-ready chicken, jointed into 8 portions
2 level tbsps. seasoned flour
beaten egg
4 oz. (2 cups) fresh white breadcrumbs
1 tbsp. cooking oil
3 oz. butter
½ oz. (1½ tbsps.) flour
½ pint (1¼ cups) chicken stock
¼ pint (⅝ cup) soured cream
salt and pepper

For corn fritters:
2 oz. (½ cup) flour
salt and pepper
1 egg, beaten
¼ pint (⅝ cup) milk
8-oz. can sweet corn, drained
fat for frying

For fried bananas:
1 banana per person

Discard the skin from the chicken joints. Dip each piece of chicken into the seasoned flour, then coat with egg and breadcrumbs, patting the crumbs firmly on to the chicken. Heat the oil in a large frying-pan and add the butter. When the butter is melted add the chicken, reduce the heat and cook slowly, allowing 35–45 minutes, until evenly browned and well cooked. Drain and keep warm.

Pour off all but 2 tablespoons of the fat. Add the flour and cook, stirring, for 2–3 minutes. Stir in the stock and soured cream, bring to the boil and check the seasoning. Serve the chicken surrounded by corn fritters and fried bananas, with the gravy in a sauceboat.

Corn fritters
Sift the flour and seasoning into a basin, make a well in the centre and add the beaten egg and 4 tablespoons of milk. Beat until smooth. Add enough milk to give a thick coating consistency, then add the sweet corn. Fry the batter in spoonfuls in shallow fat for about 5 minutes, turning once.

Fried bananas
Peel the bananas and cut into 3–4 pieces. Before you make the gravy, fry the banana in the chicken fat.

Hamburgers – a favourite lunch-time snack

HAMBURGERS
serves 4

1 lb. lean beef
½ an onion, grated (optional)
salt and pepper
melted butter or oil for coating or a little fat for shallow frying

Mince the meat very finely and mix well with the onion and a generous amount of salt and pepper. Shape lightly into 4 round flat cakes.

To cook, shallow fry in a little fat, allowing 4–6 minutes on each side. Hamburgers can be served rare or well done, according to personal preference.

Variations:
Traditionally, hamburgers contain no other ingredients, but they can be varied by adding any of the following when mixing the meat and seasoning:–
2–4 oz. cheese, grated
1 tbsp. sweet pickle
1–2 level tbsps. made mustard
1 level tsp. mixed herbs
1 tbsp. chopped parsley
2 oz. mushrooms, skinned and sliced
2–3 tomatoes, skinned and chopped
Alternatively, when the hamburgers are cooked, top them with a fried or poached egg or with a sprinkling of grated cheese.
Serve in a plain, soft bap with onion rings, slices of tomato and American relish on top, or accompanied by a salad.

MUSTARD STEAKS
serves 4

4 fillet steaks
salt and pepper
1 tbsp. cooking oil
2 oz. butter
¼ pint (⅝ cup) double cream
2 level tsps. French mustard

Sprinkle the steaks with salt and pepper. Heat the oil and butter and

fry the steaks for 3–5 minutes on each side. Drain and keep hot. Pour the cream into the remaining butter and meat juices and cook without boiling until thick; stir in the mustard and pour the mixture over the steaks immediately before serving.

PEPPER STEAK
serves 4

1 oz. white peppercorns
1½ lb. rump steak, cut 1 in. thick
1 tbsp. cooking oil
1 oz. butter
2 tbsps. brandy
¼ pint (⅝ cup) dry white wine
2 tbsps. double cream
salt and pepper

Crush the peppercorns roughly and coat both sides of the steak with them. Heat the oil and butter in a frying pan. Fry the steak, turning once, for 6–10 minutes, according to taste. Place on a serving dish and keep hot. Pour off the fat, leaving the peppercorns in the pan. Pour in the brandy and wine, add the cream and warm through. Taste and season; pour over the steak and serve at once.

Note: For a less pungent flavour, try canned green peppercorns.

LIVER, BACON AND MUSHROOMS
serves 4

¾–1 lb. calves' or lambs' liver
seasoned flour
4 rashers of lean bacon, rinded and chopped
1–2 onions, skinned and chopped
fat or oil
4 oz. mushrooms, sliced

Wash and trim the liver and cut into thin strips. Toss in seasoned flour to coat. Fry the bacon until the fat begins to run, add the onion and cook for 5 minutes, or until

soft, then add the sliced mushrooms and strips of liver. Add a little more fat if necessary and continue frying over a gentle heat, stirring from time to time until the meat is just cooked – about 5–10 minutes.

FRIED SWEETBREADS
serves 4

1 lb. lambs' or calves' sweetbreads
juice of ½ a lemon
1 egg, beaten
salt and pepper
2 oz. (1 cup) fresh white breadcrumbs
8 rashers streaky bacon, rinded

Soak the sweetbreads in cold water for 3–4 hours. Drain, put in a pan and cover them with cold water and the lemon juice. Bring the water slowly to the boil and simmer for 5 minutes. Drain and leave the sweetbreads in cold water until they are firm and cold, then strip off any stringy unwanted tissue.

Press the sweetbreads well between sheets of absorbent kitchen paper, slice, season and dip into the beaten egg, then the crumbs. Cut the bacon rashers into strips and fry lightly until just crisp, drain and keep hot. Fry the sweetbreads in the same fat until golden. Toss the bacon and sweetbreads together and serve at once with tartare or tomato sauce.

FRIED SCAMPI
serves 4

8 oz. shelled scampi or Dublin Bay (large) prawns
seasoned flour
4 oz. (1 cup) plain flour
pinch of salt
1 tbsp. oil
1 egg yolk
2–3 tbsps. water or milk and water
fat for deep frying

If fresh scampi or prawns are used, discard their heads and remove the dark veins; if frozen, allow to thaw then drain well.

Dip the scampi in seasoned flour. Mix together the flour, salt, oil and egg yolk with sufficient liquid to give a stiff batter which will coat the back of a spoon; beat until smooth. Dip the scampi in the batter. Heat the fat until a cube of bread dropped into it takes 20–30 seconds to brown. Fry the scampi a few at a time until they are golden brown, drain and serve with tartare or tomato sauce.

Alternatively, fry the scampi coated in egg and breadcrumbs.

FISH CAKES
serves 2

½ lb. smoked haddock
¾ lb. potatoes, peeled and
    quartered
1 oz. butter
1–2 tbsps. chopped parsley
salt and pepper
milk or beaten egg to bind
1 egg, beaten, to coat
dry breadcrumbs
fat for frying

Poach the fish in water until tender, drain, discard the skin and flake the flesh. Boil and drain the potatoes and mash with the butter. Mix the fish with the potato, parsley and salt and pepper to taste, binding if necessary with a little milk or egg. Form the mixture into a roll on a floured board, cut into 8 slices and shape into cakes. Coat with egg and crumbs. Fry in shallow fat until crisp and golden; drain well on absorbent kitchen paper.
These fish cakes are good served with tomato or parsley sauce.

FRIED FILLETS OF MACKEREL
serves 2

2 mackerel, filleted
oil for frying
a few button mushrooms,
    wiped
1 onion, skinned and thinly
    sliced
1 small clove of garlic,
    skinned and crushed
a little vinegar
grilled tomatoes
parsley, chopped

Fry the fillets quickly in very hot shallow oil, then arrange them on a dish and keep hot. Cook the mushrooms, onion and garlic in the reheated oil, browning them well, and spoon over the fillets. Heat the vinegar until very hot, pour over the fillets and surround with grilled tomatoes. Sprinkle with chopped parsley.

FISH PUFFS
serves 2

½ lb. potatoes, peeled
½ lb. white fish – haddock or
    cod
½ a small onion, grated
2 level tsps. curry powder
salt and pepper
1 oz. butter, melted
2 eggs, beaten
deep fat for frying

Some of the nicest fritters have a sweet filling

Boil and drain the potatoes and mash them. Poach and flake the fish, mix it with the potatoes and remaining ingredients (except the fat for frying) and beat until smooth.
Heat the fat until it will brown a cube of bread in 40 seconds. Drop the fish mixture into it with a teaspoon, fry quickly until golden, drain on crumpled kitchen paper and serve with a well-flavoured sauce, such as tomato or tartare.

CHIPPED POTATOES

allow 6–8 oz. potatoes per person

Peel the potatoes and cut into ¼–½ in. slices, then into strips ¼–½ in. wide. (For speed, several slices can be put on top of one another and cut together, or use a special 'chipper'.) Place in cold water and leave for at least ½ hour; drain well and dry with a cloth.
Heat oil in a deep fat fryer until when one chip is dropped in it rises to the surface straight away, surrounded by bubbles. Put enough chips into the basket to about quarter-fill it and lower carefully into the fat. Cook for 6–7 minutes, remove and drain on absorbent paper. Repeat this procedure until all the chips have been cooked.
Just before serving, reheat the fat, test to make sure it is hot enough and fry the chips rapidly for about 3 minutes, until crisp and brown. Drain well on absorbent paper and serve at once in an uncovered dish, sprinkled with salt.
Note: The initial soaking helps to remove the excess starch from the potatoes, making the chips crisp.

DOUGHNUTS
makes 10–12

1 level tsp. sugar
4 tbsps. milk (approx.)
¼ oz. dried yeast
8 oz. (2 cups) plain flour
½ level tsp. salt
2 oz. butter or margarine
1 egg, beaten
jam
deep fat for frying
sugar and ground cinnamon
    to coat

Dissolve the sugar in the milk, warm slightly and whisk in the yeast. Leave in a warm place until frothy – about 15 minutes. Mix the flour and salt and rub in the fat. Add the yeast and egg and mix to a soft dough, adding a little more milk if necessary. Beat well until smooth and leave to rise until doubled in size. Knead lightly on a floured board and divide into 10–12 pieces. Shape each into a round, put 1 teaspoon of jam in the centre and draw up the edges to form a ball, pressing firmly to seal them together. Put on a greased baking sheet and leave to prove for about 15 minutes.
Heat the fat until it will brown a cube of bread in 40 seconds. Fry the doughnuts fairly quickly until golden brown – 5–10 minutes, according to size. Drain on crumpled kitchen paper and toss in sugar mixed with a little cinnamon (if liked). Serve really fresh.
Alternatively, shape the doughnuts into rings, removing a small circle from the centre of each ring. In this case, do not add the jam but prove and bake plain. Roll in sugar and cinnamon as for the jam-filled doughnuts.

FRUIT FRITTERS WITH LIQUEUR
Serves 4

8 canned pineapple rings,
    drained
2 tbsps. Kirsch
4 oz. (1 cup) plain flour
pinch of salt
1 egg
¼ pint (⅝ cup) milk
fat for deep frying
caster sugar and ground
    cinnamon

Soak the pineapple rings in the Kirsch. Make up a coating batter by sifting the flour and salt into a basin. Make a well in the centre and break in the egg. Add half the milk gradually and beat the mixture until smooth. Add the rest of the milk and beat until well mixed. Heat the fat until it is hot enough to brown a cube of bread in 1 minute.
Dip the pineapple rings in the batter and fry in the fat until golden. Drain on crumpled kitchen paper, toss in caster sugar and a little ground cinnamon.

CONTROLLED PAN FRYING
There are now available electric frying pans and deep-fat fryers with built-in thermostatic controls. Any food that can be fried in the normal way can be fried in a temperature-controlled pan and they are particularly useful for foods which need a high degree of accuracy in the fat temperature to achieve the correct result. Once the desired temperature is reached, the thermostat maintains it automatically with only small variations.
The deep-fat fryers are most useful if you cook in any quantity, as you can generally cook larger amounts more quickly than by the ordinary deep frying method. These fryers prevent the fat spitting in your face or spattering over the hob. Although they take a rather larger quantity of fat than the normal deep fryers, it can, of course, be used repeatedly.
Shallow-fat frying in a controlled-temperature pan is often more satisfactory than in an ordinary pan, as the heat is evenly spread, giving a more level temperature overall. Dry-frying (i.e. with little or no fat) can be very successful in this type of frying-pan, in particular those with a 'non-stick' or easy-clean finish.
Controlled-temperature pans can also be used for braising, pot roasting and stewing.

STEWS AND CASSEROLES

A casserole can be anything from an inexpensive, tasty meal for the family to the richest of dinner party dishes. The long, slow cooking method breaks down the fibres of the meat and draws out the full flavour.

In the main, casserole dishes use the cheaper, tougher cuts that require long cooking to make them tender, but these cuts often have the most taste. Add vegetables and a rich, home-made stock and the result is a meal to be proud of. For a party dish, add cream or soured cream to the cooking liquid to make a really delicious sauce. For many casserole recipes, the ingredients are fried first. This can either be done in a frying pan, transferring the food to a casserole afterwards, or it can be done in a flameproof casserole, using the same pan for top-of-the-stove and oven cooking.

If you are using 1 pan only, be careful to discard the excess fat before adding liquid.

PAUPIETTES OF PORK
serves 2

2 6-oz. pork escalopes
1 level tbsp. flour
1 tbsp. cooking oil
1 oz. butter
3 oz. onion, skinned and chopped
3 tbsps. dry white wine
¼ level tsp. paprika
½ pint (1¼ cups) chicken stock
1 tbsp. cream

For forcemeat :
1 oz. butter
2 oz. lean streaky bacon, rinded and diced
1 oz. onion, skinned and chopped
2 oz. (1 cup) fresh white breadcrumbs
4 oz. pork sausage meat
¼ level tsp. dried thyme
salt and freshly ground black pepper

Place the escalopes between sheets of non-stick paper and bat out with a meat bat or a heavy knife until fairly thin.

For the forcemeat melt the butter in a small pan, add the bacon and the onion and fry until soft. Allow to cool.

Combine the mixture with the breadcrumbs, sausage meat and thyme; season and spread the forcemeat over the meat. Roll up the meat and tie with string.

Toss the pork rolls in the flour. Heat the oil in a small pan, add the butter and when beginning to colour, fry the pork until evenly browned. Transfer the meat to a small casserole.

Reheat the pan juices and add the onion. Fry until transparent. Stir in the excess flour with the wine, paprika, stock and cream. Bring to the boil and pour it over the meat. Cook in the oven at 350°F. (mark 4) for about 1½ hours. Skim off any excess fat with kitchen paper and remove the string from the meat before serving. Serve with creamed potatoes and green beans.

PORK RIBS WITH SPICED SAUCE
serves 4

2 lb. spare ribs, English cut
1 tbsp. cooking oil
1 oz. butter
½ lb. onions, skinned and finely chopped
1 level tbsp. flour
½ level tsp. ground ginger
½ pint (1¼ cups) chicken stock
2 tbsps. white wine vinegar
8-oz. can cranberry sauce
¼ level tsp. dried rosemary
salt and freshly ground black pepper
chopped parsley for garnish

Trim the spare ribs of excess fat. Heat the oil in a large frying pan, add the butter and on the point of browning add the meat. Fry briskly and brown on both sides. Transfer to a casserole. Add the onions to the pan and fry until tender, stir in the flour and ginger and cook for a minute.

Add the stock, vinegar, sauce

rosemary and seasoning and bring to the boil, stirring. Pour over the meat. Cover the casserole and cook at 325°F. (mark 3) for about 1½ hours.

Remove the meat from the casserole. Lift off the fat by laying sheets of absorbent paper over the top of the liquid. Reduce the juices by one-third by boiling hard in a pan, or in the casserole if it is flameproof. Return the meat to the casserole and reheat. Sprinkle with fresh parsley before serving.

SCANDINAVIAN PORK
serves 4

4 pork chops
2 fresh herrings (or other small oily fish)
4 medium-sized potatoes, peeled
4 onions, skinned
butter
2 eggs
1 pint (2½ cups) milk
1 oz. (¼ cup) flour
salt and pepper
parsley for garnish

Trim the chops of excess fat and rind. Cut the heads and tails off the herrings and fillet them. Slice the potatoes and onions thinly. Butter a large ovenproof dish, put in a layer of potato, a layer of onion, then 2 chops and 2 herring halves and a further layer of potato and onion. Add the remaining 2 chops and 2 herring halves, then fill in round the sides and cover the top with the rest of the onion and potato. Put a few small knobs of butter on top and cook, uncovered, at 350°F. (mark 4) near the top of the oven for 1 hour. Slake the flour with a little of the measured milk to a smooth cream, beat in the eggs and gradually add the rest of the milk. Season to taste, then pour this mixture over the contents of the casserole. Return the dish to the oven for a further ½ hour, until the savoury custard topping is set. Garnish with parsley.

VEAL AND RICE PAPRIKA
serves 4

1 oz. butter
1 lb. pie veal, cut into small pieces
6 oz. onion, skinned and finely sliced
1 level tsp. paprika
1 level tbsp. tomato paste
¾ pint (1⅞ cups) stock
6 oz. (¾ cup) long grain rice
¼ pint (⅝ cup) soured cream
salt and pepper
chopped parsley for garnish

Melt the butter in a frying pan. When on the point of turning brown, add the veal and fry briskly. Transfer the meat to a casserole and fry the onion until tender. Stir in the paprika, tomato paste and stock. Pour over the veal, cover and cook in the oven at 325°F. (mark 3) for about 1 hour, or until tender. Add the rice, cover and return to the oven for a further 30 minutes.

Gently heat the soured cream in a small pan and fork it through the rice. Season and sprinkle with chopped parsley.

VEAL AND OLIVE CASSEROLE
serves 5–6

2 lb. stewing veal, cubed
1 oz. (¼ cup) flour
1 oz. butter
2 tbsps. cooking oil
1 clove garlic, skinned and finely chopped
2¼-oz. can tomato paste
1 beef bouillon cube
1 pint (2½ cups) boiling water
1 bay leaf
pinch of thyme
pinch of marjoram
12 black olives, stoned
¼ lb. mushrooms, sliced
4–6 oz. (½–¾ cup) long grain rice
12 small stuffed olives
salt and pepper
For glazed onions :
12 small onions, skinned
butter
2 level tbsps. soft brown sugar
2 tbsps. vinegar
2 tbsps. port

Coat the veal cubes with flour and brown on all sides by frying in the mixed butter and oil. Transfer to a casserole. Add the garlic, tomato paste, the bouillon cube dissolved in the boiling water and the herbs. Cook in the centre of the oven at 350°F. (mark 4) for 1½ hours. After the first hour, add the black olives and sliced mushrooms. Adjust seasoning.

To glaze the onions, cook them gently in butter in a pan with the lid on, shaking occasionally. Meanwhile, put the sugar, vinegar, and port in a pan and cook until a thick syrup is formed. When the onions are cooked, put them into the syrup and boil it for a few minutes, until the onions are well coated. Cook the rice in plenty of boiling salted water for 12–15 minutes. Drain well.

Serve the casserole with the boiled rice and garnish with the stuffed olives and glazed onions.

Veal and rice paprika, finished with soured cream

POULET A L'ORANGE
serves 4

4 chicken portions, halved
2 tbsps. cooking oil
1 pkt. white sauce mix
½ pint (1¼ cups) milk
2 medium oranges
white grapes for garnish

Fry the chicken pieces in the oil until well browned. Remove from the pan and place in a 4-pint casserole. Make up the sauce according to directions on the packet, using the milk. Thinly pare the rind (free of all pith) from 1½ oranges and cut in thin strips. Add these to the sauce, together with the juice of 1 orange. Pour the sauce over the chicken, cover and cook in the oven at 375°F. (mark 5) for about 45 minutes, or until the chicken is tender.

Cut the remaining orange in slices and use it for garnish along with the grapes.

CHICKEN AND WALNUTS
serves 6

3½–4 lb. roasting chicken, jointed and skinned
2 tbsps. sherry
2 level tsps. caster sugar
3 tbsps. oil
8 oz. button mushrooms, wiped and sliced
6-oz. can water chestnuts, drained and diced (optional)
1 pint (2½ cups) chicken stock
2 level tbsps. cornflour
4 oz. halved walnuts
1 oz. butter

Place the chicken joints in a dish, pour the sherry and caster sugar over them and leave to marinade

Chicken, cooked with orange and garnished with grapes

Marinaded beef with olives for a French style casserole

for 1–2 hours.

Heat the oil in a frying pan. Drain the chicken pieces and brown in the oil. Place the mushrooms and water chestnuts in a large casserole and arrange the chicken pieces on top. Pour over the chicken juices and stock, cover the casserole and cook in the oven at 350°F. (mark 4) for 2 hours.

Drain off the liquor, keeping the chicken hot, and thicken it with the cornflour, slaked with a little water. Brown the walnuts in melted butter for 4–5 minutes and drain.

Arrange the chicken, mushrooms and water chestnuts on a serving plate and pour some of the thickened gravy over them. Garnish with the browned walnuts. Serve the remaining gravy separately in a sauce boat.

Rabbit is delicious in a casserole

POULET EN COCOTTE
serves 4

For stuffing :

4 oz. sausage meat
2 level tbsps. fresh white
 breadcrumbs
1 chicken liver, chopped
2 level tbsps. chopped parsley

3–3½ lb. oven-ready chicken
salt and freshly ground black
 pepper
2½ oz. butter
8 oz. lean back bacon, in the
 piece, rinded
1 lb. potatoes, peeled
6 oz. shallots, skinned
1 lb. small new carrots,
 scraped
chopped parsley to garnish

Mix together all the stuffing ingredients in a bowl until well blended. Adjust seasoning. Stuff the chicken at the neck end, plump up and secure with a skewer. Truss the bird as for roasting and season well.

Melt the butter in a large frying pan, add the chicken and fry, turning until browned all over. Place the chicken and butter in a large casserole. Cut the bacon into ¾-in. cubes, add to the casserole, cover and cook at 350°F. (mark 4) for 15 minutes. Meanwhile, cut the potatoes into 1-in. dice.

Remove the casserole from the oven and baste the chicken. Surround with the potatoes, shallots and carrots, turning them in the fat. Season, return to the oven and cook for a further 1½ hours. Garnish with chopped parsley.

Have a hot plate to hand for carving the bird, but serve the vegetables and juices straight from the casserole.

FRENCH BEEF AND OLIVE CASSEROLE
serves 4

For marinade :

3 tbsps. cooking oil
1 carrot, peeled and sliced
1 onion, skinned and sliced
2–3 sticks of celery, scrubbed
 and cut in 1-in. pieces
¼ pint (⅝ cup) red wine
¼ pint (⅝ cup) wine vinegar
bunch of fresh herbs
1 clove of garlic, skinned
 and crushed
few peppercorns
salt and pepper

1½ lb. rump steak, trimmed
6 oz. fat bacon, rinded
6 oz. lean bacon, rinded
¼ pint (⅝ cup) red wine
¼ lb. black and green olives
3–4 tomatoes, skinned and
 sliced

Make up the marinade as follows. Heat the oil and add the vegetables. Fry until brown, then add the remaining ingredients, bring to the boil and simmer for 15 minutes. Allow to cool. Cut the meat into thick chunks and cover with the marinade.

Fry the fat bacon to extract the fat, then remove from the pan. Fry the meat on both sides in the bacon fat and put it in a casserole. Dice the lean bacon and add to the casserole with the marinade, wine and olives. Cover with greased greaseproof paper, then with a lid and cook in the oven at 325°F. (mark 3) for 1½–2 hours.

Shortly before serving, remove any excess fat and add the sliced tomatoes. Serve with buttered noodles and grated cheese.

MARINADED STEAK POT
serves 6

2 lb. chuck steak
2 tbsps. garlic vinegar
2 oz. dripping
1½ oz. (⅜ cup) flour
¼ lb. button onions, skinned
¼ lb. button mushrooms,
 wiped and stalked
¼ lb. streaky bacon, rinded
 and diced
1 pint (2½ cups) beef stock
1 bay leaf
1 level tbsp. tomato paste
bouquet garni
chopped parsley

Cut the meat into neat pieces, put it in a polythene bag and add the vinegar. Toss the meat well, place the bag in a deep bowl and leave the meat overnight to marinade.

Melt the dripping in a frying pan. Drain the meat, reserving the juices, and coat with the flour. Fry it until sealed and brown on all sides. Remove the meat from the pan, add the onions, mushrooms and bacon and fry for 5 minutes. Place the mixture together with the meat and juices in a tightly-lidded casserole.

Pour the stock into the frying pan, stir to loosen the sediment and add the bay leaf, tomato paste and bouquet garni. Bring to the boil and pour over the meat. Cover tightly and cook in the oven at 325°F. (mark 3) for about 1½ hours. Discard the bay leaf and bouquet garni and serve sprinkled generously with chopped parsley.

BROWN CASSEROLE OF RABBIT
serves 4

1 rabbit, jointed
2 oz. (½ cup) seasoned flour
2 oz. dripping
1 onion or leek, skinned and
 sliced
1 meat extract cube or 2
 level tsps. powdered meat
 extract
1 pint (2½ cups) stock or water
2 carrots, peeled and diced
1 stalk of celery, scrubbed
 and chopped
bouquet garni
1 tbsp. tomato ketchup
pinch of ground nutmeg
fried croûtons to garnish

Soak the rabbit joints in cold salted water to remove the blood. Dry the pieces and toss in flour, then fry in the dripping, several joints at a time, until lightly browned. Remove from the pan, add the onion or leek and fry gently for a few minutes; add the remaining flour and fry until lightly browned. Add the meat extract with the liquid and stir until boiling. Put the rabbit and the vegetables into a casserole and pour the sauce over. Add the bouquet garni, ketchup and nutmeg, cover and cook in the centre of the oven at 350°F. (mark 4) for about 2 hours. Remove the herbs, adjust seasoning and serve the casserole garnished with fried croûtons.

SUMMER LAMB CASSEROLE
serves 4

2 lb. neck of lamb
2 level tsps. salt
½ level tsp. pepper
1 lb. new carrots, scraped and sliced
1 lb. small new potatoes, scraped
½ lb. frozen peas or fresh peas, shelled
1 level tbsp. tomato paste
fresh mint, chopped

Place the meat in a shallow flameproof casserole, cover with cold water and bring to the boil. Pour off the water, rinse the meat and return it to the casserole with 1 pint (2½ cups) cold water, to which the salt and pepper has been added. Bring to the boil, add the carrots, cover and cook in the oven at 325°F. (mark 3) for about 1½ hours, until the meat is fork tender.
Add the potatoes to the casserole with the peas, if fresh are used; cover and cook for a further 20 minutes. Remove the meat and strip the flesh from the bones. Cut it roughly and return it to the casserole with the peas and tomato paste. Adjust seasoning and return the casserole to the oven for a further 10–15 minutes.
To serve, sprinkle with chopped mint.

NAVARIN OF LAMB
serves 4

2 lb. middle neck of lamb, trimmed
2 oz. lard or dripping
2 level tbsps. flour
2 level tsps. salt
½ level tsp. pepper
3 level tbsps. tomato paste
1 pint (2½ cups) hot water
bouquet garni (including cut clove of garlic)
4 onions, skinned and sliced
4 carrots, peeled and sliced
4 small turnips, peeled and sliced
8 small potatoes, peeled

Cut the meat into serving-size pieces. Melt 1 oz. fat in a pan and brown the meat a few pieces at a time. Dredge with seasoned flour and brown again. Gradually stir in the tomato paste and hot water, add the bouquet garni, bring to the boil, reduce heat, cover and simmer for 1 hour.
Melt 1 oz. fat in a pan and fry all the vegetables except the potatoes. When lightly browned add to the meat and simmer for a further 30 minutes. Discard the bouquet garni, add the potatoes and simmer for a further 30 minutes.
Adjust seasoning and skim off fat.

A fish casserole makes a pleasant change from meat and poultry

LAMB JULIENNE
serves 6

3 level tbsps. flour
1 level tsp. curry powder
2 level tsps. salt
freshly ground black pepper
2 lb. boned shoulder lamb, cubed
oil for frying
1½ pints (3¾ cups) water or chicken stock
8 small onions, skinned
8 carrots, peeled

For crispy dumplings :
1½ oz. butter
2 oz. (1 cup) fresh white breadcrumbs
8 oz. (2 cups) self-raising flour
1 level tsp. salt
½ level tsp. dried onion
3 tbsps. corn oil
milk

Sift together the flour, curry powder, salt and pepper. Toss the lamb cubes in this mixture. Fry the meat in the oil until well browned. Stir in any excess flour. Gradually add the water or stock, stirring, and bring to the boil. Transfer to a casserole and add the onions. Cover and cook in the oven at 325°F. (mark 3) for 1 hour. Cut the carrots into long thick matchsticks and add to the meat. For crispy dumplings, melt the butter in a pan, stir in the crumbs and cook gently, stirring frequently, until golden. Sift together the flour, salt and onion powder. Stir in the oil and enough milk to give a soft but manageable dough. Shape into balls, coat with crumbs and arrange in the casserole. Cover and cook for a further hour.

CIDERED HADDOCK CASSEROLE
serves 4–6

1–1½ lb. haddock or cod fillet, skinned
½ lb. tomatoes, skinned and sliced
2 oz. button mushrooms, sliced
1 tbsp. chopped parsley
salt and freshly ground black pepper
¼ pint (⅝ cup) cider
2 tbsps. fresh white breadcrumbs
2 tbsps. grated cheese

Wipe the fish, cut into cubes and lay these in an ovenproof dish. Cover with the sliced tomatoes and mushrooms, the parsley and seasonings and pour the cider over. Cover with foil and cook in the centre of the oven at 350°F. (mark 4) for 20–25 minutes. Sprinkle with the breadcrumbs and cheese and brown in a hot oven, 425°F. (mark 7), or under a hot grill.

FISH AND BACON CASSEROLE
serves 6

4 oz. bacon, rinded and chopped
3 onions, skinned and chopped
½ oz. butter
1½ lb. white fish, free of skin and bones
salt
cayenne pepper
1 tsp. Worcestershire sauce
¼ pint (⅝ cup) tomato sauce
¼ pint (⅝ cup) water

Fry the bacon and onion in the butter. Put alternate layers of bacon and onion and the fish into a casserole, sprinkling each layer with salt and very little cayenne pepper.
Mix the Worcestershire and tomato sauces with the water and pour over the fish. Cover and cook in the oven at 350°F. (mark 4) for 45 minutes.

SWEETBREAD HOTPOT
serves 4

1 lb. sweetbreads
1 onion, skinned and chopped
8 oz. peas, shelled
4 oz. mushrooms, wiped and sliced
1 oz. butter
2 oz. (½ cup) plain flour
1 pint (2½ cups) white stock
salt and freshly ground black pepper
1 tsp. mixed herbs
toast to garnish

Soak the sweetbreads in salted water until free from blood – about 1 hour. Cover with fresh water, bring slowly to the boil, then pour off the liquid.
In a flameproof casserole, fry the onion, peas and mushrooms slowly for 5 minutes in the butter. Add the flour and stir until cooked. Add the liquid slowly, season, sprinkle in the herbs and bring to the boil.
Chop the sweetbreads and add to the casserole. Cook at 325°F. (mark 3) for about 2 hours. Serve garnished with triangles of toast.

Lamb julienne

BRAISING

Braising is a combination of baking and steaming. It is suitable for both the less expensive roasting cuts and stewing meats—particularly such cuts as leg of mutton, rib, brisket or silverside of beef, best end of neck of lamb or knuckle of veal, pork spare ribs and, of course, poultry and game (especially the tougher, boiling birds). It gives a delicate flavour to the food and a tender, moist consistency. A split calf's foot added to the pan will make it even more succulent. Start with a fairly generous joint, as it will shrink a little in the cooking. Many vegetables can also be successfully braised.

Meat is cooked by laying it on a bed of vegetables (called a mirepoix), just covered with liquid, and is either cooked in the oven at 300–325°F. (mark 2–3), or simmered on top of the stove. The liquid may be stock, wine or cider. The meat may be braised either as a whole joint, or boned and stuffed, or sliced. Prepare the vegetables you plan to use in the mirepoix— e.g. an onion, a carrot, a small turnip, 2 stalks of celery—by peeling and trimming in the usual way and cutting into pieces. Use enough to make a 2-in. layer in the bottom of the pan.

Put about 1 oz. dripping into a flameproof casserole along with a few bacon rinds. Fry the meat in the hot fat until well browned all over. Take out the meat, add the vegetables, seasoning and a bouquet garni to the pan and place the meat on top. Add sufficient stock or water to half-cover the mirepoix. Bring to the boil, cover and simmer gently, basting every 15–20 minutes for half the cooking time until the meat is tender. (For a joint under 3 lb. allow 2 hours.) Slice the meat and serve with vegetables, in the cooking juices. Alternatively, coat the meat in seasoned flour and fry in the melted dripping; remove the meat from the pan before frying the vegetables and continuing as in the first method. Cover, and cook in the oven at 325°F. (mark 3) until the meat is tender.

To serve, the vegetables are usually piled round the meat and the liquor (made into a sauce) is poured over them.

To braise vegetables, fry lightly first, then season, add a little liquid and cook slowly in the oven.

Chicken absorbs the flavours of herbs and vegetables braised with it

BRAISED CELERY
serves 4

4 small heads of celery, trimmed and scrubbed
2 oz. butter
stock
salt and pepper

Tie each head of celery securely to hold the shape. Fry lightly in 1½ oz. butter for 5 minutes until golden brown. Put in an ovenproof dish, add enough stock to come half-way up the celery, sprinkle with salt and pepper and add the remaining butter. Cover and cook in the centre of the oven at 350°F. (mark 4) for 1–1½ hours.
Remove the string and serve with the cooking liquid poured over.

BRAISED CHICORY
serves 4

1½ lb. chicory, washed and trimmed
1 oz. butter
¼ level tsp. grated nutmeg
juice of ½ a lemon
¼ pint (⅝ cup) chicken stock
1½ level tsps. cornflour
1 tbsp. cold water
2 tbsps. cream
salt and black pepper
chopped parsley

Plunge the trimmed chicory into boiling water for 1 minute. Drain and rinse with cold water. Drain again. Butter a large casserole. Lay the chicory in the base in a single layer, and dot with butter. Stir the nutmeg and lemon juice into the stock and pour it over the chicory. Cover with buttered foil or a lid and cook at 325°F. (mark 3) for about 1½ hours. Blend the cornflour with the water. Drain the juices from the casserole into a small saucepan, add the cornflour and bring to the boil, stirring; allow it to bubble for 1 minute. Adjust the seasoning and pour the sauce over the chicory. Sprinkle with parsley.

SWEET-SOUR RED CABBAGE
serves 4

2 lb. red cabbage, shredded
2 medium onions, skinned and sliced
2 cooking apples, peeled and chopped
2 level tsps. sugar
salt and pepper
bouquet garni
2 tbsps. water
2 tbsps. red wine vinegar
1 oz. butter or margarine

In a casserole, layer the cabbage with the onions, apples, sugar and seasoning. Put the bouquet garni in the centre.
Pour the water and vinegar over the mixture, cover tightly and cook at 300°F. (mark 2) for about 2½ hours.
Just before serving, add the butter and mix well into the other ingredients.

CHICKEN IN A POT
serves 6

4 oz. pork sausage meat
2 level tbsps. fresh white breadcrumbs
1 chicken liver, chopped
2 tbsps. chopped parsley
3½-lb. oven-ready chicken
3 tbsps. cooking oil
salt and freshly ground black pepper
4 sticks celery, scrubbed and thickly sliced
2 leeks, washed and thinly sliced
½ lb. small turnips (or swedes), peeled and quartered
½ lb. carrots, peeled and roughly sliced
juice of ½ a lemon
bouquet garni
a little stock made from the giblets
chopped parsley to garnish

In a bowl, combine the sausage meat, breadcrumbs, liver and measured parsley. Stuff the chicken with this mixture and truss with skewers or string. Heat the oil in a large pan, season the skin of the bird with salt and pepper and fry lightly in the oil until golden brown on all sides.
Transfer the chicken to a large casserole. Put the celery, leek, turnip and carrot in the oil, cover and cook gently for 5 minutes, stirring often. Drain and pack round the chicken. Add the lemon juice and just enough stock to give a depth of about 1 in. in the base of the casserole. Add the bouquet garni.
Cover tightly, place on a baking sheet and cook in the oven at 350°F. (mark 4) for about 1½ hours, until both the chicken and vegetables are fork tender.
Arrange the chicken and drained vegetables on a large plate. Keep them warm in the oven. Skim off any surplus fat from the juices using a spoon and crumpled kitchen paper and reduce slightly. Adjust the seasoning and sprinkle in the parsley.
Pour the juice over the chicken and serve at once.

BRAISED PORK AND RED CABBAGE

serves 6

**2 lb. unsalted belly pork,
 rinded
½ oz. butter
1 tbsp. cooking oil
1 lb. cooking apples, peeled
 and cored
1 lb. red cabbage, trimmed
 and finely shredded
2 level tbsps. flour
3 tbsps. wine vinegar
1 pint (2½ cups) stock
salt and freshly ground black
 pepper**

Cut the pork away from the bone in one piece, then cut it into strips ½ in. wide. Cut each strip in half. In a frying pan, melt the butter with the oil and heat until bubbling. Season the pork and fry until well browned on both sides. Reduce heat and cook for a further 10–15 minutes. Slice the apples roughly.

Place a good third of the red cabbage in a deep casserole, add some apple and half of the meat. Continue to layer up, finishing with the apple. Blend the flour with the vinegar, gradually add the stock until blended and adjust the seasoning. Bring to the boil, stirring, and cook for 2–3 minutes before pouring over the casserole. Cook, covered, at 350°F. (mark 4) for about 2 hours, or until the pork is tender.

BRAISED BEEF WITH SOURED CREAM AND MUSHROOMS

serves 6

**3½ lb. thick flank beef,
 trimmed free of fat
14-oz. can plum tomatoes
2 beef stock cubes
½ lb. onions, skinned and
 quartered
½ lb. carrots, peeled and
 halved
1 lb. button mushrooms,
 washed and stalks removed
2 oz. butter
1 or 2 5-fl. oz. cartons soured
 cream
chopped parsley for garnish**

Cut the lean meat into thin strips. Pour the tomatoes into a large, flameproof casserole and crumble in the stock cubes. Arrange the meat in the centre with the onions, carrots and mushroom stalks round the sides. Cover tightly, preferably with foil and a lid. Cook at 325°F. (mark 3) for about 2 hours.

Remove the lid and gently turn the meat in the juice. Cover, reduce heat to 300°F. (mark 2) and cook for a further hour, or until tender.

Slice the mushrooms. Melt the butter and fry the mushrooms. Discard the vegetables from the casserole. On top of the cooker, add the mushrooms to the beef and stir in the contents from 1 carton of soured cream. Reheat carefully, without boiling. Adjust the seasoning; if wished, stir in another carton of soured cream and garnish with chopped parsley.

BRAISED DUCKLING WITH TURNIPS

serves 4

**3½ lb. oven-ready duckling,
 cut into 4 joints
salt and freshly ground black
 pepper
2 large onions, skinned and
 chopped
1 lb. small turnips (or swedes),
 peeled and quartered
2 stalks celery, scrubbed and
 chopped
1 level tsp. dried thyme
1 pint (2½ cups) brown stock
1 level tbsp. cornflour
1 tbsp. chopped parsley**

Place the duckling joints in a roasting pan and season well. Cook, uncovered, at 400°F. (mark 6) for about 20 minutes, until well browned. Remove from the tin and set on kitchen paper to absorb any excess grease.

Place the onions, turnips and celery in the base of a flameproof casserole. Sprinkle thyme over and lay the joints on top. Pour the stock over the duckling, cover and cook at 375°F. (mark 5) for about 1 hour.

Blend the cornflour to a creamy consistency with a little water. Stir into the casserole juices, bring to the boil and cook for 1 or 2 minutes. Arrange the duckling and vegetables on a hot serving plate, pour the juices over and garnish with chopped parsley.

BRAISED VEAL CUTLETS

serves 4

**2½ oz. butter
4 veal cutlets, neatly trimmed
4 oz. cooked ham, chopped
1 tbsp. chopped onion
1 tbsp. chopped parsley
salt and pepper
¼ pint (⅝ cup) red wine**

Melt 2 oz. of the butter and in it fry the cutlets until golden brown. Fry the ham and onion, add the parsley and season well. Cover the

cutlets with this mixture, place carefully in a casserole and add the wine and sufficient water to come halfway up the meat.

Cook in the oven at 350°F. (mark 4) with a lid on for about 45 minutes. Take out the cutlets and keep them hot while boiling the liquid to reduce it slightly.

Just before serving, add the re-maining knob of butter to this liquor and replace the cutlets in it.

BRAISED GAMMON

serves 12

**½ a gammon, either bottom or
 knuckle end (about 7 lb.)
1 onion, skinned and halved
1 carrot, peeled and halved
1 turnip (or swede), peeled
 and halved
bouquet garni
2 pints (5 cups) stock
3 tomatoes, skinned and sliced
a few mushrooms, washed
 and sliced (optional)
½ pint (1¼ cups) rich brown
 sauce
¼ pint (⅝ cup) sherry
 (optional)**

Soak the gammon overnight in cold water.

Place it in a large pan with the vegetables and herbs and add just sufficient fresh cold water to cover. Bring to the boil and simmer for half the calculated cooking time. (Allow 15–20 minutes per lb. and 15 minutes over.) Remove the gammon and peel off the rind.

Place the gammon in a braising pan or a deep, flameproof casserole and add the stock, tomatoes and mushrooms. Cover tightly and place in the oven at 350°F. (mark

Preparing braised chicory

4) for the remainder of the cooking time.

Place the gammon on a warm dish, strain the stock and reduce to a half-glaze by boiling. Brush over the gammon. Add the sauce and sherry to the remaining stock, boil up and serve as gravy.

BRAISED SWEETBREADS

serves 4

**1 lb. frozen lambs' sweet-
 breads, thawed
1 large carrot, peeled and
 diced
1 onion, skinned and diced
2 stalks celery, scrubbed and
 diced
1 tbsp. cooking oil
salt and pepper
½ pint (1¼ cups) white stock
2–3 oz. green streaky bacon
 rashers, rinded
2 level tsps. cornflour
parsley for garnish**

Soak the sweetbreads for at least 4 hours, changing the water several times. Put into fresh cold water and bring to the boil; lift the sweetbreads out and rinse under running cold water. Remove the black veins and skin, wrap lightly in a cloth or muslin and cool, pressed between 2 weighted plates. Fry the prepared vegetables in the oil until half cooked. Place them in the base of a casserole which is just large enough to take the sweet-breads. Add the seasoning and stock (just enough to cover the vegetables) and arrange the sliced sweetbreads on top. Overlap the rashers of bacon on top.

Cover and cook in the oven at 375°F. (mark 5) for ½–¾ hour, bast-ing occasionally with the juices.

Vermouth is the ideal flavour with this delicious brill

Increase the oven temperature to 425°F. (mark 7) and remove the lid for the last 10 minutes.

Strain the liquor from the casserole. Thicken it with the cornflour and pour over the sweetbreads. Garnish with parsley.

BRAISED PIGEONS WITH GOLDEN SPAGHETTI

serves 4

2 oz. bacon, rinded and diced
1 carrot, peeled and diced
a piece of turnip (or swede), diced
2–3 sticks of celery, scrubbed and chopped
1 onion, skinned and chopped
4 pigeons, halved
1½ pints (3¾ cups) stock
bouquet garni
salt and pepper
1 level tbsp. cornflour
6 oz. spaghetti
2 oz. butter
tomatoes or watercress to garnish

Put the bacon and vegetables into a flameproof casserole and lay the 8 portions of pigeon on top. Add enough stock to almost cover, the bouquet garni and seasonings, cover tightly and cook on top of the stove for 1 hour until the pigeons are almost tender.

Transfer the casserole to the oven and cook uncovered at 350°F. (mark 4) for 45 minutes until the stock is reduced and the pigeons are browned. Thicken the stock with cornflour if necessary.

Meanwhile, boil the spaghetti in salted water until tender and then drain. Add the butter to the spaghetti in small pieces, making it golden and glistening. Serve the pigeons on a hot dish, surrounded by the spaghetti and garnished with tomatoes or watercress.

BOEUF EN DAUBE

serves 6

2½ lb. top rump of beef
1 oz. butter
2 tbsps. cooking oil
½ lb. onions, skinned and finely sliced
1 lb. carrots, peeled and finely sliced
½ lb. salt pork, rinded and cubed
½ pint (1¼ cups) dry white wine
¼ pint (⅝ cup) beef stock
1 level tsp. dried basil
½ level tsp. dried rosemary
1 bay leaf
½ level tsp. powdered mixed spice
salt and pepper
6 black olives, stoned

Secure the beef firmly with string. Melt the butter with the oil and fry the meat quickly on all sides to seal. Drain on absorbent paper and place in a casserole. Fry the vegetables and salt pork until golden brown, drain and place round the beef. Pour over the wine and stock and stir in the herbs and seasonings. Bring to the boil, cover and cook at 325°F. (mark 3) for 2½–3 hours until fork tender. About ½ hour before the end of the cooking time, add the olives. When cooked, remove the string from the meat and slice. Skim the fat from the juices and serve from the casserole.

ORANGE-BRAISED PORK CHOPS

serves 4

3 oz. butter
½ lb. onions, skinned and sliced
4 pork chops
salt and pepper
1 level tsp. dry mustard
2 level tsps. Demerara sugar
1 level tbsp. plain flour
3 large oranges
¼ pint (⅝ cup) dry white wine

In a frying pan, heat 1 oz. of the butter, add the onions and fry gently until light golden brown. Remove them from the pan. Trim any excess fat from the chops.

In a small bowl, mix together the salt and pepper, mustard, sugar and remaining 2 oz. butter. Spread on one side of each chop. Fry the chops until golden on both sides.

Remove from pan, add flour to the juices and mix well. Coarsely grate the rind from 2 oranges and add to the pan with the onions. Squeeze the juice from 2 oranges and make up to ¼ pint (⅝ cup) with water. Add to the pan, stirring, then add the wine and bring to the boil.

Peel remaining orange and cut it into segments. Arrange the chops in a flameproof pan, add the orange segments. Pour on the sauce. Cover and simmer on top of the stove for 40 minutes.

BRAISED BRILL

serves 4

2¼ lb. brill (or sole or whiting), filleted
salt and pepper
2½ oz. butter
fresh white breadcrumbs
2 shallots, skinned and chopped
1½ tsps. finely chopped parsley
6 tbsps. dry vermouth

Season the brill. Melt 1 oz. of the butter and dip the fillets in it, then coat them with the breadcrumbs. Mix together the chopped shallots and parsley and spread over the base of a greased baking dish. Lay the fillets on top. Melt the rest of the butter and use to glaze the fish. Spoon the vermouth carefully round the fish (not over it).

Cook, uncovered, at 450°F. (mark 8) for 10–15 minutes. Transfer the fish to a hot serving plate and keep warm. Pour cooking juices into a small pan, and boil rapidly to reduce. Pour over the fish.

HERRINGS BRAISED IN WINE

serves 6

½ bottle Mâcon (red)
thick slices of onion, carrot and celery
1 bay leaf
bouquet garni
6 peppercorns
salt and pepper
6 herrings (or other small oily fish), cleaned
sauté button mushrooms, small onions and parsley

Place the wine, sliced vegetables, herbs, peppercorns and seasoning in a saucepan. Cover and simmer for 30 minutes.

Arrange the herrings in a single layer in an ovenproof dish. Strain the liquor over them, adding a little water, if necessary, almost to cover them. Cover and cook at 325°F. (mark 3) for 1 hour. Garnish with sauté mushrooms, small onions and parsley. ●

Boeuf en daube is a classic braised dish

COOKING WITH OFFAL

Ragoût of liver

LIVER

Ox liver has a strong flavour and is often rather tough and coarse-textured. Best used for casseroles.
Calf's liver is very tender and has a delicate flavour. It can be lightly grilled or fried, but over-cooking makes it hard and dry.
Lamb's liver has a slightly stronger flavour than calf's, but is also suitable for grilling or frying.
Pig's liver has a pronounced distinctive flavour and a softer texture. It is best casseroled and makes an excellent pâté.
Allow 4 oz. liver per person.

SAVOURY LIVER
serves 4

1 lb. lambs' liver
2 oz. (1 cup) fresh white
   breadcrumbs
1 tbsp. chopped parsley
1 level tsp. mixed dried herbs
1 oz. suet, chopped
salt and pepper
grated rind of ½ lemon
little egg or milk to mix
4 rashers streaky bacon,
   rinded
¼ pint (⅝ cup) stock or water

Wash and slice the liver and

arrange it in a casserole. Mix together the breadcrumbs, parsley, herbs, suet, seasoning and lemon rind. Bind with a little egg or milk. Spread the stuffing on the liver and place the bacon on top. Pour in the stock or water and cover.
Cook in the oven at 350°F. (mark 4) for 30–45 minutes, until the liver is tender, removing the lid for the final 15 minutes to crisp the bacon.

RAGOUT OF LIVER
serves 4

1 lb. lambs' liver
4 level tbsps. seasoned flour
1 onion, skinned and sliced
4 rashers of bacon, chopped
1 oz. fat or oil
¾ pint (1⅞ cups) stock
1 oz. sultanas
1 apple, peeled and grated
1 level tsp. tomato paste
8 oz. (1 cup) long grain rice

Wash and trim the liver, cut it into small pieces and coat with the seasoned flour. Fry the liver, onion and bacon in the fat or oil until golden brown. Add the stock to the pan and bring to the boil, stirring constantly. Add the sultanas, apple and tomato paste and simmer for 20 minutes.
Cook the rice in boiling salted water

until tender and serve separately.

LIVER MARSALA
serves 4

1 lb. calves' or lambs' liver
lemon juice
seasoned flour
2 oz. butter
3 tbsps. Marsala
¼ pint (⅝ cup) stock
grilled tomatoes, matchstick
   potatoes and parsley to
   garnish

Slice the liver, sprinkle with the lemon juice and coat with seasoned flour. Melt the butter in a frying pan and fry the liver quickly on both sides until lightly browned. Stir in the Marsala and stock and simmer until the meat is just cooked and the sauce syrupy. Arrange the liver on a serving dish and garnish with the tomatoes, potatoes and parsley.

KIDNEY

Ox kidney has a fairly strong flavour. It needs slow, gentle cooking to make it tender. It is usually cooked with steak in casseroles and pies, or curries. Allow 4 oz. kidney to 1 lb. steak.

Calf's kidney is more tender and delicate in flavour than ox kidney, but is used in the same ways. One kidney will serve 1–2 people and is usually sold chopped.
Lamb's kidneys are usually the best, being small, well-flavoured and tender enough to grill or fry, either whole or in halves. The skin and white 'core' should be removed for cooking. Allow 2 per person.
Pig's and sheep's kidneys are similar to lamb's but are slightly larger and not quite so tender. Pig's kidney has a strong flavour. They can be halved and grilled or fried, or used in stews, curries, or casseroles. Allow 1–2 per person, depending on size.

KIDNEYS IN RED WINE
serves 4

2 oz. butter
1 onion, skinned and chopped
4–6 sheeps' kidneys
3 level tbsps. flour
¼ pint (⅝ cup) red wine
¼ pint (⅝ cup) stock
bouquet garni
1 level tbsp. tomato paste
salt and pepper
2 oz. mushrooms, sliced

Melt the butter and fry the onion until golden brown. Wash, skin and core the kidneys and cut them into small pieces; add to the pan and cook for 5 minutes, stirring occasionally.

Stir in the flour, add the wine and stock and bring slowly to the boil, then add the bouquet garni, tomato paste and some salt and pepper. Simmer for 5 minutes. Add the mushrooms and simmer for a further 5 minutes.

Remove the bouquet garni before serving and check the seasoning.

KIDNEY ROYALE
serves 4

8 lambs' kidneys
1½ oz. butter
1 medium-sized onion, skinned and chopped
2 canned red pimiento caps
salt and freshly ground black pepper
2 tbsps. Irish whiskey
4 tbsps. soured cream
8 oz. (1 cup) long grain rice
chopped parsley

Halve the kidneys, remove and discard the skin and cores, then cut into pieces. Melt the butter in a frying pan and fry the onion gently for about 5 minutes, till transparent but not coloured. Add the kidneys and fry for about 10 minutes.

Stir in the pimiento, season and simmer for a further 5 minutes. Pour the whiskey over and ignite. When the flames have died remove the pan from the heat, stir in the cream and then reheat without boiling.

Cook the rice in boiling salted water until tender. Arrange it round the edge of a serving dish and pile the kidneys in the centre. Garnish generously with chopped parsley.

HEART

Ox heart is the largest and tends to be rather tough unless cooked long and slowly. It can be parboiled whole and then roasted, or cut up and braised or stewed, but in any case it needs strong seasonings and flavourings. An ox heart weighs about 3–4 lb. and serves 4–6 people. It can be bought sliced.

Calf's heart is small and more tender, but still needs slow cooking. It may be roasted, braised or stewed. 1 calf's heart will serve 2 people.

Lamb's heart is more tender than ox or calf's and has a fine flavour. It is usually stuffed and either roasted or braised. Allow 1 per person.

RICH CASSEROLED HEART
serves 4

1 ox heart, 2½–3 lb.
2 oz. fat or oil
2 onions, skinned and sliced
1 oz. (¼ cup) flour
½ pint (1¼ cups) stock
½ lb. carrots, peeled and grated
½ a small swede, peeled and grated
pared rind of 1 orange
6 walnuts, chopped

Slice the heart, removing the tubes, and wash it well. Fry in the fat or oil till slightly brown, then put into a casserole. Fry the onions and add to the casserole. Add the flour to the remaining fat and brown slightly. Pour in the stock, bring to the boil, stirring, and simmer for 2–3 minutes, then strain over the meat in the casserole. Cover and cook at 300°F. (mark 2) for 2½–3 hours. Add the carrots and swede and cook for a further hour.

Shred the orange rind and boil for 10–15 minutes; drain. Add the walnuts and orange rind to the casserole for the last 15 minutes.

STUFFED HEART CASSEROLE
serves 4

4 small lambs' hearts
2 level tbsps. seasoned flour
1 oz. fat or oil
1 pint (2½ cups) stock
1 onion, skinned and sliced
4 sticks of celery, scrubbed and sliced
¼ lb. carrots, peeled and sliced
1 tbsp. cider (optional)

For stuffing :

4 oz. (2 cups) breadcrumbs
1 medium-sized onion, skinned and finely chopped
3 tbsps. melted butter
2 level tsps. mixed dried herbs
salt and pepper

Wash the hearts, slit open, remove any tubes and wash again. Mix the ingredients for stuffing and fill the hearts with it. Tie them into their original shape with string, coat with seasoned flour and brown quickly in the hot fat or oil.

Place in a casserole with the stock, cover and cook in the oven at 350°F. (mark 4) for 2½ hours, turning them frequently. Add the onion, celery, carrots and cider (if used) for the last 45 minutes.

SWEETBREADS

Ox sweetbreads need slow,

Try lambs' kidneys flamed in Irish whiskey – kidney royale

gentle cooking in a casserole.

Calf's sweetbreads are more tender than ox, but are also best stewed or casseroled.

Lamb's sweetbreads are tender, with a fine delicate flavour. They can be fried, or casseroled. Allow 4 oz. sweetbreads per person.

FRIED SWEETBREADS
serves 4

1 lb. lambs' or calves' sweetbreads
juice of ½ lemon
beaten egg
breadcrumbs for coating
oil for deep frying
tomato slices and onion rings

Soak the sweetbreads for 3–4 hours in cold water, then drain and put in a pan. Cover with cold water and lemon juice and bring slowly to the boil. Simmer for 5 minutes. Drain and leave in cold water until they are firm and cold; strip off any stringy unwanted tissues.

Press the sweetbreads well between absorbent paper, slice and dip in the beaten egg and crumbs. Fry the sweetbreads in the hot fat until golden. Serve at once with tartare or tomato sauce and garnished with tomato slices and onion rings.

CREAMED SWEETBREADS
serves 4

1 lb. sweetbreads, prepared (see fried sweetbreads)
½ an onion, skinned and chopped
1 carrot, peeled and chopped
few parsley stalks
½ bay leaf
salt and pepper
1½ oz. butter
1½ oz. (⅜ cup) flour
½ pint (1¼ cups) milk
squeeze of lemon juice
chopped parsley for garnish

Put the sweetbreads, vegetables, herbs and seasonings in a pan with water to cover and simmer gently until tender–about ¾–1 hour. Drain and keep hot, retaining ½ pint (1¼ cups) of the cooking liquid.

Melt the butter, stir in the flour and cook for 2–3 minutes. Remove the pan from the heat and gradually stir in the sweetbread liquid and milk. Bring to the boil and continue to stir until it thickens. Season well and add the lemon juice.

Reheat the sweetbreads in the sauce and serve sprinkled with parsley.

Sweetbreads are delicious coated with egg and breadcrumbs and fried

POULTRY AND GAME

Poultry is the term used for all birds reared specially for the table. It includes chicken, duck, goose and turkey. Game refers to wild birds and animals that are hunted for food, but which are protected by law at certain seasons. The most common game birds are grouse, partridge, pheasant, wild duck, black game and ptarmigan; the only protected animals are deer. Hare, pigeon and rabbit are usually grouped with game although they are not protected. Pigeon and rabbit are sometimes reared specially for the table; both are prepared in much the same ways as game and it is therefore convenient to include them.

CHICKEN

A very young chicken (6–8 weeks old, weighing 1–2 lb.) is known as a poussin and is usually grilled, fried or baked. A broiler (12 weeks old, weighing 2½–3½ lb.) is cooked in the same way. (Frozen chickens are usually broilers.) There is of course no reason why these birds should not be casseroled or braised. A roaster (4–5 lb.) and a capon (up to 10 lb.) both look and taste very appetizing when stuffed and roasted. Boiling fowl (18 months old, weighing 4–7 lb.) are boiled or casseroled; the meat is too tough to roast.

TURKEYS, DUCKS, GEESE

Whole turkeys are most commonly roasted, stuffed with 1 or 2 kinds of forcemeat. Cut joints may be made into a variety of casserole dishes.

Ducks may be roasted, casseroled or braised. They are rich and are therefore usually served with a sharp-flavoured sauce or accompaniment such as apple sauce or orange salad. Ducklings are more commonly eaten than fully grown ducks. Buy a duck or duckling weighing at least 3 lb., otherwise the proportion of bone is too high.

Geese (average weight 9–10 lb.) are usually roasted, though they can be casseroled. Again they are rich in fat and need something to offset this.

Game birds tend to dry out when roasting, so bard them with bacon

GAME BIRDS

Generally speaking, the more simply game is cooked, the better. For young birds there is no better way than roasting. For older birds that are likely to be tough, braising or casseroling are better. Since game birds lack fat, it is usual to bard the breast before roasting with pieces of fat bacon and to baste frequently with fat during cooking. Sometimes a knob of butter or a piece of juicy steak is put inside the bird before it is cooked, to keep it moist.

HARE AND RABBIT

Hares may be roasted (if young), fricasseed or braised. They are usually hung for 7–10 days before cooking. Rabbits may be cooked almost any way suitable for other kinds of meat, but only young, tender ones should be roasted or fried; they also make a good pie filling and adapt well to jellied moulds.

VENISON

This is the meat of the red deer. The haunch is the prime cut and this and the other better-quality cuts roast and fry well. Venison, which should be well hung, does tend to be rather dry; so bard or lard it and marinade before cooking. The back and breast may be casseroled or braised.

PREPARATION

Most poultry and game are now sold ready for cooking, that is hung, cleaned or drawn where appropriate, and plucked or skinned. However, since many of the birds are stuffed before cooking, you need to be able to truss them at home (trussing keeps the bird a good shape, so that it looks attractive and is easy to carve).

Note: Poultry are cooked without the feet, but game feet are left on for cooking.

TRUSSING

There are 2 ways of trussing, using either a trussing needle and fine string or a skewer and string. First stuff the bird if required, then fold the neck skin under the body and fold the wing tips back towards the backbone so that they hold the neck skin in position. Make a slit in the skin above the vent and put the tail (the 'parson's nose') through.

If you are using a trussing needle, thread it with fine string and insert it close to the second joint of the right wing; push it right through the body, passing it out to catch the corresponding joint on the other side. Then insert the needle in the first joint of the left wing, pass it through the flesh at the back of the body, catching the wing tips and the neck skin, and bring it out through the first joint of the wing on the right side. Tie the ends of the string in a bow. To secure the legs, re-thread the needle, insert it through the gristle beside the parson's nose and tie the legs and tail firmly together. If you are using a skewer, insert it right through the body just below the thigh bone and turn the bird over on its breast. Catching in the wing tips, pass the string under the ends of the skewer and cross it over the back. Turn the bird over and tie the ends of the string round the tail, at the same time securing the drumsticks.

FROZEN BIRDS

Both poultry and game are frequently sold frozen. *The bird must be thoroughly thawed before cooking starts.* A single joint of chicken will take 2–3 hours to thaw; a whole chicken or game bird 12–24 hours, depending on size. A large turkey may take up to 3 days.

ROAST CHICKEN

Wipe the inside of the bird with a clean, damp cloth and stuff the neck end. Don't stuff too tightly as the forcemeat mixture tends to swell and might split the skin. To add flavour if left unstuffed, put a knob of butter with some herbs, an onion or a wedge of lemon in the body. Truss. Brush the chicken with oil or melted butter and sprinkle with salt and pepper. Place a few strips of streaky bacon over the breast if you wish.

Cook at 375°F. (mark 5), allowing 20 minutes per lb. plus 20 minutes. Baste occasionally and put a piece of greaseproof paper over the breast if it seems to be browning too quickly.

Alternatively, wrap the bird in foil before cooking, with the join along the top or use a transparent roasting bag, following the instructions. Allow the same cooking time but open the foil for the final 15–20 minutes to allow the bird to brown.

Serve with roast potatoes and green vegetables or a tossed green salad; also bacon rolls, chipolata sausages, bread sauce and thin gravy made from the giblets.

To roast a very small bird, spread with softened butter and put a knob of butter inside. Wrap in buttered paper and cook for only about $\frac{1}{2}$–$\frac{3}{4}$ hour, according to size. Remove the paper for the last 15 minutes to brown the breast.

ROAST TURKEY

Stuff and truss and spread with softened butter or dripping. Cover the breast with strips of fat bacon. Cook either at 325°F. (mark 3), basting regularly, or at 450°F. (mark 8) wrapping the bird in foil first and unwrapping it for the last 30 minutes. In either case turn it once, for even browning.

Cooking times – at 325°F. (mark 3)

6–8 lb.	3–3$\frac{1}{2}$ hours
8–10 lb.	3$\frac{1}{2}$–3$\frac{3}{4}$ hours
10–12 lb.	3$\frac{3}{4}$–4 hours
12–14 lb.	4–4$\frac{1}{4}$ hours
14–16 lb.	4$\frac{1}{4}$–4$\frac{1}{2}$ hours
16–18 lb.	4$\frac{1}{2}$–4$\frac{3}{4}$ hours

Cooking times – at 450°F. (mark 8)

6–8 lb.	2$\frac{1}{4}$–2$\frac{1}{2}$ hours
8–10 lb.	2$\frac{1}{2}$–2$\frac{3}{4}$ hours
10–12 lb.	2$\frac{3}{4}$ hours
12–14 lb.	3 hours
14–16 lb.	3–3$\frac{1}{4}$ hours
16–18 lb.	3$\frac{1}{4}$–3$\frac{1}{2}$ hours

If preferred, use a large roasting bag and follow directions.
Serve with roast potatoes and brussels sprouts; sausages, forcemeat balls, bacon rolls, thin gravy, bread sauce, cranberry sauce.

ROAST DUCK

allow 12–14 oz. per person

Stuff at the tail and truss as for chicken, except that the wings are not drawn across the back. Prick the skin all over with a fine skewer and sprinkle the breast with salt and pepper.
Cook at 375°F. (mark 5) for 20 minutes per lb.
Serve with apple sauce, new potatoes, peas and thin brown gravy, or orange salad, or with bigarade sauce.

ROAST GOOSE

serves 8

Stuff and truss. Sprinkle with salt and place in a roasting tin on a wire rack, as goose tends to be fatty. Cover the breast with greaseproof paper or foil. A sour apple put in the roasting tin will add extra flavour to the gravy.
Cook at 400°F. (mark 6) for 15 minutes per lb. plus 15 minutes, without basting. Alternatively cook at 350°F. (mark 4) for 25–30 minutes per lb. Remove the paper for last 30 minutes to brown skin. Serve with gravy and apple or gooseberry sauce.

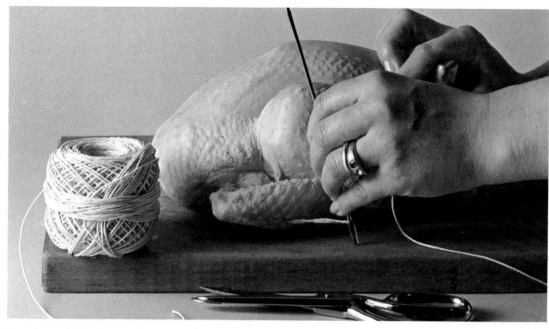

Trussing a chicken for roasting, using fine string and a special trussing needle

ROAST GROUSE

serves 2–3

Truss, season inside and out and lay some fat bacon over the breast. Put a knob of butter inside and place the bird on a slice of toast. Cook at 400°F. (mark 6) for 30 minutes, basting frequently. After 20 minutes, remove the bacon, dredge the breast with flour, baste well and cook for a further 10 minutes. Serve the grouse on the toast on which it was roasted, with thin gravy, bread sauce, fried crumbs and matchstick potatoes.

ROAST PARTRIDGE

serves 1–2

Season the inside with salt and pepper, replace the liver and add a knob of butter. Truss. Cover the breast with pieces of bacon fat. Cook at 450°F. (mark 8) for 10 minutes, then reduce the temperature to 400°F. (mark 6) and cook for a further 10–20 minutes, according to size. Partridge should be well cooked.
Serve with fried crumbs, game chips, clear gravy, watercress, bread or orange sauce and quarters of lemon.

ROAST PHEASANT

serves 4–5

Wipe the bird inside and out and put a knob of butter, flavoured with herbs and lemon juice, inside. Truss and cover the breast with strips of fat bacon. Cook at 450°F. (mark 8) for 10 minutes, then reduce the temperature to 400°F. (mark 6) and continue cooking for 30–40 minutes, according to size. Baste frequently with butter.

15 minutes before the end, remove the bacon, dredge with flour and baste well. Serve as for partridge.

ROAST WILD DUCK

Mallard serves 4–5
Pintail serves 2
Widgeon serves 2
Teal serves $\frac{1}{2}$–1

Truss like a domestic duck and spread with softened butter. Cook at 425°F. (mark 7), basting frequently. Allow 20 minutes for teal, 30 minutes for mallard and widgeon – they should on no account be overcooked. Halfway through the cooking time, pour a little port or orange juice over the bird. Serve with thin gravy, and orange salad or bigarade sauce.

ROAST VENISON

For marinade :
2 carrots, peeled and chopped
2 small onions, skinned and chopped
1 stick of celery, scrubbed and chopped
6 peppercorns
parsley stalks
1 bay leaf
3 blades of mace
red wine

The best joint for roasting is the saddle, but for a small piece use the loin or a fillet cut from the saddle. Place the vegetables and flavourings for the marinade in a large container, put in the venison and add sufficient wine to half cover it. Leave to marinade for 12 hours, turning the meat 2–3 times.
It was traditional to cover the meat with a paste made by mixing flour and water to a stiff dough (allow

about 3 lb. flour to a saddle) and rolling it out to $\frac{1}{2}$-in. thickness. Nowadays, however, the meat is usually brushed generously with oil and wrapped loosely in foil. Roast in the centre of the oven at 325°F. (mark 3), allowing 25 minutes per lb. ; 20 minutes before the end of cooking time, remove foil or paste, dredge joint with flour and return to oven to brown. Serve hot with thick gravy and redcurrant or cranberry jelly.

GAME CHIPS

Scrub and peel the potatoes and slice very thinly into rounds. Soak the slices in cold water, dry them and fry in deep fat for about 3 minutes (fill the frying basket only $\frac{1}{4}$ full). Remove the chips from the fat and drain well.
Just before serving, reheat the fat and fry the chips rapidly for a further 3 minutes, until crisp and brown. Drain well on kitchen paper and serve in an open dish.

FRIED CRUMBS

2–4 oz. fresh white breadcrumbs
1 oz. butter

Fry the crumbs in the butter until golden brown.

REMOULADE SAUCE

$\frac{1}{4}$ pint ($\frac{5}{8}$ cup) mayonnaise
1 tbsp. filely chopped mixed pickles
1 tbsp. made mustard

Combine all the ingredients and allow to stand a while for the flavours to mellow.

The richness of duck can be offset by the sharp orange tang of bigarade sauce

CRANBERRY SAUCE

6 oz ($\frac{3}{4}$ cup) sugar
$\frac{1}{4}$ pint ($\frac{5}{8}$ cup) water
$\frac{1}{2}$ lb. cranberries

Gently heat the sugar with the water in a pan until the sugar dissolves. Add the cranberries and cook uncovered over a medium heat for about 10 minutes; cool. Add sherry to taste.

BIGARADE SAUCE

3 oranges (use bitter ones, e.g. Seville, when available)
1 lemon
1 level tbsp. sugar
1 tbsp. vinegar
2 tbsps. brandy
1 level tbsp. cornflour

Grate the rind from 1 orange and squeeze the juice from all of the oranges and the lemon. Melt the sugar in a pan with the vinegar and heat until it is a dark brown caramel. Add the brandy, orange and lemon juice to the caramel and simmer gently for 5 minutes. Drain the excess fat from the tin in which the duck was roasted and add the grated rind and the orange sauce to the sediment. Stir in the cornflour blended with a little water, return the tin to the heat, bring to the boil and cook for 2–3 minutes, stirring.
Adjust seasoning.

ORANGE SALAD

2 oranges, peeled
chopped tarragon or mint
French dressing
endives or crisp lettuce leaves, washed

Divide the oranges into segments, removing all the skin, pith and pips. Alternatively, cut across in thin slices, using a saw-edged knife.
Put the orange into a shallow dish, sprinkle with tarragon or mint and pour the dressing over; allow to stand for a short time.
Spoon the orange on to a bed of endives or lettuce to serve.

VEAL FORCEMEAT
for turkey

8 oz. lean veal, trimmed and diced
6 oz. lean bacon, rinded and diced
2 onions, skinned and finely chopped
2 oz. butter
6 oz. fresh white breadcrumbs
2 large mushrooms, wiped and chopped
2 tsps. finely chopped parsley
salt and freshly ground black pepper
pinch of cayenne pepper
pinch of ground mace
2 eggs, beaten
milk (optional)

Mix the veal and bacon and pass twice through a mincer, then beat them well in a bowl. Fry the onion lightly in a little of the butter until soft but not coloured – about 2–3 minutes. Add to the meat.
Add the breadcrumbs, mushrooms, remaining butter, seasoning and spices and bind with the beaten eggs. Mix well together; if the mixture is too stiff, add a little milk.
Use as required.

APPLE AND CELERY STUFFING
for duck; use double the quantity for goose

2 oz. bacon, rinded and chopped
1 oz. butter
2 onions, skinned and chopped
2 sticks of celery, scrubbed and chopped
4 medium cooking apples, peeled and cored
3 oz. fresh white breadcrumbs
2 tbsps. chopped parsley
sugar to taste
salt and pepper

Fry the bacon in the butter for 2–3 minutes until golden brown and remove from the pan with a slotted spoon. Fry the onions and celery for 5 minutes and remove from the pan with a slotted spoon. Slice the apples into the pan and fry for 2–3 minutes until soft. Add the breadcrumbs, parsley, sugar and seasoning and mix well together.

APRICOT STUFFING
for chicken; make double this quantity to stuff the neck end of a turkey

3 oz. dried apricots
3 oz. fresh white breadcrumbs
$\frac{1}{4}$ level tsp. mixed spice
$\frac{1}{4}$ level tsp. salt
$\frac{1}{4}$ level tsp. pepper
1 tbsp. lemon juice
1 oz. butter, melted
1 egg, beaten

Soak the apricots overnight in cold water. Drain off the liquid, chop the fruit, stir in the remaining ingredients and bind with the egg.

POULET AU GRAND MARNIER
serves 4–6

For stuffing:
3 oz. butter
4 oz. onions, skinned and finely chopped
4 oz. celery, scrubbed and finely chopped
1 level tsp. dried marjoram or oregano
$\frac{1}{2}$ lb. cooked ham, minced or finely chopped
$\frac{1}{2}$ level tsp. grated orange rind
6 oz. fresh white breadcrumbs
1 tbsp. Grand Marnier
salt and freshly ground black pepper

$3\frac{1}{2}$–4 lb. oven-ready chicken
$\frac{1}{2}$ oz. butter
salt and pepper
juice of 2 medium oranges
2 tbsps. Grand Marnier
$\frac{1}{2}$ lb. cherries, stoned
2 oz. ($\frac{1}{4}$ cup) caster sugar
1 level tbsp. flour
$\frac{1}{2}$ pint ($1\frac{1}{4}$ cups) water
parsley sprigs

Melt 1 oz. butter in a large pan. Add the onion and celery, cover with a lid and simmer for 10 minutes. Add remaining 2 oz. butter and allow it to melt. Stir in the herbs, ham, orange rind, breadcrumbs and Grand Marnier. Mix well together, adjust seasoning and use this to stuff the bird, then truss in the usual way.
Smear the $\frac{1}{2}$ oz. butter over the bird. Sprinkle with salt and pepper. Put the chicken and its washed giblets in a roasting tin. Pour the juice of 1 orange over the bird. Roast at 375°F. (mark 5) for about $1\frac{1}{2}$–2 hours. 15 minutes before the end of cooking time spoon 2 tablespoons Grand Marnier over the breast and complete the cooking.
Meanwhile squeeze the juice from the remaining orange and put it in a small pan with the cherries and the sugar. Cook over gentle heat. Remove the bird from the roasting pan. Discard the trussing string and keep the bird warm on a serving dish.
On top of the stove, reduce the pan juices to about 2 tablespoons by boiling rapidly. Stir in the flour and add the water. Bring to the boil and let it bubble for 1–2 minutes. Season well.
Drain the cherries and arrange them round the bird. Add the cherry juice to the thickened pan juices. Pass all through a sieve. Garnish with parsley and serve the gravy separately.

Poulet au Grand Marnier, generously garnished with cherries

GROUSE A L'AMERICAINE

serves 4

2 young grouse
2 oz. butter
salt and pepper
4 oz. fresh breadcrumbs
cayenne pepper
4 rashers of bacon, rinded
4 tomatoes, halved
¼ lb. button mushrooms, washed
watercress

Slit the grouse down the back and flatten. Brush them with melted butter and dust with salt and pepper. Grill lightly for 5 minutes under a medium heat, sprinkle with the breadcrumbs and dust sparingly with cayenne. Continue to grill for about 20 minutes, turning the birds frequently.

Roll the bacon and grill, with the tomatoes and mushrooms, for 3–5 minutes, until cooked. Serve round the grouse on the serving dish.

SALMI OF PARTRIDGE OR PHEASANT

serves 4

2 partridges or 1 pheasant, lightly roasted
1 shallot, skinned and chopped
1 orange, peeled and segmented
¼ pint (⅝ cup) stock
½ pint (1¼ cups) espagnole sauce
¼ pint (⅝ cup) red wine
a few white grapes, skinned and pipped
red-currant jelly

Remove the skin from the birds; cut off the breast and leg joints; set aside. Break up the remaining carcasses into small pieces and put in a pan with the shallot, orange rind and stock. Simmer together for ½ hour. Strain the stock from the pan, put it together with the espagnole sauce, wine and joints into a saucepan and simmer until the meat is heated through – about 10 minutes. Arrange the joints on a serving dish and boil the sauce until it is reduced to a syrupy consistency. Pour it over the game and garnish with the grapes, orange segments and red-currant jelly.

Grilled grouse à l'américaine makes a quick 'company' dish

HUNTER'S CASSEROLE

serves 4

3½-lb. rabbit, skinned and jointed into small pieces (2½ lb. meat when skinned)
salt and freshly ground black pepper
2 tbsps. cooking oil
½ oz. butter
¼ pint (⅝ cup) dry white wine
1 clove of garlic, skinned and crushed
3 tbsps. chopped parsley

Season the rabbit joints. Heat the oil and butter in a heavy pan and fry the rabbit briskly on all sides until golden brown. Remove the rabbit pieces and place in a casserole. Drain the excess fat from the pan juices and add the wine, garlic and 2 tablespoons chopped parsley. Adjust the seasoning and heat for a few minutes. Pour the sauce over the rabbit and cook in the centre of the oven at 375°F (mark 5) for about 45 minutes, until the flesh is tender.

Remove the flesh from the bones, return to the sauce and cook for a further 15 minutes. Sprinkle with remaining chopped parsley.

CHICKEN CHASSEUR

serves 4

4 chicken joints
seasoned flour
1 tbsp. cooking oil
1 oz. butter
1 onion, skinned and chopped
2 oz. mushrooms, washed and sliced
2 tomatoes, skinned and seeded
½ pint (1¼ cups) espagnole sauce or rich gravy
4 tbsps. dry white wine
salt and pepper
chopped parsley

Coat the chicken joints in seasoned flour and fry until golden in the oil and butter. Arrange in a casserole in a single layer. Add the onion and mushrooms to the pan and fry gently for 5 minutes. Drain off the fat. Dice the tomatoes and add to the onion and mushrooms, and add the espagnole sauce or gravy, the wine and seasoning. Pour over the chicken. Cover and cook in the oven at 350°F. (mark 4) for about 1¼ hours, until tender. Sprinkle with chopped parsley before serving.

TURKEY A LA KING

serves 4

8 oz. button mushrooms
1 small green pepper (capsicum), seeded
2 oz. butter
1½ oz. (⅜ cup) flour
6½-oz. can pimiento (sweet red pepper), drained and diced
¼ pint (⅝ cup) turkey stock
¼ pint (⅝ cup) milk
Tabasco sauce
12 oz. cooked turkey, diced
salt and pepper
1–2 tbsps. sherry

Wipe the mushrooms and remove the stalks but do not peel. Slice thickly. Slice the pepper thinly. Melt the butter and saute the mushrooms and pepper for 10 minutes. Stir in the flour and cook for 2–3 minutes. Add the pimiento caps, and slowly stir in the stock and milk. Bring to the boil, reduce heat, add a few drops of Tabasco and the turkey. Season and simmer for 15 minutes. Add sherry, reheat and serve with rice.

PIGEONS IN CREAM

serves 6

6 pigeons
4 oz. butter
¼ pint (⅝ cup) stock
2 tbsps. red-currant jelly
½ pint (1¼ cups) double cream
1 tbsp. brandy
chopped parsley

Wash the pigeons and trim away the claws and undercarriage bones. Fry in the butter until well browned. Place in a casserole, breast side down in the butter and juices; add the stock and cover tightly. Cook in the oven at 325°F. (mark 3) for about 2 hours until really tender. Remove the birds from the casserole and keep warm. Boil the juices rapidly to reduce by half. Stir in the red-currant jelly and cream. Adjust seasoning.

Bring to the boil and reduce the heat. Warm the brandy, ignite and pour flaming over the sauce. Pour the sauce over the birds, and sprinkle with chopped parsley.

COOKING WITH VEGETABLES

Vegetables add interest and flavour to the day's meals and many of them are also a good source of vitamins and minerals. For example, a helping of potatoes and a green vegetable will supply most (if not all) of the daily Vitamin C requirements.

Storing and preparation

Buy vegetables in prime condition and store in a cool, airy place – a vegetable rack in a well ventilated larder is ideal, or the vegetable compartment of a refrigerator. Green vegetables should be used as soon as possible after gathering, while their Vitamin C value is at its highest.

All vegetables should be prepared with care and as near to the time of cooking as possible, to retain both flavour and Vitamin C content.

Serving

Serve vegetables as soon as they are cooked – they tend to deteriorate when they are kept hot and some develop unpleasant, strong smells. Serve them slightly under-rather than over-cooked, and drain them well if they have been boiled. Serve all vegetables really hot, especially if fried. Don't cover them with a lid or they will become soggy.

A sprinkling of salt and pepper improves most vegetables – especially fried ones, where no salt is used in the cooking process. Add a knob of butter to boiled or steamed vegetables when serving.

JERUSALEM ARTICHOKES

Scrub the artichokes; using a stainless steel knife or peeler, peel them quickly and immediately plunge them into cold water, to prevent discolouration. A squeeze of lemon juice or a few drops of vinegar added to the water helps to keep them a good colour.

Cook in boiling salted water to which a little lemon juice or vinegar has been added for about 30 minutes, until just soft. Drain, garnish with finely chopped parsley and serve with melted butter or a white, cheese, or hollandaise sauce.

Allow 6–8 oz. per person.

GLOBE ARTICHOKES

Cut off the stem close to the base of the leaves and take off the outer layer of leaves and any others which are dry or discoloured. Soak the artichokes in cold water for about 30 minutes to ensure they are clean; drain well (upside-down).

Cook them in boiling salted water until the leaves will pull out easily – about 20–40 minutes, depending on size – and drain up-side-down. Serve them with melted butter or hollandaise sauce. Globe artichokes may also be served cold, with a vinaigrette dressing.

Allow 1 artichoke per person as a starter.

ASPARAGUS

Cut off the woody end of the stalks and scrape the white part lightly, removing any coarse spines. Tie in bundles with all the heads together and place upright in a deep saucepan or special asparagus pan of boiling salted water. Boil for 10 minutes, then lay them flat and continue cooking until just soft – a further 10–15 minutes (this does not apply when cooking in a special pan).

Alternatively, lay the bundles in the bottom of a saucepan with the heads all pointing in the same direction and have one side of the pan slightly off the heat, so that the heads are in the cooler part allow about 15 minutes.

Drain well and untie the bundles before serving with melted butter or hollandaise sauce.

Don't overcook asparagus – it is better to have to discard more of the stem part than to have the tips mushy.

Allow 8–12 stems per person.

AUBERGINE (EGGPLANT)

Aubergines should be of a uniform purple colour, free from blemishes. Cut off the stem and small 'leaves' which surround it; wash the vegetables but do not peel them.

Aubergines are usually fried or stuffed and baked. If frying, slice the aubergines, spread them out

on a plate and sprinkle with salt. Leave for 30 minutes, then dry with kitchen paper and dip in flour, if wished, before frying. Allow about 6 oz. per person.

BROAD BEANS

Shell and cook the beans in boiling salted water until soft – 20–30 minutes. Serve with butter or parsley sauce. When broad beans are very young and tender – that is, when the pods are only a few inches long and the beans inside very small – the whole pods may be cooked and eaten.

Allow 8–12 oz. per person (weight including pods).

FRENCH AND RUNNER BEANS

Top and tail the beans. String runner beans if they seem coarse. Slice runner beans thinly; French beans may be left whole or broken in half. Cook in boiling salted water for about 10–15 minutes, until soft. Remove any scum that rises to the top with a spoon. Drain and toss with pepper and a knob of butter before serving. French beans may be cooked and served cold, with vinaigrette dressing.

Allow 6 oz. per person.

BEETROOT

Cut off the stalks 1 in. or so above the root, then wash the beetroots, taking care not to damage the skins or they will 'bleed' while boiling. Boil in salted water until the skin will rub off easily with your thumb – the time depends on age and freshness, but 2 hours is about average. When they are ready, peel off the skin and cut the beets into cubes or slices. Serve hot, coated with a white sauce, or cold plain or in a little vinegar.

Allow 4–6 oz. per person when served as an accompaniment.

GLAZED BEETROOTS

serves 4

12 small beetroots, cooked
1 oz. butter
1 level tsp. sugar
salt and pepper
grated rind of 1 lemon
1 tsp. chopped chives
2 tsps. chopped parsley
juice of ½ lemon
1 tbsp. capers

Remove the skin, stalks and root end from the beetroots. Melt the butter in a saucepan and add the beetroots, sugar, salt, pepper and lemon rind. Toss the beetroots in the pan over a medium heat

Sauté courgettes and tomatoes, finished au gratin

until they are well coated; add the remaining ingredients, heat through and serve.

BROCCOLI
(purple-headed or Cape and sprouting)

White and purple-headed broccoli are cooked like cauliflower, but take only 15–20 minutes. Serve plain, buttered, or with hollandaise sauce.

Cook sprouting broccoli as for asparagus – set upright in the pan and boil for about 15 minutes.

Allow 6–8 oz. per person.

BRUSSELS SPROUTS

Wash the sprouts, removing any discoloured outer leaves, and cut a cross in the stalks. Cook in boiling salted water until tender – 8–10 minutes. Drain, return them to the pan and reheat with pepper and a knob of butter.

Allow 6–8 oz. per person.

SAVOY AND DUTCH CABBAGE

Remove the coarse outer leaves, cut the cabbage in wedges and take out the hard centre stalk. Wash thoroughly and cook rapidly in about 1 in. of boiling salted water for about 12 minutes. Take care

not to overcook. Drain well, chop roughly if wished and toss with a knob of butter, sprinkling of pepper and a pinch of grated nutmeg (optional). Serve at once.

Allow 4 oz. prepared cabbage per person.

Spring greens

Separate the leaves and discard any thick stems. Wash well and shred roughly. Cook as for cabbage.

Allow ½ lb. per person.

Red cabbage

Wash and shred the cabbage and braise with apple and onions, until tender.

CARROTS

New

Trim off the leaves and any root, wash, then scrape lightly with a sharp knife. Boil the whole carrots in salted water for about 15 minutes, or until tender. Serve tossed with a little butter, pepper and chopped parsley.

Old

Peel thinly and cut into ¼- or ½-in. strips, lengthwise, or into strips and then across into small squares, or into thin rounds. Cook and serve as for new carrots, but simmer for about 20 minutes.

Allow 4–6 oz. per person.

CAULIFLOWER

Remove the coarse outside leaves, cut a cross in the stalk end and wash the cauliflower. Boil it stem side down in salted water for 20–30 minutes, depending on size. Drain well and serve coated with white or cheese sauce.

The cauliflower can be divided into individual florets and cooked in fast-boiling salted water for about 10 minutes. Drain well and serve tossed with butter and a sprinkling of pepper or coated with sauce.

A medium-sized cauliflower serves 4 people.

CELERIAC
(the root of turnip-rooted celery)

Cut away leaves and root fibres. Do not peel. Boil in salted water for 40–60 minutes. To serve, drain, peel and slice; add butter, salt, pepper and parsley. Celeriac may also be served raw, cut into julienne strips and mixed with other salad vegetables.

Allow 4–8 oz. per person.

CELERY

Wash, scrub and cut the stalks into even 1½–2 in. lengths. Cook in boiling salted water until tender – about 20 minutes, depending on the coarseness of the celery. Add a stock cube for extra flavour. Drain well and serve with a white, parsley or cheese sauce. Celery is also very good braised.

Allow 1 head of celery per person if small, 2–3 sticks if large.

CHICORY

Generally eaten raw as a salad plant, but chicory may also be cooked. Cut off a thin slice from the base. Pull away any damaged outer leaves and wash quickly under cold water.

To cook, plunge the whole heads into boiling water and blanch for 5 minutes. Drain and cook in the minimum of water with a knob of butter, lemon juice and seasoning for about 20 minutes. Serve sprinkled with chopped parsley or a little paprika.

Allow 1–2 heads per person when chicory is being cooked.

CORN ON THE COB

Choose the cobs when they are plump, well formed and of a pale golden yellow colour. Remove the outside leaves and silky threads, put the cobs into boiling unsalted water (salt toughens the corn) and cook for about 15 minutes, depending on their size.

Drain well and serve with melted butter, salt and freshly ground pepper.

Allow 1–2 cobs per person.

COURGETTES (ZUCCHINI)

Cut away the stalk end and ¼ in. from the rounded end; do not peel. If small, blanch whole, otherwise slice thickly; blanch in salted water for 5 minutes. Drain, then sauté in a little butter, lemon juice and chopped parsley for a few minutes. Season before serving.

Allow ¼ lb. per person, when served as an accompaniment.

courgettes. Cook gently until soft and slightly transparent and put them in an ovenproof dish. Melt the remaining ½ oz. butter and cook the tomatoes, parsley, garlic, pepper and sugar until a thickish purée forms.

Re-season the mixture if necessary and pour it over the courgettes. Sprinkle with the cheese and breadcrumbs and grill until golden brown.

LEEKS

Remove the coarse outside leaves and cut off the roots and most of the green. Wash very thoroughly,

dripping round the meat or stuffed and baked, either whole or in rings.

Allow 8 oz. per person when served as an accompaniment.

ONIONS

Onions vary considerably in both size and flavour from the small white 'cocktail' onion to the large, mild Spanish onion.

Both the leaves and the bulbs of the young plants, known as spring onions, may be eaten in salads, but in the case of the ordinary mature onions the stems and skin are discarded.

Chop the centres finely, mix with the crumbs, seasoning and 1 oz. cheese. Fill the onions and place them in a greased ovenproof dish. Put small knobs of butter on top and sprinkle with the remaining cheese. Bake in the centre of the oven at 400°F. (mark 6) for 20–30 minutes, till the onions are cooked and browned.

Serve with tomato sauce.

PARSNIPS

Wash the parsnips, peel, quarter and remove the hard centre cores if the parsnips are at all woody. Quarter or slice and cook in boiling salted water for 20–40 minutes, until soft. Drain and toss in butter, salt, pepper and a little grated nutmeg.

To roast parsnips, par-boil them (halved or quartered) for 5 minutes in salted water, drain and cook as for roast potatoes for about 1 hour. Allow 6–8 oz. per person.

PEAS

The season for fresh peas lasts for about 6 weeks only, but they are sold preserved in various ways – canned, dried, dehydrated and frozen. Frozen and dehydrated peas are very similar to fresh ones when they are properly cooked and presented.

Allow 8–12 oz. fresh peas (as bought), 3 oz. drained canned or frozen peas, or 2 oz. dehydrated peas, per person.

Fresh peas

Shell and wash, place in boiling salted water with about 1 level teaspoon sugar and a sprig of mint and cook until tender – 15–20 minutes. Drain them, remove the mint and toss the peas with a knob of butter before serving.

Frozen, dehydrated and canned peas

Follow the manufacturer's directions.

Onions, stuffed with cheesy crumbs, baked and served with tomato sauce

COURGETTES (ZUCCHINI) A LA GRECQUE

serves 4

2 small onions, skinned and thinly sliced
3 tbsps. olive oil
1 clove of garlic, skinned and crushed
just over ¼ pint (⅝ cup) dry white wine
salt and freshly ground black pepper
1½ lb. courgettes (zucchini)
½ lb. tomatoes
pinch of dried chervil (optional) or 1 tbsp. chopped fresh chervil

Variation:

Firm button mushrooms which have been cleaned and trimmed can be used in place of the courgettes.

Sauté the onions in the hot oil until soft but not coloured; add garlic, wine and a little seasoning. Wipe courgettes and discard a slice off each end. Cut remainder into rings. Skin and quarter the tomatoes, discarding the seeds. Add courgettes and tomatoes to the pan and cook gently, without covering, for 10 minutes. Cool quickly. Add a little chervil if liked (or add fresh chervil, if available, when serving).

VEGETABLE MARROW

Large marrows must be peeled, the seeds removed and the flesh cut into even-sized pieces. Cook in boiling salted water until tender – about 20 minutes – and drain well. Serve coated with a white or cheese sauce.

Marrow can also be roasted in the

Chopped onions are included in many savoury dishes as flavouring. As a separate vegetable, they are best braised, fried, or stuffed and baked.

BAKED STUFFED ONIONS

serves 4

4 medium-sized onions, skinned
2 level tbsps. fresh white breadcrumbs
salt and pepper
2 oz. cheese, grated
butter

Cook the onions in boiling salted water for 15–20 minutes, removing them before they are quite soft; drain and cool. Scoop out the centres, using a pointed knife to cut the onion top and a small spoon to remove the centres.

SAUTE OF PEAS

serves 4

few spring onions, trimmed
1 oz. butter
2 lb. peas, shelled
salt and freshly ground black pepper
¼–½ pint (⅝–1¼ cups) white stock
1 tsp. chopped parsley

Lightly fry the onions in the butter for about 2 minutes, then add the peas, salt and pepper and just enough stock to cover the peas. Cover with a tightly fitting lid and cook gently for 15–20 minutes, until the peas are tender

remove the lid after 10–15 minutes to allow the cooking liquid to evaporate.
Sprinkle with chopped parsley just before serving.

POTATOES

Peel old potatoes as thinly as possible; new potatoes are scraped, or brushed and cooked with the skins on and peeled before serving. Cook the potatoes as soon as possible after peeling. Allow 6–8 oz. per person.

Boiled potatoes

Cut the prepared potatoes into even-sized pieces (leave new potatoes whole), put into cold water, add ½ level teaspoon salt per lb., bring to the boil and simmer until tender but unbroken – 15–20 minutes for new potatoes, 20–30 minutes for old.
Drain well, add a knob of butter and serve sprinkled with chopped parsley.

Creamed potatoes

Boil old potatoes as above; using a fork or potato masher, mash with a knob of butter, salt and pepper to taste and a little milk. Beat them well over a gentle heat with a wooden spoon or hand-held electric mixer until fluffy.
Serve in a heated dish, mark with a fork and sprinkle with chopped parsley.

Baked or 'jacket' potatoes

Choose even-sized old potatoes, free from 'eyes' and blemishes. Scrub well, dry and prick all over with a fork. Bake near the top of the oven at 400°F. (mark 6) for about ¾–1 hour for small potatoes, 1–1¼ hours for larger ones, or until soft when pinched. Cut a cross in the top of each potato and put in a knob of butter or a spoonful of soured cream.

Roast potatoes

Using old potatoes, peel in the usual way and cut into even-sized pieces. Cook in boiling salted water for about 7 minutes and drain well. Transfer them to a roasting tin containing 4 oz. hot lard or dripping, baste well and cook near the top of a hot oven – 425°F. (mark 7) – for about 20 minutes; turn them and continue cooking until soft inside and crisp and brown outside – about 40 minutes altogether. Alternatively, place potatoes in the tin round a roasting joint. Drain well on kitchen paper and serve uncovered, sprinkled with salt.

LYONNAISE POTATOES
serves 4

½ lb. onions, skinned and
   sliced
1–2 tbsps. cooking oil
1 lb. sauté potatoes
chopped parsley

Fry the onions slowly in the oil until golden brown – about 10 minutes. Serve in layers with the potatoes and sprinkle with chopped parsley.

SEAKALE

Wash well, cut off ends and tie into neat bundles. Cook for 20–

This is a hot curry and is good served with boiled rice

30 minutes in boiling salted water to which a squeeze of lemon juice has been added. Drain well and remove the strings before serving. Serve coated with béchamel or hollandaise sauce.
Seakale may also be braised or served au gratin, served cold with a vinaigrette dressing or eaten raw with cheese and in salads.
Allow 4–8 oz. per person.

SPINACH

Wash well in several waters to remove all grit and strip off any coarse stalks. Pack into a saucepan with only the water that clings to the leaves after washing. Heat gently, turning the spinach occasionally, then bring to the boil and cook gently for 5–15 minutes until soft. Drain thoroughly, chop roughly or purée and reheat with

a knob of butter and a sprinkling of salt, pepper and nutmeg.
Allow 6–8 oz. per person.

SWEDES
(Swedish turnips)

Peel thickly and slice, dice or cut into julienne strips. Keep covered with water and cook as soon as possible after peeling. Boil in a little salted water with the lid on for about 20 minutes, according to size and age. Drain well, and mash them with a little salt, pepper, grated nutmeg and a knob of butter.
Alternatively, cut them in chunks or fingers and roast them round the joint allowing 1–1¼ hours.
Allow 4–6 oz. per person.

SWEET PEPPERS
(CAPSICUMS)

Both red and green peppers can be sliced or chopped and eaten raw in a salad. Small amounts of raw or blanched peppers may be included in savoury dishes made with rice and macaroni. Peppers may be fried or stuffed and baked. To prepare them, remove stem, seeds and membrane. For stuffing and baking, leave whole, parboil for 5 minutes and bake at 350°F. (mark 4) for 25–30 minutes. Or cut in rings and sauté in butter for 5 minutes.
Allow 1 medium-sized pepper per person for cooked dishes such as stuffed or fried peppers.

SWEET PEPPERS WITH TOMATOES
serves 4

2 tbsps. cooking oil
½ an onion, skinned and
   chopped
1 clove of garlic, skinned and
   crushed
4 tomatoes, skinned and
   sliced
2 level tbsps. tomato paste
¼ pint (⅝ cup) dry white wine
4 medium-sized peppers,
   seeded and thinly sliced
salt and pepper

Heat the oil and lightly fry the onion and garlic for 5 minutes without colouring. Add the tomatoes, tomato paste and wine and simmer for 5 minutes. Add the peppers, cover and simmer for 30 minutes. Adjust seasoning.

TURNIPS

Peel thickly to remove the outer layer of skin and put under water to prevent discolouration. Young turnips can be left whole, older ones should be sliced, diced or cut in strips. Cook whole in salted water for 20–30 minutes, if sliced or diced cook for 15–20 minutes. Toss young turnips in butter or a little top of the milk, with added seasoning, or serve in white sauce. Mash old ones with salt, pepper, nutmeg and a knob of butter.
Allow 4–6 oz. per person.

VEGETABLE CURRY
serves 4

1 cauliflower, cut in large
   sprigs
6 tomatoes, skinned and
   sliced
6–8 small potatoes, peeled and
   quartered
¼ lb. shelled peas
¼ lb. French beans, sliced
1 level tbsp. turmeric
1½ level tbsps. mild curry
   powder
½ level tsp. salt
2 oz. butter
6 small onions, skinned
1 clove of garlic, skinned and
   crushed
½ pint (1¼ cups) stock

Place the raw cauliflower, tomatoes, potatoes, peas and beans on a large plate. Mix the spices and salt and sprinkle over the vegetables. Melt the butter in a heavy pan and sauté the small onions and garlic. Add the spiced vegetables, then the stock; cover, bring to the boil and simmer for about 20 minutes, until all the vegetables are tender. Serve with boiled rice.

SALADS

Serve crisp, cool salads for main courses, starters and accompaniments. Full of vitamins and minerals for your family, quick and easy to prepare for guests – salads are the answer to many a 'what shall we eat?' situation. Above: Dutch salad, based on cheese, apples and spinach.

MAIN COURSE SALADS

PORK AND BEAN SALAD
serves 4

2 tbsps. chopped parsley
1 small onion, skinned and
    very finely chopped
1 level tsp. dry mustard
1 level tsp. French mustard
1 level tsp. paprika pepper
1 level tsp. salt
freshly ground black pepper
¼ level tsp. grated nutmeg
2 level tsps. caster sugar
juice of 1 orange
4 tbsps. salad oil
2 tbsps. tarragon vinegar
7-oz. can red kidney beans,
    drained
2 large cooked potatoes, diced
1 lb. cold, cooked pork
    sausages
2 eating apples, cored and
    diced
2 tomatoes, skinned and
    seeded

Put the parsley, onion, seasonings, spices, sugar, orange juice, oil and vinegar in a lidded container, close and shake to make a dressing.

In a bowl, lightly toss together the beans, potatoes, sausages (cut into ¼-in. slices) apples and chopped tomatoes. Fold the dressing through and leave to marinade for 30 minutes, giving the mixture an occasional stir. Turn into a salad bowl for serving.

CHICKEN SALAD
serves 6

3½-lb. oven-ready boiling fowl
1 small onion, skinned
2–3 strips of lemon rind
2 tbsps. lemon juice
blade of mace
2 sprigs of parsley
6 peppercorns
2 cloves
salt
4 oz. (½ cup) long grain rice
2 oz. sultanas
1 oz. seedless raisins
8 oz. white and black grapes,
    skinned and pipped
¼ pint (⅝ cup) mayonnaise
1 tomato, sliced, for garnish
1 egg, hard-boiled and sliced,
    for garnish
watercress for garnish

Put the fowl in a casserole with the onion, lemon rind and juice, the herbs and spices, tied in muslin, salt to taste and sufficient water to cover; cook slowly on top of the stove or in the oven until tender – about 3 hours.
Remove all bones and skin from the fowl and dice the flesh. Boil the rice in the strained chicken stock until tender, drain if necessary and leave until cold. Mix the diced fowl, rice, dried fruit and half the grapes, adding the mayonnaise. Pile high in a deep dish and garnish with a border of alternating black and white grapes; on top place a few tomato and egg slices and a tuft of watercress.

SWEDISH CHICKEN SALAD
serves 6

3½-lb. oven-ready chicken,
    roasted
6 oz. (¾ cup) long grain rice
1 green eating apple
1 red eating apple
2 bananas
lemon juice
¼ pint (⅝ cup) double cream
7 fl. oz. (⅞ cup) mayonnaise
1 level tsp. curry powder
salt and pepper
watercress for garnish

Allow the chicken to cool. Meanwhile cook the rice in boiling, salted water for about 12 minutes, drain and cool. Carve the chicken into slices and cut these into strips. Halve and core the apples and slice thinly. Peel the bananas and slice thickly. Sprinkle both with lemon juice.
Whip the cream to the same consistency as the mayonnaise and fold it in. Add the curry powder. Fold in the chicken, apple and banana. Add more lemon juice and adjust the seasoning. Pile on a bed of rice, or combine with the rice. Garnish with watercress.

BEEF SALAD
serves 4

8 oz. (1 cup) long grain rice
2–3 tomatoes, skinned and
    sliced
8 oz. cold, cooked beef, thinly
    sliced and cut in strips
1 tbsp. finely chopped onion
1 level tsp. made mustard
3 tbsps. French dressing
1 lettuce, washed and
    separated
4 tomatoes, sliced, to garnish

Cook the rice in boiling, salted water for about 12 minutes and allow to cool. Mix with the tomatoes, meat and onion.
Add the mustard to the French dressing and stir into the salad ingredients. Serve with the lettuce and remaining sliced tomatoes.

CHEESE SALAD BOWL
serves 4

1 lettuce, washed and
    separated
bunch of watercress, washed
    and trimmed
½ lb. tomatoes, skinned and
    sliced
4 oz. small, new potatoes,
    boiled and diced
6–8 oz. Cheddar cheese, diced
¼ pint (⅝ cup) mayonnaise
a little made mustard
chopped chives or parsley

Line a salad bowl with lettuce and

watercress. Combine the tomatoes, potatoes and cheese. Mix the mayonnaise with a little mustard and combine with the potato mixture. Put into the centre of the salad bowl and sprinkle with chives or parsley.

SALAMI SALAD
serves 4

4 oz. Danish salami, thinly sliced
4 oz. Samsoe cheese, diced
French dressing
small bunch of radishes, trimmed and sliced
1 clove of garlic, skinned and cut
1 lettuce, washed and roughly shredded
½ cucumber (or 1 small, ridge cucumber), thinly sliced
bunch of watercress, washed and trimmed
4 oz. Gruyère cheese, thinly sliced

Put 8 slices of salami to one side and cut the rest into strips, using scissors. Toss the Samsöe cheese in 2 tablespoons of the dressing, mix in a bowl with the salami and radishes. Add the garlic. Leave for a little time for the flavours to mellow.
Cut half way through each slice of the reserved salami and curl into cones.
To serve, remove the garlic, lightly toss the lettuce, cucumber and half the watercress in a little dressing. Arrange in a shallow flat dish. Tuck in the slices of Gruyère round the edge and pile the dressed cheese and salami mixture in the centre. Surround with salami cones and watercress sprigs.

PIQUANT EGG SALAD WITH YOGHOURT DRESSING
serves 4

For dressing :

½ pint (1¼ cups) low-fat natural yohourt
1 level tsp. paprika pepper
1 level tsp. sugar
1 tbsp. lemon juice
1 tbsp. orange juice
pepper
1 tbsp. finely chopped parsley

1 head of celery, scrubbed and finely sliced
4 eggs, hard-boiled and sliced
4 carrots, peeled and grated
a few radishes, washed and sliced
½ cucumber (or 1 whole, small, ridge cucumber)

Salami salad, served continental style on a wooden board

For the dressing combine the natural yoghourt with the paprika pepper, sugar, strained lemon and orange juices, a little pepper and the finely chopped parsley.
Fold the celery through half the dressing and spoon into a salad bowl. Arrange the eggs on top, cover with the grated carrot and surround with sliced radishes and cucumber.
Spoon the remaining yoghourt dressing over the top. Chill before serving.

AVOCADO, TOMATO AND ONION SALAD

For dressing :

4 tbsps. salad oil
2 tbsps. wine vinegar
½ level tsp. caster sugar
¼ level tsp. salt
¼ level tsp. dry mustard
¼ level tsp. Dijon mustard
freshly ground black pepper

1 avocado
juice of ½ a lemon
½ medium green pepper (capsicum), seeded and thinly sliced
2 tomatoes, skinned and sliced
1 small onion, skinned and thinly sliced
chopped parsley

To make the dressing, place all the ingredients in a screw-top jar and shake vigorously.
Cut the avocado in half lengthwise, discard the stone, peel and slice the fruit. Squeeze a little lemon juice over the flesh.
Combine the avocado with the pepper, tomatoes, and onion, moisten with dressing and garnish with chopped parsley.

SIDE SALADS

DUTCH SALAD
serves 6

1½ tbsps. lemon juice
3 firm, green, eating apples
8 oz. Edam cheese, rinded
7-oz. can pimientos (sweet red peppers), drained
¾ lb. spinach

For dressing :

1½ tbsps. cider vinegar
3 tbsps. corn oil
salt and freshly ground black pepper
½ level tsp. dry mustard
½ level tsp. caster sugar

Put the lemon juice in a bowl. Dice the apples, discarding the core; turn at once in the lemon juice. Cut the cheese into dice the same size as the apples. Cut the pimiento into small strips. Carefully wash the spinach and remove all the stems; roughly break the drained leaves into manageable pieces.
Whisk together the dressing ingredients and toss the spinach in the dressing until it glistens. Drain, and arrange round the edge of the salad bowl. Toss the apple, cheese and pimiento in the remaining dressing and pile in the centre of the spinach.

TUNA-FILLED TOMATOES
serves 4

4 large tomatoes
2 oz. butter
1 onion, skinned and chopped
4 oz. button mushrooms, wiped and sliced
7-oz. can tuna, drained and flaked
2 tbsps. chopped parsley

Remove the top from each tomato, cutting in a zig-zag fashion with a small, sharp-pointed knife. Using a teaspoon, scoop out the soft core and seeds and discard. Put the tomato cases on a baking sheet. Heat the butter in a frying pan, add the onion and cook until soft, without colouring. Add the mushrooms, continue cooking for a few minutes. Add the flaked tuna, together with the parsley. Mix well together and divide the filling between the tomatoes. Cover with kitchen foil and bake in the centre of the oven at 350°F. (mark 4) for 20–30 minutes.

BEAN AND CELERY SALAD
serves 4

½ lb. French beans, trimmed and halved
1 celery heart, scrubbed and finely sliced
½ dill cucumber, roughly chopped
7½-oz. can butter beans, drained
3–4 tbsps. well-seasoned French dressing
chopped chives to garnish

Cook the French beans in boiling salted water for about 5 minutes, drain and leave to cool. Toss the celery, dill cucumber, butter beans and French beans in enough dressing to moisten them.
Chill slightly and serve sprinkled with chopped chives.

SPINACH SLAW
serves 4

½ lb. fresh spinach
6 oz. white cabbage, washed and trimmed
2 oz. seedless raisins
4 tbsps. lemon juice
3 tbsps. salad oil
salt and freshly ground black pepper
caster sugar
1 dessert apple, cored and chopped but not peeled

Remove any coarse stems from the spinach and wash thoroughly; pat the leaves dry on a clean cloth. Finely shred the spinach and cabbage. Soak the raisins in half the lemon juice until soft and swollen, then add to the spinach and cabbage.
Whisk together the oil, remaining lemon juice, salt, pepper and sugar to taste. Add the apple and pour over the spinach and cabbage. Blend with 2 forks until the vegetables glisten with the dressing.

TOMATO AND ANCHOVY SALAD

serves 6

rind of ½ a lemon
3 tbsps. lemon juice
3 tbsps. salad oil
½ level tbsp. caster sugar
salt and freshly ground black
  pepper
2-oz. can anchovy fillets,
  drained and finely chopped
1½ oz. shallots, skinned and
  chopped
1½ lb. tomatoes, skinned and
  sliced

Using a potato peeler, thinly pare the lemon rind, free of the white pith, and chop it. Whisk together the chopped rind, juice, oil, sugar and seasoning. Add the anchovies and shallots. Turn the tomatoes in this dressing and leave in a cool place for 1–2 hours.

SALADE BASQUE

serves 4

6 eggs, hard-boiled and sliced
7-oz. can tuna, drained and
  flaked
2 dill cucumbers, finely sliced
8 tomatoes, skinned and
  sliced
2-oz. can anchovy fillets,
  drained
3–4 tbsps. salad oil
1 tbsp. wine vinegar
1 level tsp. French mustard
2 level tbsps. tomato ketchup
1 level tsp. dried mixed herbs

Layer the sliced eggs, flaked tuna, cucumber and tomatoes in a salad bowl. Split the anchovy fillets in half lengthwise and arrange in a lattice over the tomato layer. Whisk the remaining ingredients together to make a dressing and pour over the salad. Chill.

CABBAGE AND PINEAPPLE SALAD

1 firm cabbage (e.g. Dutch or
  Savoy)
4 eating apples, peeled and
  cored
1 large can of pineapple
  pieces
4 sticks of celery, scrubbed
  and chopped
½ pint (1¼ cups) mayonnaise
salt and pepper

Wash the cabbage, shred it and soak in really cold water for about 15 minutes to crisp it. Dice the apples.
Drain the cabbage and mix with the drained pineapple, apples and celery. Season the mayonnaise well, pour over and toss until everything is well coated.

FRANKFURTER ROKA SALAD

serves 4

12-oz. can frankfurters,
  drained
12½-oz. can new potatoes,
  drained
4-fl. oz. bottle blue cheese
  dressing (such as Kraft
  Roka)
1 tsp. chopped parsley
2½-fl. oz. jar stuffed olives,
  drained and halved
1 lettuce, washed
paprika pepper

Cut the sausages into ½-in. pieces, halve the potatoes and mix well together in a bowl, with the dressing, parsley and olives. Arrange on a bed of lettuce on a serving dish and sprinkle with paprika.

COURGETTE AND RICE SALAD

8 courgettes (zucchini)
8 oz. (1 cup) long grain rice
4 tomatoes
16 black olives
French dressing
fresh mint
4 tsps. chopped basil

Slice the courgettes, discarding a thin slice from the top and bottom, and cook (without peeling) in boiling salted water until just tender but still crisp. Drain well. Boil the rice, drain and allow to dry a little. Slice the tomatoes; stone and halve the olives. Mix the courgettes and olives with the rice, toss in the dressing and pile into a dish; surround with tomato slices. Spoon a little more dressing over the tomatoes and garnish with herbs.

WALDORF SALAD

2 lb. crisp eating apples
lemon juice
2 level tsps. sugar
½ pint (1¼ cups) mayonnaise
1 head of celery, chopped
4 oz (1 cup) walnuts, chopped
1 lettuce
few whole walnuts

Peel and core the apples, slice 2 and dice the rest; dip the slices in lemon juice to prevent discolouration. Toss the diced apples with 4 tablespoons lemon juice, the sugar and 2 tablespoons mayonnaise and leave to stand for about ½ hour. Just before serving, add the celery, walnuts and remaining mayonnaise and toss together. Serve in a bowl lined with lettuce leaves and garnish with the apple slices and a few whole walnuts.

Celery and beans make a sophisticated side salad

SALAD DRESSINGS

FRENCH DRESSING

¼ level tsp. salt
⅛ level tsp. pepper
¼ level tsp. dry mustard
¼ level tsp. sugar
1 tbsp. vinegar or
  lemon juice
2–3 tbsps. salad oil

Put the salt, pepper, mustard and sugar in a bowl, add the vinegar and stir until well blended. Whisk in the oil gradually with a fork. The oil separates out on standing, so if necessary whisk the dressing again immediately before use. Alternatively, make a larger quantity and store it in a salad cream bottle, shaking it up vigorously just before serving.

Note: The proportion of oil to vinegar varies with individual taste, but use vinegar sparingly. Wine, tarragon or other herb flavoured vinegar may be used.

FOAMY MAYONNAISE

2 egg yolks
salt
pepper
¼ pint (⅝ cup) salad oil
2 tbsps. lemon juice
1 egg white, stiffly
  whisked

Cream the egg yolks and seasonings and add the oil drop by drop, stirring hard all the time, until the mayonnaise is thick and smooth, then stir in the lemon juice. Put in a cool place until required just before serving, fold in the egg white.

MAYONNAISE

1 egg yolk
½ level tsp. dry mustard
½ level tsp. salt
¼ level tsp. pepper
½ level tsp. sugar
¼ pint (⅝ cup) salad oil
1 tbsp. vinegar or lemon
  juice

Put the egg yolk into a basin with the seasonings and sugar. Mix thoroughly, then add the oil drop by drop, stirring briskly with a wooden spoon the whole time, or using a whisk, until the sauce is thick and smooth.
If it becomes too thick, add a little of the vinegar. When all the oil has been incorporated, add the vinegar gradually and mix thoroughly until smooth and evenly combined.

THOUSAND ISLANDS MAYONNAISE

¼ pint (⅝ cup) mayonnaise
1 tbsp. finely chopped stuffed
  olives
1 tsp. finely chopped onion
1 egg, hard-boiled and
  chopped
1 tbsp. finely chopped green
  pepper (capsicum)
1 tsp. chopped parsley
1 level tsp. tomato paste
  or purée

This popular American salad dressing is very easy to make. Simply put all the ingredients in a bowl and mix them together until they are evenly combined. This mayonnaise can be served as a hamburger relish or with prawn cocktail as well as with fresh green salads.

Pork and bean salad

SAVOURY SAUCES

A good sauce can make a dish. It enhances the flavour of the food and adds new dimensions of texture and moisture. A sauce is not difficult to make, either, once the basic principles are mastered—the right amount of flour to liquid and careful regulation of the heat while blending are probably the two factors that have the greatest bearing on the texture of the finished sauce.

Most savoury sauces are thickened with either flour or egg. Flour sauces are based on a roux, made by melting the butter (or other fat), adding the flour, mixing thoroughly and cooking until they are well combined. For a brown sauce the roux is cooked until it is an even golden brown colour; the roux for a white sauce is not allowed to colour. The liquid is then added gradually and the sauce is stirred and cooked after each addition until it reaches the required consistency. (Beginners will find it easier if they take the pan off the heat to add the liquid.)

For white sauces the liquid used is usually milk or milk and white stock. For brown sauces, meat stock or vegetable water give a good flavour (stock made from a bouillon cube is adequate for most

but beware of over-seasoning) and for fish sauces you can use the bones from the fish to make a stock, combining this with milk for a sauce.

If you are entertaining, it helps the last minute rush if you can make the sauce earlier in the day—but the one thing worse than a lumpy sauce is one with a skin on top. If you make a sauce well in advance, press a piece of damp greaseproof paper on to its surface to stop this happening, and reheat it when needed. The basic white sauce recipes given here show how to vary the proportion of flour and fat to liquid to give sauces of different consistencies for different purposes.

WHITE SAUCES

1 Pouring consistency
¾ oz. butter
¾ oz. (approx. 2 level tbsps.) flour
½ pint (1¼ cups) milk or milk and stock
salt and pepper

Melt the fat, add the flour and stir with a wooden spoon until smooth. Cook over a gentle heat for 2–3

minutes, stirring until the mixture begins to bubble. Remove from the heat and add the liquid gradually, beating and stirring rapidly after each addition to prevent lumps forming. Bring the sauce to the boil, stirring continuously, and when it has thickened, cook for a further 1–2 minutes. Add salt and pepper to taste.

2 Coating consistency
1 oz. butter
1 oz. (3 level tbsps.) flour
½ pint (1¼ cups) milk or milk and stock
salt and pepper

Make the sauce as for pouring consistency.

3 Binding (panada) consistency
2 oz. butter
2 oz. (6 level tbsps.) flour
½ pint (1¼ cups) milk or milk and stock
salt and pepper

Melt the fat, add the flour and stir well. Cook gently for 2–3 minutes, stirring. Add the liquid gradually, beating well. Bring to the boil, stirring all the time, and cook for 1–2 minutes after it has thickened. Add salt and pepper to taste. This thick sauce is used for binding mixtures such as croquettes.

There are many variations on a basic white sauce—those given here are perhaps the most popular. These may also be made with béchamel.

MUSHROOM SAUCE Wash and slice 2–3 oz. button mushrooms. Fry in ½–1 oz. butter until soft but not coloured and fold into ½ pint (1¼ cups) white sauce. Season to taste.
Serve with fish, meat and eggs.

PARSLEY SAUCE Make ½ pint (1¼ cups) white sauce, using half milk and half stock, if available. When the sauce thickens, stir in 1–2 tablespoons chopped parsley and a little salt and pepper. Don't reboil or the parsley may turn the sauce green.
Serve with fish, boiled or braised bacon, or vegetables.

SHRIMP SAUCE Simmer the rind of 1 lemon and a bay leaf for 5 minutes in ½ pint (1¼ cups) liquid from which the sauce is to be made (milk or milk and fish stock). Strain and use to make the white sauce. When it thickens, stir in 2 oz. frozen, canned or potted shrimps, season to taste and reheat for 1–2 minutes. Serve with fish.

ANCHOVY SAUCE Make ½ pint (1¼ cups) white sauce with half milk and half fish stock. When it thickens, remove it from the heat and stir in 1–2 teaspoons anchovy essence (to taste), then a squeeze of lemon juice. (Anchovy essence is very salty and you will not need extra seasoning.) If you wish to tint the sauce a dull pink, add a few drops of red colouring. Serve with fish.

CAPER SAUCE Make the white sauce using ½ pint (1¼ cups) milk, or ¼ pint (⅝ cup) milk and ¼ pint cooking liquid from the meat. When the sauce thickens, stir in 1 tablespoon capers, and 1–2 teaspoons vinegar from the capers or lemon juice. Season well. Re-heat for 1–2 minutes.
Serve with boiled mutton or lamb.

BÉCHAMEL SAUCE
A classic, rich, white sauce

½ pint (1¼ cups) milk
1 shallot, skinned and sliced (or a small piece of onion, skinned)
a small piece of carrot, peeled and cut up
½ a stick of celery, scrubbed and cut up
½ a bay leaf
3 peppercorns
1 oz. butter
1 oz. (¼ cup) flour
salt and pepper

Put the milk, vegetables and flavourings in a saucepan and bring slowly to the boil. Remove from the heat, cover and leave to infuse for about 15 minutes. Strain the liquid and use this with the butter and flour to make a white sauce. Season to taste before serving.

AURORE SAUCE

½ pint (1¼ cups) béchamel sauce
1–2 level tbsps. tomato paste
1 oz. butter
salt and pepper

Make the sauce and when it has thickened stir in the tomato paste. Add the butter a little at a time and season to taste.
Serve with egg dishes, chicken or fish.

MORNAY SAUCE

½ pint (1¼ cups) béchamel sauce
2 oz. Parmesan, Gruyère or mature Cheddar cheese, grated
paprika pepper
salt and pepper

Chicken chaudfroid, garnished with radishes, angelica and lemon rind

White sauce, made to a pouring consistency

Make the béchamel or plain white sauce and when it thickens, remove from the heat and stir in the cheese and seasonings. Do not reheat or the cheese will become overcooked and stringy.
Serve with eggs, chicken or fish.

WHITE CHAUDFROID SAUCE

¼ pint (⅝ cup) normal strength liquid aspic made from aspic jelly powder
¼ oz. (1½ level tsps.) powdered gelatine
½ pint (1¼ cups) béchamel sauce
⅛–¼ pint (⅜–⅝ cup) single cream
salt and pepper

While the aspic is still warm stand it, in a basin, in a pan of hot water. Sprinkle in the gelatine and stir until it has dissolved, taking care not to overheat the mixture. Stir in the warm béchamel sauce, beat well and add the cream. Adjust the seasoning.
Strain the sauce and leave to cool, stirring frequently so that it remains smooth and glossy. Use when at the consistency of thick cream, for coating chicken, fish or eggs.

SOUBISE SAUCE

½ lb. onions, skinned and chopped
1 oz. butter
a little stock or water
½ pint (1¼ cups) béchamel sauce
salt and pepper

Cook the onions gently in the butter and a small amount of stock or water until soft–about 10–15 minutes. Sieve and stir the purée into the sauce, with seasoning to taste; reheat for 1–2 minutes.
Serve with lamb or veal.

VELOUTE SAUCE

¾ oz. butter
¾ oz. (2 level tbsps. approx.) flour
¾ pint (1⅞ cups) chicken or other light stock
2–3 tbsps. single cream
a few drops of lemon juice
salt and pepper

Melt the butter, stir in the flour and cook gently, stirring well, until the mixture is a pale fawn colour. Stir in the stock gradually, bring to the boil, stirring all the time. Simmer until slightly reduced and syrupy. Remove from the heat and add the cream, lemon juice and seasoning.
Serve with poultry, fish and veal.

TOMATO SAUCE
(made from fresh tomatoes)

1 small onion, skinned and chopped
1 small carrot, peeled and chopped
1 oz. butter
½ oz. flour
1 lb. cooking tomatoes, quartered
½ pint (1¼ cups) chicken stock (made from a cube)
½ a bay leaf
1 clove
1 level tsp. sugar
salt and pepper
2 level tsps. tomato paste (optional)
1–4 tbsps. white wine or sherry (optional)

Melt the butter in a pan and lightly fry the onion and carrot in the butter for 5 minutes. Stir in the flour and add the tomatoes, the stock and flavourings. Bring to the boil, cover and simmer for about 30 minutes, or until the vegetables are cooked. Sieve, reheat and re-season if necessary.
Tomato paste may be added to give a fuller flavour and a better colour. The wine or sherry may be added just before serving. Adjust seasoning after rather than before adding these optional ingredients.
Serve with croquettes, cutlets, réchauffés or any savoury dish.

TOMATO SAUCE
(made from canned tomatoes)

½ an onion, skinned and chopped
2 rashers of bacon, rinded and chopped
½ oz. butter
½ oz. flour
15-oz. can of tomatoes
1 clove
½ a bay leaf
a few sprigs of rosemary (or 1 level tsp. mixed dried herbs)
salt and pepper
pinch of sugar (optional)

Melt the butter in a pan and fry the onion and the bacon in the butter for 5 minutes. Stir in the flour and gradually add the tomatoes, also the flavourings and seasonings. Simmer gently for 15 minutes, then sieve and re-season if necessary. Add sugar if the flavour is too acid.
Serve with made-up meat dishes such as rissoles or stuffed peppers, and with cutlets.

HOLLANDAISE SAUCE

2 tbsps. wine or tarragon
   vinegar
1 tbsp. water
2 egg yolks
3–4 oz. butter
salt and pepper

Put the vinegar and water in a small pan and boil until reduced to about 1 tablespoon. Cool slightly.

Put the egg yolks in a small basin and stir in the vinegar. Put over a pan of hot water and heat gently, stirring all the time, until the egg mixture thickens (never let the water go above simmering point or the sauce will curdle). Divide the butter into small pieces and gradually whisk into the sauce; season to taste.

If the sauce is too sharp add a little more butter–it should be slightly piquant, almost thick enough to hold its shape and warm rather than hot when served.

Serve with salmon and other fish dishes, asparagus or broccoli. (The vinegar may be replaced by lemon juice–this tends to give a slightly blander sauce.)

MAYONNAISE
makes about ⅓ pint (¾ cup)
1 egg yolk
½ level tsp. dry mustard
½ level tsp. salt
¼ level tsp. pepper
½ level tsp. sugar
¼ pint (⅝ cup) oil
1 tbsp. white vinegar

Make sure that all ingredients are at room temperature. Put the egg yolks into a basin with the seasonings and sugar. Mix thoroughly, then add the oil drop by drop, beating briskly with a wooden spoon the whole time, or use a whisk. Continue adding oil until the sauce is thick and smooth –if it becomes too thick too quickly, add a little of the vinegar. When all the oil had been added, add the vinegar gradually and mix thoroughly.

TARTARE SAUCE

¼ pint (⅝ cup) mayonnaise
1 tsp. chopped tarragon or
   chives
2 tsps. chopped capers
2 tsps. chopped gherkins
2 tsps. chopped celery
1 tbsp. lemon juice or
   tarragon vinegar

Mix all the ingredients well, then leave the sauce to stand at least 1 hour before serving, to allow the flavours to mellow. Serve with fish.

Add oil very gradually for a mayonnaise, whisking all the time

BROWN SAUCES

GRAVY

A rich, brown gravy is served with all roast joints–thin with roast beef and thick with other meats. If the gravy is properly made in the roasting tin, there should be no need to use extra colouring. Remove the joint from the tin and keep it hot while making the gravy.

THIN GRAVY

Pour the fat very slowly from the tin, draining it off carefully from one corner and leaving the sediment behind. Season well with salt and pepper and add ½ pint (1¼ cups) hot vegetable water or stock (stock made from a bouillon cube is adequate but extra seasoning will not be required). Stir thoroughly with a wooden spoon until all the sediment is scraped from the tin and the gravy is a rich brown. Return the tin to the heat and boil for 2–3 minutes. Serve very hot.

This is the 'correct' way of making thin gravy, but some people prefer to make a version of the thick gravy given below, using half the amount of flour.

THICK GRAVY

Leave 2 tablespoons of the fat in the tin, stir in 1 level tablespoon flour (preferably shaking it from a flour dredger, to give a smoother result). Blend well and cook over the heat until it turns brown, stirring continuously. Carefully mix in ½ pint (1¼ cups) hot vegetable water or stock and boil for 2–3 minutes. Season well, strain and serve very hot.

ESPAGNOLE SAUCE

This classic brown sauce is used as a base for many savoury sauces

1 oz. streaky bacon, chopped
1 oz. butter
1 shallot, skinned and
   chopped (or a small piece
   of onion, chopped)
1 oz. mushroom stalks,
   washed and chopped
1 small carrot, peeled and
   chopped
¾–1 oz. (2–3 level tbsps.) flour
½ pint (1¼ cups) beef stock
a bouquet garni
2 level tbsps. tomato paste
salt and pepper
1 tbsp. sherry (optional)

Melt the butter in a pan and fry the bacon in the butter for 2–3 minutes. Add the vegetables and fry for a further 3–5 minutes, or until lightly browned. Stir in the flour, mix well and continue frying very slowly until it turns brown. Remove from the heat and gradually add the stock (which if necessary can be made from a stock cube). Stir after each addition. Return the pan to the heat and stir until the sauce thickens. Add the bouquet garni, tomato paste, salt and pepper. Reduce the heat, cover and allow to simmer very gently for 1 hour, stirring from time to time to prevent it sticking (an asbestos mat under the pan is a good idea). Alternatively, cook in the centre of the oven at 300°F. (mark 1–2) for 1½–2 hours. Strain the sauce, reheat and skim off any fat, using a metal spoon. Re-season if necessary.

If required, add the sherry just before the sauce is served, to give extra flavour.

Serve with beef dishes.

DEMI-GLACE SAUCE

¼ pint (⅝ cup) clear beef gravy
   or jellied stock from under
   beef dripping
½ pint (1¼ cups) espagnole
   sauce

Add the gravy to the sauce and boil (uncovered) until the sauce has a glossy appearance and will coat the back of the spoon with a shiny glaze.

Serve with dishes made from beef.

BROWN CHAUDFROID SAUCE

¼ pint (⅝ cup) normal strength
   liquid aspic, made from
   aspic jelly powder
¼ oz. (1½ level tsps.) powdered
   gelatine
¾ pint (1⅞ cups) espagnole
   sauce
Madeira, sherry or port to
   taste
salt and pepper

While the aspic is still warm stand it, in a basin, in a pan of hot water. Sprinkle in the gelatine and stir over a gentle heat until it dissolves. Warm the espagnole sauce and beat in the aspic and gelatine mixture. Add Madeira, sherry or port to taste and extra salt and pepper if necessary.

Strain the sauce and allow to cool, beating it from time to time so that it remains smooth and glossy. When it reaches the consistency of thick cream, use to coat game, duck or cutlets (see illustration for chicken chaudfroid, previous page).

SWEET SAUCES

Add a delicious sweet sauce to your dessert, to give it new dimensions. Whether you are serving a hot, steamy pudding or a smooth, icy sorbet a sauce will provide added flavour and texture. For a quick dessert, nothing can beat a bought ice cream with a helping of your own favourite sauce.

A true custard sauce, made with eggs, for fruit sweets

CUSTARD SAUCE
makes ½ pint (1¼ cups)

1½ level tbsps. custard powder
1½–2 level tbsps. sugar
½ pint (1¼ cups) milk

Blend the custard powder and sugar with a little cold milk to a smooth cream. Boil the rest of the milk and stir into the blended mixture. Return the sauce to the boil, stirring all the time until it thickens.
Serve hot, with puddings or pies.

EGG CUSTARD SAUCE
makes approx. ½ pint (1¼ cups)

1½ eggs or 3 egg yolks
1 level tbsp. sugar
½ pint (1¼ cups) milk
a few strips of thinly pared lemon rind

Whisk the eggs and sugar lightly. Warm the milk and lemon rind and leave to infuse for 10 minutes. Pour the milk on to the eggs and strain the mixture into the top of a double boiler or into a thick-based saucepan. Stir over a very gentle heat until the sauce thickens and lightly coats the back of the spoon. Serve hot or cold, with fruit sweets.

CHOCOLATE SAUCE
makes ½ pint (1¼ cups)

1 level tbsp. cornflour
1 level tbsp. cocoa powder
2 level tbsps. sugar
½ pint (1¼ cups) milk
a knob of butter

Blend the cornflour, cocoa and sugar with 1 tablespoon of the milk. Heat the remaining milk with the butter until boiling and pour on to the blended mixture, stirring all the time to prevent lumps forming. Return the mixture to the pan and bring to the boil, stirring until it thickens; cook for a further 1–2 minutes. Serve with steamed or baked sponge puddings.
Note: The cornflour and cocoa may be replaced by 2 level tablespoons chocolate blancmange powder.

JAM SAUCE
makes approx. ¼ pint (⅝ cup)

3 rounded tbsps. jam
¼ pint (⅝ cup) water or fruit juice
2 level tsps. arrowroot
2 tbsps. cold water
a squeeze of lemon juice (optional)

Warm the jam and water or fruit juice and simmer for 5 minutes. Blend the arrowroot and cold water to a smooth cream and stir into the jam mixture. Return the sauce to the heat, stirring, until it thickens and clears. Add the lemon juice and sieve into a sauce boat.
Serve hot with steamed or baked puddings, or cold over ice cream.
Note: A thicker sauce is made by just melting the jam on its own over a gentle heat and adding a little lemon juice.

SYRUP SAUCE
makes approx. ¼ pint (⅝ cup)

3–4 tbsps. golden syrup
3 tbsps. water
juice of ½ lemon

Warm the syrup and water, stir well and simmer, uncovered, for 2–3 minutes; add the lemon juice. Serve with steamed or baked sponge puddings.

FRUIT SAUCE
makes approx. ½ pint (1¼ cups)

15-oz. can fruit (e.g. apricots), drained
2 level tsps. arrowroot
squeeze of lemon juice or 1 tbsp. rum, sherry or fruit liqueur (optional)

Sieve the drained fruit or purée in a blender, make up to ½ pint (1¼ cups) with juice and heat until boiling. Blend the arrowroot with a little more juice until it is a smooth cream, then stir in the puréed fruit. Return the mixture to the pan and heat gently, continuing to stir, until the sauce thickens and clears. A squeeze of lemon juice or 1 tablespoon rum, sherry or a fruit liqueur may be added just before the sauce is served.
Good with meringue sweets, cold soufflés, hot baked puddings, steamed puddings and ice cream.

LEMON OR ORANGE SAUCE
makes ½ pint (1¼ cups)

grated rind and juice of 1 large lemon or orange
1 level tbsp. cornflour
2 level tbsps. sugar
1 egg yolk (optional)

Make up the fruit rind and juice with water to give ½ pint (1¼ cups). Blend the cornflour and sugar with a little of the liquid to a smooth cream. Boil the remaining liquid and stir into the mixture. Return it to the pan and bring to the boil, stirring until the sauce thickens and clears. Cool, add the egg yolk (if used) and reheat, stirring, but do not boil.

Lemon or orange sauce can be served either hot or cold, as for fruit sauce.

JUBILEE CHERRY SAUCE
makes approx. ½ pint (1¼ cups)

14-oz. can cherry pie filling
grated rind of 1 orange or lemon
a little brandy
4 portions vanilla ice cream

Heat the pie filling in a saucepan, adding the grated orange or lemon rind. Just before serving, add a little brandy; ignite it and spoon the flaming cherries over the portions of ice cream.

MOUSSELINE SAUCE
makes approx. ¼ pint (⅝ cup)

1 egg
1 egg yolk
1½ oz. sugar
1 tbsp. sherry
4 tbsps. single cream

Place all the ingredients in a basin over a pan of boiling water and whisk with a rotary whisk or electric mixer until pale and frothy and of a thick creamy consistency. Serve at once, over light steamed or baked puddings, fruit, fruit sweets or Christmas pudding.

SABAYON SAUCE
makes approx. ¼ pint (⅝ cup)

2 oz. (¼ cup) sugar
4 tbsps. water
2 egg yolks
rind of ½ lemon, grated
juice of 1 lemon
2 tbsps. rum or sherry
2 tbsps. single cream

Dissolve the sugar in the water over gentle heat and boil for 2–3 minutes, until syrupy. Pour on to the beaten yolks and whisk until pale and thick. Add the lemon rind, lemon juice and rum or sherry, and whisk for a further few minutes. Fold in the cream and chill well.
Serve with cold fruit sweets.

RUM BUTTER

3 oz. butter
3 oz. (½ cup) soft brown sugar
2–3 tbsps. rum
grated rind of ½ a lemon
1 tsp. lemon juice

Cream the butter and beat in the other ingredients carefully, as for brandy butter.

Serve with Christmas pudding and mince pies.

BRANDY BUTTER

3 oz. butter
3 oz. ($\frac{3}{8}$ cup) caster or icing sugar
2–3 tbsps. brandy

Cream the butter until pale and soft. Beat in the sugar gradually and add the brandy a few drops at a time, taking care not to allow the mixture to curdle. The finished sauce should be pale and frothy. Pile it up in a small dish and leave in a cool place to harden before serving.
Traditionally served with Christmas pudding and mince pies.

CHOCOLATE SAUCE

2 oz. plain (dark) chocolate
$\frac{1}{2}$ oz. butter
1 tbsp. milk
1 tsp. vanilla essence

Melt the chocolate and butter in a basin standing in a pan of hot water. Stir in the milk and vanilla essence and serve straight away, over ice cream.

COFFEE SAUCE

4 oz. ($\frac{5}{8}$ cup) Demerara or granulated sugar
2 tbsps. water
$\frac{1}{2}$ pint ($1\frac{1}{4}$ cups) strong black coffee

Put the sugar and water in a heavy-based pan and dissolve over a gentle heat, without stirring. Bring to the boil and boil rapidly until the syrup becomes golden in colour. Add the coffee and stir until the caramel has dissolved. Boil for a few minutes, until syrupy. Allow to cool, and serve poured over ice cream.

MELBA SAUCE

4 level tbsps. red-currant jelly
3 oz. ($\frac{3}{8}$ cup) sugar
$\frac{1}{4}$ pint ($\frac{5}{8}$ cup) raspberry purée (from $\frac{1}{2}$ lb. raspberries or a 15-oz. can)
2 level tsps. arrowroot
1 tbsp. cold water

Mix the jelly, sugar and raspberry purée and bring to the boil. Blend the arrowroot with the cold water to a smooth cream, stir in a little of the raspberry mixture, return the sauce to the pan and bring to the boil, stirring with a wooden spoon until it thickens and clears. Strain and cool.
This sauce is traditionally served over fresh peaches and ice cream.

Add a little extra to ice cream with a rich, home-made sauce

Brandy butter is a traditional 'hard' sauce for mince pies

APRICOT SAUCE

Mix some sieved apricot jam with a little lemon juice and 2 teaspoons sherry; pour it over ice cream and sprinkle with dessicated coconut or other decoration.

BUTTERSCOTCH SAUCE

1 oz. butter
1 oz. ($\frac{1}{6}$ cup) soft light brown sugar
1 tbsp. golden syrup
1 oz. nuts, chopped
a squeeze of lemon juice (optional)

Warm the butter, sugar and syrup until well blended. Boil for 1 minute and stir in the nuts and lemon juice. Serve straight away, over ice cream.

PECAN RUM SAUCE

makes $\frac{3}{4}$ pint ($1\frac{7}{8}$ cups)

6 oz. (1 cup) soft brown sugar
2 level tsps. instant coffee
6 tbsps. single cream or evaporated milk
1 oz. butter
1 tbsp. golden syrup
1 tbsp. rum
2 oz. shelled pecans (or walnuts)

Combine in a saucepan the sugar, coffee, cream or evaporated milk, butter and golden syrup. Cook over a low heat to dissolve the sugar, bring to the boil and boil gently, stirring, for 2–3 minutes, or until thickened. Stir in the rum and nuts. Serve either cold or warm, with vanilla ice cream.
This sauce may be bottled and stored for a short time.

CHERRY SAUCE

makes approx. $\frac{3}{4}$ pint ($1\frac{7}{8}$ cups)

$\frac{1}{2}$ lb. black or dark red cherries
2 oz. ($\frac{1}{4}$ cup) sugar
2 level tsps. arrowroot
almond essence
2 tsps. cherry brandy

Stone the cherries and cook in a little water with the sugar until fairly tender. Drain the fruit; make the juice up to $\frac{1}{2}$ pint ($1\frac{1}{4}$ cups) with water if necessary. Blend the arrowroot with a little juice, return it with the rest of the measured juice to the pan, and cook until transparent. Pour over the cherries and add a little almond essence and the cherry brandy.
Allow to cool. Serve with ice cream.

FLAMBE SAUCE

makes approx. $\frac{1}{3}$ pint

8-oz. can fruit cocktail
grated rind of $\frac{1}{2}$ lemon
3 oz. ($\frac{3}{8}$ cup) sugar
$1\frac{1}{2}$ oz. butter
3 level tsps. cornflour
2 tbsps. brandy

Gently heat the fruit cocktail with the grated lemon rind, sugar, butter and cornflour, stirring until the mixture thickens. Add the brandy, but do not stir. Ignite the brandy and spoon into the sauce. Pour the sauce at once over vanilla ice cream.

MARSHMALLOW SAUCE

makes $\frac{1}{2}$ pint ($1\frac{1}{4}$ cups)

4 oz. ($\frac{1}{2}$ cup) sugar
3 tbsps. water
8 marshmallows, cut up small
1 egg white
$\frac{1}{2}$ tsp. vanilla essence
red colouring (optional)

Dissolve the sugar in the water and boil for 5 minutes. Add the marshmallows and stir the mixture until they have melted. Whip the egg white stiffly and gradually fold in the marshmallow mixture. Flavour with vanilla and if you like, add a drop or two of colouring to tint it pink. Serve at once, over coffee or chocolate ice cream.

HONEY SAUCE

2 oz. butter
$1\frac{1}{2}$ level tsps. cornflour
4–6 oz. clear honey

Melt the butter in a pan and stir in the cornflour. Gradually add the honey. Bring to the boil and cook for a minute or two.

HOT DESSERTS

Brown sugared peaches with soured cream

ALMOND FRUIT PUFF

serves 6

For filling:

2 oz. butter
2 oz. ($\frac{1}{4}$ cup) caster sugar
$\frac{1}{2}$ tsp. almond essence
1 egg, beaten
$\frac{1}{2}$ oz. ($1\frac{1}{2}$ tbsps.) flour
2 oz. ($\frac{1}{2}$ cup) ground almonds
2 oz. maraschino cherries, halved
8-oz. can prunes, drained
8-oz. can sliced peaches, drained
8-oz. can apricot halves, drained
1 small apple, peeled and chopped
1 lb. frozen puff pastry, thawed
1 egg, beaten

Cream the butter and sugar until pale and fluffy. Beat in the essence, egg, flour and almonds and then lightly fold in the cherries, canned fruits and apple.

Roll out a quarter of the pastry very thinly and trim to an 8-in. diameter circle. Place on a baking sheet, prick well with a fork and brush round the rim with beaten egg. Divide the remaining pastry in half. Roll out one piece and trim it into a 9-in. circle, for the lid. Roll out the remainder into a strip 1 in. wide by about 14 in. long. Divide this strip in half and lay the strips over the egg-glazed rim to form a 'wall'. Leave pastry in a cool place to relax for 30 minutes.

Pile the fruit mixture inside the 'wall'. Brush the 'wall' with beaten egg, place the pastry lid on top and press the edges together lightly. Roll out the trimmings thinly and cut into thin, narrow strips. Arrange on the lid like the spokes of a wheel and glaze the pastry with beaten egg.

Bake at 450°F. (mark 8) for 15 minutes. Cover the puff with dampened greaseproof paper and cook for a further 45 minutes at 350°F. (mark 4). Serve warm in wedges with whipped cream.

BROWN-SUGARED PEACHES WITH SOURED CREAM

serves 4

4 large fresh peaches
2 level tbsps. soft brown sugar
$\frac{1}{2}$ level tsp. powdered cinnamon
$\frac{1}{2}$ pint ($1\frac{1}{4}$ cups) soured cream
4 level tbsps. caster sugar

Heat the grill before starting.

Dip the peaches into boiling water, count 10, then plunge them into cold water. Skin, stone and slice them. Arrange the slices evenly in individual soufflé dishes or ramekins.

Blend the soft brown sugar with the cinnamon and sprinkle the mixture over the peaches.

Spoon the soured cream over the peaches. Sprinkle each with 1 tablespoon of caster sugar and place them under a hot grill until the sugar melts and caramelizes. It is important that the grill is very hot, otherwise the cream will melt before the sugar forms a crust.

If practical, chill before serving; otherwise, serve straight from the grill.

HOT GINGER SOUFFLE

serves 4

1$\frac{1}{2}$ oz. butter
1$\frac{1}{2}$ oz. ($\frac{3}{8}$ cup) plain flour
$\frac{1}{2}$ pint ($1\frac{1}{4}$ cups) milk
3 oz. ($\frac{3}{8}$ cup) caster sugar
1 tbsp. brandy (optional)
$\frac{1}{8}$ level tsp. powdered ginger
2 oz. preserved stem ginger, chopped
4 large eggs, separated

Butter a 7-in. (2-pint) soufflé dish. Melt the butter in a saucepan, stir in the flour and gradually add the milk. Bring to the boil, reduce the heat and cook for 2 minutes. Stir in the sugar, brandy and ginger and beat in the egg yolks one at a time. Stiffly whisk the egg whites and fold into the mixture in the pan.

Turn the mixture into the soufflé dish and bake at 350°F. (mark 4) for about 40–45 minutes, until it is well risen and just firm to the touch.

Serve at once with ginger syrup and cream.

APPLE AND BRAMBLE PLATE PIE

serves 6

2 lb. cooking apples, peeled and cored
6 tbsps. water
$\frac{1}{2}$ level tsp. dried grated orange rind
3 oz. ($\frac{3}{8}$ cup) sugar
8 oz. shortcrust pastry (i.e. made with 8 oz. flour)
3–4 tbsps. bramble jelly
milk and sugar for glazing

Slice the apples fairly thickly and place in a shallow layer on the base of a large saucepan. Cover with the water and bring gently to the boil.

Reduce heat and cook for a few minutes until some of the fruit begins to break up – most of it should remain in slices and there should not be any extra juice. Stir in the orange rind and sugar and leave to cool.
Divide the pastry in half. Roll out one part into a large circle and use to line a $1\frac{3}{4}$-pint clear ovenproof glass flan dish or an 8-in. fluted flan ring placed on a baking sheet. Spread the base with bramble jelly and spoon the part-cooked apple on top.
Roll out the remaining pastry to make a lid. Damp the pastry edges, lift the lid into position and press the edges together. Knock up the edges with the back of a knife, make a slit in the lid, brush with milk and dredge with granulated sugar.
Place the flan dish on a pre-heated baking sheet. Bake in the centre of the oven at 400°F. (mark 6) for about 35–40 minutes or until the pastry is a good colour.
Serve warm with clotted cream.

APPLE DUMPLINGS WITH WALNUT SAUCE

serves 4

12 oz. shortcrust pastry (i.e. made with 12 oz. flour)
4 large cooking apples, washed and cored
6 level tbsps. mincemeat
1 egg, beaten

For sauce:
2 oz. butter
2 oz. ($\frac{3}{8}$ cup) Demerara sugar
$1\frac{1}{2}$ tbsps. cream
2 oz. ($\frac{1}{2}$ cup) walnuts, coarsely chopped

Divide the pastry into 4; knead lightly and roll each piece out into a large enough circle to wrap round an apple. Place each apple on to a pastry round and fill the centres generously with mincemeat.
Brush the pastry edges with egg and completely enclose the apples with the pastry, sealing the join. Place the dumplings on a baking sheet, join side down, and brush all over with beaten egg. Bake in the oven at 400°F. (mark 6) for about 35 minutes until golden brown.
Meanwhile make the walnut sauce by melting the butter and stirring in the sugar; when dissolved, add the cream and nuts and bring to the boil.
Serve the sauce separately in a jug to pour over the dumplings.

Golden apple dumpling, served with hot walnut sauce

APPLE FLAN

serves 6

For pastry case:
3 oz. ($\frac{3}{4}$ cup) plain flour
3 oz. ($\frac{3}{4}$ cup) self-raising flour
2 oz. butter
2 oz. margarine
1 oz. ($\frac{1}{4}$ cup) icing sugar, sifted
water

For filling:
4 tbsps. apricot jam
2 tbsps. water
juice of 1 small lemon
$1\frac{1}{4}$ lb. eating apples
1–2 level tbsps. caster sugar

Place the flours in a bowl, rub in the fats to resemble fine bread-crumbs. Stir in the icing sugar. Mix to a firm but pliable dough with cold water. Knead lightly on a floured board. Roll out and use to line a 9–$9\frac{1}{2}$ in. loose-bottomed French fluted flan tin.
Boil together the jam and water for 2–3 minutes, stirring. Sieve into a cup or small bowl. Cool; then spread half over the flan base. Squeeze the lemon juice into a bowl. Peel, core and thinly slice the apples straight into the lemon juice – for speed slice on the chisel edge of a grater. Turn apple slices in the juice to prevent discolouration. Spoon apple into the flan case, keeping the surface level. Sprinkle with sugar.
Place on a baking sheet and cook in the oven at 400°F. (mark 6) for about 35 minutes. Whilst still hot brush with the rest of the apricot glaze to which any excess lemon juice has been added.
Serve warm rather than hot, with thick cream.

RICE AND FRUIT TART

serves 8

7 oz. ($\frac{7}{8}$ cup) long grain rice
$1\frac{1}{4}$ pints (3 cups) milk
6 oz. ($\frac{3}{4}$ cup) caster sugar
2 eggs, beaten
3 firm pears, peeled and cored
12 apricots, halved and stoned
3 peaches (or large plums), halved and stoned
$\frac{1}{2}$ lb. apricot jam

Simmer the rice in boiling water for 3 minutes and drain well. Put the milk and $2\frac{1}{2}$ oz. ($\frac{1}{3}$ cup) of the sugar on to boil and when boiling add the rice. Stir well, and simmer gently until the rice is tender and most of the liquid has been absorbed.
Meanwhile, using a shallow pan, dissolve the remaining sugar in $\frac{1}{3}$ pint ($\frac{7}{8}$ cup) water, bring to the boil and boil for 2 minutes.
Beat the eggs into the rice, then mould the mixture into a well-buttered 10-in. shallow ovenproof dish, covering the base and the sides. Place the dish in the centre of the oven at 350°F. (mark 4) for 10 minutes.
Remove the dish from the oven, remould the sides if necessary and return it to the oven for a further 20 minutes, or until the rice is firm and set.
Quarter the pears and simmer them gently in the sugar syrup for about 10 minutes. Add the apricots and peaches and continue to simmer for 5 minutes until all the fruits are tender but not soft. Drain them well, and arrange them in the rice case. Keep everything warm.
Melt the apricot jam in the remaining syrup and boil until reduced by one-third. Strain and spoon a little over the fruits – just enough to glaze them.
Put the rest in a sauce boat and serve as an accompaniment to the hot tart.

CHERRY-WALNUT UPSIDE DOWN PUDDING

serves 6

For topping:
1 oz. butter
2 oz. (4 tbsps.) soft light brown sugar
3 oz. glacé cherries, halved
3 oz. walnuts, coarsely chopped
1 tbsp. coffee essence

For sponge base:
4 oz. butter or margarine
4 oz. ($\frac{1}{2}$ cup) caster sugar
2 eggs, lightly beaten
2 tbsps. coffee essence
6 oz. ($1\frac{1}{2}$ cups) self-raising flour

Lightly grease a 6-in. round cake tin. Melt the butter and brown sugar for the topping and stir in the cherries, walnuts and coffee essence. Spread the mixture evenly over the base of the cake tin.
Cream the butter and sugar until light and fluffy; beat in the eggs one at a time and stir in the coffee essence. Fold in the sifted flour, turn into the tin, level and bake at 350°F. (mark 4) for 50–55 minutes, until the sponge is firm but springy to the touch and shrinks slightly from the tin.
Turn out the pudding on to a heated serving plate and serve hot with whipped double cream or clotted cream.

PEACH COBBLER

serves 4

8 oz. (1½ cups) dried peaches
4 oz. (½ cup) granulated sugar

For topping :

4 oz. butter
8 oz. (2 cups) self-raising
  flour
1 oz. (2 tbsps.) caster sugar
¼ pint (⅝ cup) milk, approx.
1 egg, beaten
Demerara sugar

Soak the peaches for 2–3 hours in 1 pint (2½ cups) cold water. Put the peaches, sugar and water into a saucepan, bring to the boil and then simmer for about 30 minutes, or until the peaches are tender. Arrange in a 1½-pint pie dish.
Rub the fat into the flour until the mixture resembles fine breadcrumbs. Stir in the sugar and enough milk to give a soft but manageable dough. Knead the scone dough lightly on a floured board and roll out to approximately ½-in. thickness. Cut out 1½-in. diameter rounds with a fluted cutter. Arrange over the peaches.
Brush the scones with a little beaten egg or milk and sprinkle with Demerara sugar. Bake at 450°F. (mark 8) for 15 minutes until well risen and golden brown.

LEMON LAYER SPONGE

serves 4

2 eggs, separated
6 oz. (¾ cup) caster sugar
2 oz. butter
2 oz. (½ cup) flour
½ pint (1¼ cups) milk
3 tbsps. lemon juice
grated rind of 1 lemon

Beat the egg yolks with the sugar and the softened butter in a large basin. Stir in the flour, milk, lemon juice and rind. Whisk the egg whites until stiff and fold evenly into the mixture. Turn into a buttered 2-pint pie dish and place in a roasting tin with water to come half-way up the dish. Bake in the oven at 350°F. (mark 4) for 40–50 minutes until lightly set.

LEMON CANDY ALASKA

serves 4

3 oz. butter
7 oz. (⅞ cup) caster sugar
2 oz. cornflakes, crushed
½ pint (1¼ cups) vanilla ice
  cream
9 sour lemon sweets, finely
  crushed
2 egg whites
juice of ½ a lemon

Melt the butter in a saucepan, stir in 3 oz. (⅜ cup) of the sugar, heat gently until dissolved and then toss the cornflakes in the syrup.
Use to line a 7-in. pie plate and chill. Soften the ice cream in a basin and beat in the lemon sweets. Refreeze. Whisk the egg whites until stiff, add half the remaining sugar and whisk again until stiff. Fold in the rest of the sugar. Scoop the lemon ice cream into the chilled pie shell, sprinkling it with lemon juice.
Pile the meringue over the ice cream, covering it completely. Cook on the top shelf of a preheated oven at 450°F. (mark 8) for about 5 minutes until light brown. Serve at once.

PEACH AND ALMOND UPSIDE-DOWN

serves 4

butter
½ oz. caster sugar
15-oz. can peach halves
½ oz. whole almonds, blanched
6½-oz. pkt. sponge mix
1 level tsp. cornflour

Butter a 7½-in. round ovenproof dish. Sprinkle caster sugar around the dish. Drain the peaches, reserving the syrup, and cut each in half. Arrange with the almonds over the base of the dish. Make up the sponge according to the directions on the packet. Spoon the sponge mixture over the fruit, making sure it runs between the peaches. Bake at 375°F. (mark 5) for 35–40 minutes, until golden brown and firm. Invert onto a serving plate and top with peach glaze made from ¼ pint (⅝ cup) syrup blended with the cornflour. Bring gradually to the boil, stirring continuously.

PEAR AND ALMOND CREPES

For batter :

4 oz. (1 cup) plain flour
pinch of salt
1 egg
½ pint (1¼ cups) milk
1 tbsp. brandy
½ oz. butter, melted

For filling :

4 oz. butter
2 oz. (⅜ cup) icing sugar
2 oz. (½ cup) ground almonds
¼ tsp. almond essence
grated rind of 1 lemon
15-oz. can pears, drained and
  diced
melted butter
lemon wedges

Pancakes with a difference   filled with pear and almond

Sift the flour and salt into a bowl. Break the egg into the centre, add 2 tablespoons of milk and stir well. Gradually add the rest of the milk, stirring. Beat until the batter has the consistency of single cream, then add brandy and melted butter. Heat a 7-in. frying pan and brush the surface with a little butter. Raise the handle side of the pan slightly and pour in the batter from the raised side so that a very thin skin of batter flows over the pan. Place pan over a moderate heat and leave until the pancake is golden brown; turn it and repeat. Turn the pancake out on to a plate and keep warm. Make 8 pancakes, stacking them up as you go, separated with sheets of greaseproof paper.
Cream the butter and sugar until light and fluffy. Stir in the ground almonds, almond essence, lemon rind and diced pears. Spread a little of the filling over one half of each pancake; fold the other half over and then in half again to form a triangle.

Arrange the pancakes in an ovenproof dish overlapping each other; brush lightly with butter and quickly flash under a hot grill. Serve with lemon wedges.

BANANAS EN CROUTE

serves 4

4 large bananas, peeled
grated rind and juice of 1
  lemon
1 level tbsp. caster sugar
½ level tsp. powdered
  cinnamon
8 slices brown bread
1½ oz. butter
1 oz. (¼ cup) walnuts, chopped

Halve bananas lengthwise and leave to soak in lemon juice for 1 hour. Blend together caster sugar, lemon rind and cinnamon. Remove crusts from the bread. Melt ½ oz. butter in a frying pan and fry bananas on both sides until golden. Toast and butter the bread; sprinkle with cinnamon sugar. Lay banana on top and sprinkle with the chopped nuts.

A simple apple flan, served warm, is always popular

PARTY PUDDINGS

PISTACHIO APPLE FLAN

serves 6

For flan case:

2 large eggs
2 oz. (¼ cup) caster sugar
2 oz. (½ cup) plain flour

For filling:

½ pint (1¼ cups) milk
2 oz. (¼ cup) caster sugar
1 oz. (¼ cup) plain flour
¼ oz. cornflour
1 large egg
1 oz. butter

For decoration:

2 sharp eating apples
½ pint (1¼ cups) water
juice of ½ lemon
2 oz. (¼ cup) caster sugar
5 tbsps. apricot jam
1½ oz. pistachio nuts, peeled and chopped

Grease an 8½-in. sponge flan tin well, placing a disc of greased greaseproof paper on the raised base to prevent any sticking. Put the eggs and sugar in a large deep bowl, stand this over a pan of hot water and whisk until light and creamy – the whisk should leave a trail when lifted from the mixture. Remove from the heat and whisk until cool. If an electric mixer is used, do not place over hot water. Sift half the flour over the mixture and fold in very lightly, using a tablespoon. Add the remaining flour in the same way. Turn the mixture into the flan tin and bake towards the top of the oven at 425°F. (mark 7) for 12–15 minutes, until well risen and golden brown.

Turn out carefully and cool on a wire rack.

Meanwhile heat the milk in a pan. Mix the sugar, flour, cornflour, egg and a little milk and stir in the hot milk. Allow the mixture to thicken and just come to the boil, then add the butter and beat well. Cover and cool.

Peel, core and slice the apples in rings. Poach until soft but not broken in a light syrup made from the water, lemon juice and sugar. Drain the apple rings and leave to cool.

Brush the outside and top rim of the flan case with warm sieved apricot jam to which a little water has been added. Coat the outer edges with pistachio nuts. Fill the flan case with pastry cream and arrange apple ring on top. Glaze with more jam and chill before serving.

STRAWBERRY PALMIERS

makes 6 pairs

8 oz. frozen puff pastry, thawed
sugar to dredge
¼ pint (⅝ cup) double cream
4 tbsps. (⅜ cup) single cream
1 tbsp. orange liqueur
2 level tsps. icing sugar
¾ lb. strawberries

Roll the pastry into a rectangle 12 in. by 10 in. Dredge with caster sugar. Fold the long sides to meet in the centre and dredge again; fold in half lengthwise. Press lightly with a rolling pin. Cut into 12 equal slices, place well apart on a baking sheet, cut-side down. Open the tip of each.

Bake near the top of the oven at 425°F. (mark 7) for about 8 minutes, until the sugar is a light caramel colour. Turn each one over and bake for a further 4 minutes. Cool on a wire rack.

Whip the creams together until light and fluffy. Add the liqueur and icing sugar and use to sandwich the palmiers in pairs. Tuck halved strawberries into each.

TRANCHE AUX FRUITS

serves 6

For pastry case:

5 oz. (1¼ cups) plain flour
3 oz. butter or margarine
1½ level tsps. caster sugar
1 egg yolk
4 tsps. cold water (approx.)

For filling:

1 small eating apple, peeled, cored, quartered and thinly sliced
1 medium orange, peeled and sliced
1 banana, peeled and sliced
7½-oz. can prunes, drained and stoned
3 tbsps. Grand Marnier

For confectioner's custard:

½ pint (1¼ cups) milk
2 oz. (¼ cup) caster sugar
1 oz. (¼ cup) plain flour
½ level tbsp. cornflour
1 large egg
icing sugar
2 tbsps. apricot jam

Sift the flour, rub in the fat and sprinkle the sugar over the mixture. Blend the yolk with the water and stir into the rubbed-in ingredients. Add a little more water if necessary to give a firm dough. Knead lightly and roll out on a floured surface.

Use this dough to line a 14 in. by 4½ in. tranche frame, or a 9 in. loose-bottomed French fluted flan tin. Bake blind, using dried beans, at 400°F. (mark 6) for about 20 minutes. Remove the beans, then cook for a further 5 minutes. Leave the pastry case to cool on a wire rack.

Meanwhile prepare the apple, orange, banana and prunes. Macerate them in separate bowls, each containing ½ tablespoon Grand Marnier.

Prepare the confectioner's custard by bringing the milk to the boil; whisk together the sugar, flour, cornflour and egg, stir half the milk into the whisked ingredients then pour the whole back into the pan. Bring to the boil, stirring constantly.

Remove from the heat and stir in 1 tablespoon Grand Marnier. Cool slightly and pour into the pastry case. Dust with icing sugar to prevent a skin forming.

When completely cold, arrange the fruits in alternate rows over the surface.

Heat the apricot jam with the left-over fruit juices and liqueur, in a small pan. Bubble until thickened. Sieve and brush the glaze over the fruit. Serve with thick cream.

BLACKBERRY AND PINEAPPLE BRIOCHE

serves 6–8

**8 oz. (2 cups) strong plain
 flour**
¼ level tsp. salt
½ oz. (1 tbsp.) caster sugar
½ oz. fresh baker's yeast
1½ tbsps. warm water
2 eggs, beaten
**2 oz. melted butter, cooled
 but still liquid**
**1 egg, beaten with 1 tsp. water
 for glaze**

For filling :

16-oz. can pineapple pieces
3 tbsps. Kirsch
¼ pint (⅝ cup) single cream
¼ pint (⅝ cup) double cream
1 level tbsp. icing sugar
**½ lb. blackberries or
 raspberries**

Sift together the flour, salt and
sugar. Blend yeast with the water
and add to the dry ingredients,
together with the eggs and butter.
Work into a soft dough and knead
well for about 5 minutes. Place in
an oiled polythene bag and allow
to rise at room temperature for
1–1½ hours, until the dough has
doubled in size.
Brush a 2-pint fluted brioche
mould with oil. On a lightly
floured surface, thoroughly knead
the risen dough. Make a ball with
three-quarters of it and place in
the bottom of the mould. Press a
hollow in the centre and place the
remaining piece of dough in the
middle. Put the mould in a large
polythene bag and stand it in a
warm place to let the dough rise
again until light and fluffy – about
1 hour.
Brush with egg glaze and bake at
450°F. (mark 8) for 15–20 minutes,
until brown. When cooked, the
brioche should sound hollow when
tapped on the base. Allow to cool,
then cut a thin slice from the top
and scoop out some of the crumb.
Drain the pineapple and mix 3
tablespoons of the juice with 3
tablespoons of Kirsch; spoon the
liquid over the inside of the brioche
and let it soak for 5 minutes. Whip
the creams until they just hold their
shape, then beat in the sugar.
Reserve a little for decoration. Fold
in the pineapple, reserving a few
pieces for decoration.
Spoon layers of the cream mixture
and blackberries into the brioche,
again reserving some for decoration, and decorate the top with
piped cream, blackberries and
pieces of pineapple and, if liked,
top with the lid of brioche.

MELON AND PINEAPPLE SALAD

serves 6

1 honeydew melon
**2 16-oz. cans pineapple
 chunks, drained**
4 tbsps. Cointreau or curaçao
caster sugar (optional)
few glacé cherries

Slice the melon in half lengthwise,
scoop out and discard the seeds.
Scoop out the flesh in large pieces
and keep to one side. Using
scissors or a sharp knife serrate the
edge of one of the melon halves.
Cut the melon flesh into chunks
and pile these and the drained
pineapple chunks into the decorated melon half.
Sprinkle over the liqueur and
sugar, if used. Decorate with
glacé cherries.

MANDARIN LIQUEUR GATEAU

serves 8

3 large eggs
3 oz. (⅜ cup) caster sugar
3 oz. (¾ cup) plain flour
**2 11-oz. cans mandarin
 oranges, drained**
2 tbsps. maraschino liqueur
**8-oz. can red cherries,
 drained**
apricot glaze
**½ pint (1¼ cups) double cream,
 lightly whipped**
icing sugar
angelica

Grease and line a 10-in. by 1½-in.
deep sandwich tin. Put eggs and
sugar in a bowl over a pan of hot
water and whisk until thick and
pale in colour. If using an electric
mixer do not place over hot water.
Sift the flour over the whisked
eggs and fold in lightly and quickly
with a metal spoon. Turn the mixture into the prepared sandwich
tin and bake at 375°F. (mark 5) for
about 30 minutes. Cool on a wire
rack.
Macerate the oranges in maraschino for 30 minutes. Remove
stones from all but 12 of the
cherries. Split the cake in two and
place one half cut side up on a
serving plate. Spoon over the
strained maraschino and spread
with a little apricot glaze.
From the centre of the second half,
stamp out 3 2-in. circles, close to
each other. Brush remaining surface with apricot glaze. Arrange
groups of mandarins round the
edge; chop the remainder. Spread
most of the cream over the first
half and top with chopped mandarins and stoned cherries.

A brioche loaf filled with pineapple and blackberries

Carefully lift the second half on
top of the first. Fill the holes with
the remaining cream and top with
the sponge circles, dredged with
icing sugar. Finish with a cluster of
whole cherries and angelica leaves.

NUTTY CARAMEL PIES

serves 4

4½ oz. (⅝ cup) caster sugar
¼ pint (⅝ cup) milk
1 egg
1 egg yolk
**¼ pint (⅝ cup) double cream,
 lightly whipped**

For base :

3 oz. (¾ cup) plain flour
2 oz. butter
2 oz. plain (dark) chocolate

For decoration :

¼ pint (⅝ cup) honey sauce
2 oz. broken walnuts

Dissolve 2 oz. sugar in a heavy pan
and allow to caramellize to a pale
golden brown. Remove from the
heat and pour on 3 tablespoons of
boiling water, very slowly. Return
to the heat, simmer to dissolve the
caramel, add the milk and stir.
Beat the whole egg and yolk with
1½ oz. sugar, add the caramel-milk
and strain back into the saucepan.
Cook very gently until the custard
coats the back of a spoon. Pour
into a basin and allow to cool.
When it is cold, transfer the
custard to a freezing tray and
freeze it to a slush in the ice-
making compartment of the refrigerator or a home freezer. Beat
well, and fold in the cream. Return
to the tray and freeze until firm.
Knead the flour, butter and remaining 1 oz. of sugar to a
manageable dough. Roll out thinly

Caramel ice cream on a pastry base, with nuts and a honey sauce

Strawberry galette and whipped cream

and line 4 3½-in. shallow patty pans. Bake blind for 15 minutes at 375°F. (mark 5) until light golden brown. Allow to cool.

Melt the chocolate in a bowl over hot water and dip the edges of the pies into soft chocolate.

To serve, pile ice cream into the pastry shells, and spoon over honey sauce and walnuts.

ICED CHARLOTTE RUSSE
serves 12

For ice cream layers :
½ pint (1¼ cups) milk
15 oz. (1⅞ cups) sugar
1 vanilla pod
2 eggs, beaten
½ pint (1¼ cups) double cream
1 pint (2½ cups) water
1 lb. raspberries
8 tbsps. lemon juice
½ pint (1¼ cups) hazelnut yoghourt

For sponge case :
3 level tbsps. sugar
4 tbsps. water
4 tbsps. sherry
28 boudoir biscuits or sponge fingers (2 packets)

Heat the milk with 3 oz. sugar and the vanilla pod and pour on to the beaten eggs, stirring. Return to the saucepan and cook over a low heat, stirring, until the custard thickens. Strain and remove the vanilla pod. Allow to cool.

Half-whip the cream and fold into the cold custard. Pour the mixture into an ice tray and freeze until slushy. Turn into a chilled bowl and whisk thoroughly. Freeze again until slushy.

For the raspberry layers, dissolve 12 oz. sugar in the water, bring to the boil and reduce by boiling to 1 pint. Cool. Sieve the berries to remove the pips and make a purée; add the lemon juice, yoghourt and sugar syrup, turn into an ice tray and freeze to a slush.

Screw up some kitchen foil and make it into a collar to fit inside the base of an 8½-in. round cake tin, leaving a small gap between the tin side and foil to support the biscuits.

Dissolve the 3 level tablespoons of sugar in the water in a small pan and simmer for 5 minutes. Blend with the sherry in a flat dish, then soak the biscuits briefly in the mixture, removing them before they become soggy. Place the biscuits side by side in the gap made by the foil. Chill the tin.

Layer the vanilla and raspberry ice cream, starting with half the vanilla. Lift the foil ring as the vanilla layer is spooned in, but leave it in position above the vanilla layer to give support to the biscuits. Freeze the vanilla layer until solid; remove the foil.

Continue by adding half the raspberry ice cream, freezing, then repeating with the remaining vanilla and raspberry. Leave in the freezer until required. Turn out on to a serving dish, leave in a cool place to soften a little, then cut with a knife dipped in warm water.

Note : This large iced charlotte is best made in a home freezer; if you are using the ice-making compartment of a refrigerator, make the mixture in 2 lots.

PUDDING GLACE
serves 8–10

For coffee ice :
10 egg yolks
12 oz. (1½ cups) caster sugar
½ pint (1¼ cups) water
1 pint (2½ cups) double cream, whipped
3 level tbsps. instant coffee
4 tsps. water

For whisked sponge :
2 large eggs
2 oz. (¼ cup) caster sugar
2 oz. (½ cup) plain flour
3 tbsps. rum
juice of 1 small orange

For decoration :
glacé fruits (e.g. cherries and angelica)
¼ pint (⅝ cup) double cream, whipped

For coffee sauce :
½ pint (1¼ cups) water
8 oz. (1 cup) sugar
4 tbsps. instant coffee
2 level tbsps. cornflour

First make the ice cream. Beat the yolks thoroughly. Dissolve the sugar in the water in a small saucepan and boil to 217°F. – about 5 minutes. Cool slightly, beat the egg yolks in a deep bowl then pour the syrup slowly on to the egg yolks in a thin stream, beating. Place the bowl over a pan of hot water and continue to beat until thick. When cold, fold in the whipped cream and the coffee blended with the water. Pour into ice trays and freeze until slushy.

Meanwhile, grease and line the base of a shallow 8½-in. cake tin. Whisk together the whole eggs and caster sugar for the sponge until pale and fluffy and the whisk leaves a trail. Sift the flour over the mixture and fold in with a metal spoon. Pour the mixture into the prepared cake tin and bake at 375°F. (mark 5) for about 15 minutes. Turn out and cool on a wire rack; remove the paper.

Split the cake in half. Blend together the rum and orange juice and spoon over the sponge halves. Line either a 4-pint charlotte mould or an 8-in. deep cake tin with greaseproof paper. If necessary, trim half the sponge to fit the base of the mould and ease into place. Spoon the slushy ice cream over this half of the sponge.

Top with the remaining sponge half and return to the freezer compartment until firmly set – about 2 hours. Unmould and decorate with whipped cream and glacé fruits.

To make the coffee sauce, dissolve the sugar in the water in a small saucepan over gentle heat. Stir in the coffee. Blend the cornflour to a thick cream with a little cold water, pour on some of the coffee syrup, stirring, and return to the pan. Stir over the heat to thicken. Serve the sauce separately.

STRAWBERRY GALETTE
serves 8

9 oz. (2¼ cups) plain flour
6 oz. butter
3 oz. (⅜ cup) caster sugar
1–1½ lb. strawberries, hulled
6 oz. red-currant jelly
3 level tsps. arrowroot

Stand a 9-in. plain flan ring on a baking sheet. Sift the flour and rub in the butter and add the sugar. Lightly knead the mixture until it forms a dough.

Roll out the dough and use to line the flan ring, drawing the sides up to make a wall. Press into shape with the fingertips and crimp the edge with finger and thumb. Prick the base and bake at 350°F. (mark 4) for about 30 minutes until lightly browned.

Allow to cool for 15 minutes on the tray, then remove the ring and with a palette knife lift on to a wire rack. Leave until cold.

Cut strawberries in half. Brush the base of the galette with red-currant jelly and arrange strawberries cut side uppermost over the red-currant jelly.

Make up a glaze by heating ¼ lb. red-currant jelly with ¼ pint (⅝ cup) water. Bring to the boil, sieve and blend in the arrowroot mixed with a little water. Return to the pan and cook until the arrowroot clears.

Coat the strawberries with the warm glaze and leave to set. Serve with lightly whipped cream.

A frozen sponge, sandwiched with coffee ice cream

HOME-MADE ICES

Although bought ices are very good, the variety achieved by making your own is well worth the little extra trouble.

The only equipment necessary is an ordinary domestic refrigerator with a frozen food compartment, or a home freezer, and a rotary whisk. An electric ice cream machine makes the process easier still, but is not essential. There are several varieties of both cream and water ices. The most common types are:

Cream ices *These are seldom made entirely of cream, but any of the following mixtures give good results: equal parts cream and custard (egg custard, made with yolks only); cream and fruit purée; cream and egg whites. The cream may be replaced by unsweetened evaporated milk and flavouring and colouring ingredients are added as required.*

Water ices *The foundation is a sugar and water syrup, usually flavoured with fruit juice or purée; wine or liqueur is frequently added.*

Sherbets *A true sherbet is a water ice with whipped egg white added, to give a fluffy texture.*

Sorbets *Semi-frozen ices, sometimes flavoured with liqueur.*

Because they are soft, they are not moulded but served in tall glasses or goblets.

Bombes *Iced puddings frozen in a special bomb-shaped mould; bombes may be made of a single ice cream mixture known as a parfait or of two or more. They are often elaborately decorated after unmoulding.*

MAKING ICE CREAM

To obtain the best results, use a rich mixture, with plenty of flavouring. A flavour that tastes quite strong at room temperature will become much less so when frozen. See that the mixture is well sweetened, too, as this helps to accentuate the flavour of the frozen ice. But don't go to the other extreme and over-sweeten, as too much sugar will prevent the mixture freezing properly (too much alcohol used as flavouring will also prevent freezing). Colouring is not affected by freezing, so use sparingly, a drop at a time.

FREEZING

If you are using the frozen food compartment of a refrigerator, set the dial at the lowest setting about 1 hour before the mixture is ready. Put the mixture into a polythene ice cube tray and place in the frozen food compartment. To improve the texture, either stir the mixture at 20-minute intervals until it is half frozen and then leave it undisturbed until frozen, or allow it to half-freeze, turn it into a cool bowl and whisk thoroughly with a rotary whisk, then replace it in the freezing compartment and leave until hard. The time required will vary with the refrigerator, but usually it takes several hours. Once the mixture is frozen the temperature may be returned to normal storage temperature. The ice cream develops a better, more mellow flavour if left for a while. If you have a home freezer, use the same method, but the mixture will of course freeze much more quickly.

USING AN ELECTRIC ICE CREAM MAKER

An electric ice cream maker (like the one pictured above) will give you a more even-textured ice more quickly. It has a central motor attached to 2 paddles, which move continually while it is freezing. Put the whole machine in the refrigerator or freezer, making sure that the contact between the base and the freezer shelf is good.

Shut the door—you will find that the flex will not seriously affect the seal—plug in and switch on. If you intend making much ice cream this is well worth the small investment.

RICH VANILLA ICE CREAM
serves 4

¼ pint (⅝ cup) milk
1½ oz. sugar
2 egg yolks, beaten
½–1 tsp. vanilla essence
¼ pint (⅝ cup) double cream, partially whipped

Heat the milk and sugar and pour on to the egg yolks, stirring. Return the mixture to the pan and cook it over a very gentle heat, stirring all the time until the custard thickens; strain it and add the vanilla essence. Allow to cool, fold in the partially whipped cream, pour into a polythene ice cube tray and freeze.

ORANGE ICE CREAM
serves 4

½ pint (1¼ cups) double cream
½ pint (1¼ cups) orange juice
caster sugar
mandarin orange sections
wafers

Serve strawberry liqueur ice cream with luscious strawberry sauce

Pear sorbet with meringue is light and refreshing

Whip the cream until it holds its shape. Stir in ¼ pint orange juice and add remaining ¼ pint a little at a time. Add sufficient sugar to make the mixture taste slightly over-sweet. Pour into a polythene ice cube tray and freeze. Serve with mandarin sections and wafers.

FRUIT ICE CREAM
serves 4

small can evaporated milk
8 oz. fresh raspberries or a 15-oz. can, drained, or other fruit such as strawberries, pears, bananas
2 oz. sugar (if fresh fruit is used)

Place the unopened can of milk in a pan of boiling water and keep on the boil for 15 minutes. Remove from the pan, cool and chill thoroughly for several hours. Sieve the fruit to make ¼ pint purée; add the sugar if required. Open the can of milk and whip until stiff. Fold in the purée. Pour into a polythene ice cube tray and freeze.

STRAWBERRY LIQUEUR ICE CREAM
serves 4

¼ pint (⅝ cup) double cream, lightly whipped
8 oz. strawberries, puréed
½ tsp. vanilla essence
1 tbsp. rum or maraschino
2 oz. (¼ cup) sugar

Mix the cream with all the other ingredients, pour into a polythene ice cube tray and freeze for ¾–1 hour. Turn out and whisk until smooth. Return mixture to the tray and freeze until firm.

CHOC-DE-MENTHE

Make up the basic vanilla ice cream recipe, replacing the vanilla essence by 2 teaspoons crème de menthe and a few drops of green colouring. When the mixture is half frozen, turn into a chilled bowl and whisk. Crumble a small bar of flake chocolate and fold in. Return to the tray and freeze.

BERRY ICE CREAM
serves 8

2 level tsps. powdered gelatine
2 tbsps. water
15-oz. can strawberries or raspberries, puréed or 1 lb. fresh fruit, puréed
1–3 oz. soft brown sugar
1½ tbsps. lemon juice
¼ pint (⅝ cup) single cream
2 oz. biscuit crumbs
½ pint (1¼ cups) double cream

Dissolve the gelatine in the water in a basin held over a pan of hot water. Pour the fruit pulp into a bowl, add sugar to taste and the lemon juice. Stir in the dissolved gelatine, single cream and crushed biscuit crumbs. Two-thirds fill a polythene ice cube tray and freeze until fairly stiff. Beat again and fold in the whipped double cream. Freeze again.

TOASTED ALMOND ICE
serves 4

½ pint (1¼ cups) milk
3 oz. (⅜ cup) sugar
a pinch of salt
4 egg yolks
¼ pint (⅝ cup) double cream
vanilla essence
2 oz. crushed praline (see below)
2 egg whites
3 level tbsps. icing sugar
1 tbsp. chopped toasted almonds

Boil the milk. Mix the sugar, salt and egg yolks and stir in the milk. Cook over a very gentle heat, stirring constantly, until thick, then allow to cool. Pour into a polythene ice cube tray and freeze for 20–30 minutes.
Turn the mixture out, whip until creamy and add the cream, a little vanilla essence and the crushed praline. Pour the mixture back into the freezing tray and freeze until firm, stirring it after the first half hour.
Serve with a sauce made by whipping the egg whites and icing sugar together until just stiff enough to drop from a spoon, then adding the chopped nuts.

PRALINE

2 oz. (¼ cup) caster sugar
2 oz. chopped toasted almonds

Heat the sugar in a pan until a deep amber colour, stir in the chopped almonds and pour the mixture on to a greased tin or slab. When it is cool, pound in a mortar or crush with a rolling pin.

HONEY ICE CREAM
serves 8

1 lb. raspberries
¼ pint (⅝ cup) double cream
¼ pint (⅝ cup) plain yoghourt
3 egg whites
2 tbsps. lemon juice
10 level tbsps. clear honey
a pinch of salt

Sieve the raspberries to give ½ pint purée. In a bowl, blend together the raspberry purée, cream, yoghourt, lemon juice, honey and salt. Turn the mixture into a polythene ice cube tray and freeze until firm. Turn out into a bowl and beat until smooth. Stiffly whisk the egg whites and fold in. Return the mixture to the tray and freeze.

LEMON ICE CREAM

serves 6

½ pint (1¼ cups) double cream
2 eggs
grated rind and juice of 2
    lemons
10 oz. (1¼ cups) caster sugar
½ pint (1¼ cups) milk

Beat together the cream and eggs until smooth. Add the lemon rind, the juice, sugar and milk and mix thoroughly. Pour into polythene ice cube tray and freeze for about 2 hours. Do not stir while freezing.

LEMON SHERBET

serves 4

8 oz. (1 cup) caster sugar
1 pint (2½ cups) water
rind and juice of 3 lemons
1 egg white

Dissolve the sugar in the water over a low heat, add the thinly pared lemon rind and boil gently for 10 minutes; leave to cool. Add the lemon juice and strain the mixture into a polythene ice cube tray. Half-freeze, then turn into a bowl, whisk the egg white and fold it in, mixing thoroughly. Return to the tray and freeze.

ORANGE SHERBET

serves 4

4 oz. (½ cup) caster sugar
½ pint (1¼ cups) water
1 tbsp. lemon juice
rind of 1 orange, grated
rind of 1 lemon, grated
juice of 3 oranges and 1 lemon
1 egg white

Dissolve the sugar in the water over a low heat, bring to the boil and boil gently for 10 minutes. Add 1 tablespoon lemon juice. Put the grated fruit rinds in a basin, pour the boiling syrup over and leave until cold. Add the mixed fruit juices and strain into a polythene ice cube tray. Half-freeze the mixture then turn it into a bowl, whisk the egg white and fold it in, mixing thoroughly. Return to the tray and freeze. Other flavours of sherbet may be made by adding ½ pint (1¼ cups) fruit purée and the juice of ½ a lemon to ½ pint syrup.

A crunchy cornflake crust coats this lemon freeze

FRUIT SORBET

Follow the recipe for lemon sherbet but add 2 egg whites, which will give a much softer consistency. Freeze the mixture only until it is stiff enough to serve. Spoon into glasses.

LEMON FREEZE

serves 8

2 oz. cornflakes, crumbled
5 level tbsps. caster sugar
1 oz. butter, melted
2 eggs, separated
small can of sweetened
    condensed milk
4 tbsps. lemon juice

Blend together the cornflake crumbs, 2 tablespoons sugar and butter until well mixed. Press all but 4 tablespoons into the base of a polythene ice cube tray. Beat the egg yolks in a deep bowl until really thick and creamy. Combine with the condensed milk. Add the lemon juice and stir until thickened. Beat the egg whites until stiff but not dry. Gradually beat in remaining sugar; fold through the lemon mixture. Spoon into the polythene tray and sprinkle with the remaining cornflake crumbs. Freeze.

FRESH PINEAPPLE SORBET

2¾-lb. pineapple
6 tbsps. lemon juice
4 tbsps. orange juice
¼ pint (⅝ cup) water
11 oz. (1⅜ cups) sugar
whipped cream, for serving

Peel the pineapple, remove the core and discard. Pulp the flesh in a blender. Put the pineapple pulp through a sieve to give ¾ pint (2 cups) purée. Mix the purée with the lemon and orange juice, water and sugar, stirring until the sugar has completely dissolved. Pour into polythene ice cube trays and freeze without stirring until crystals have formed but the spoon still goes in.
Serve accompanied by whipped cream, either in sundae glasses or returned to the empty shell.

PEAR SORBET MERINGUE

serves 6

15½-oz. can pears, drained
12 oz. (1½ cups) caster sugar
½ pint (1¼ cups) water
3 tbsps. lemon juice
3 egg whites
1 fresh pear, sliced and cored
melted chocolate

Place the pears in a measure and make up to ½ pint with some of the juice. Purée in a blender or put through a sieve. Dissolve half the sugar in the water, bring to the boil and reduce to ½ pint (1¼ cups) syrup. Pour on to the pear purée, add the lemon juice and stir well. Freeze until firm.
Meanwhile, draw a 9-in. circle on a sheet of waxed paper; divide into 6 segments. Whisk the egg whites until stiff, add 3 oz. sugar and whisk again until stiff. Fold in the remaining 3 oz. sugar. Spoon the meringue into a forcing bag fitted with a large star vegetable nozzle. Following pencilled lines as a guide, pipe a scalloped edge round the circle indenting each section. Fill in the base with more meringue, then build up the scalloped edge and outline each section. Dry in the oven on the lowest setting for 3–4 hours, until crisp and firm. Cool and remove the paper.
To serve, spoon the sorbet into the meringue nests. Arrange slices of fresh pear dipped in lemon juice between them and drizzle with melted chocolate.

APRICOT SHERBET

serves 4

2 eggs, separated
1 oz. caster sugar
16-oz. can of apricots, puréed
pinch of ground nutmeg
4 tbsps. single cream

Beat the egg whites until stiff and continue whisking while gradually adding half the sugar. Fold in remaining sugar. Mix the puréed fruit, egg yolks, nutmeg and cream. Fold carefully into the egg whites, then pour immediately into a polythene ice cube tray and freeze for 3–4 hours.

APRICOT BOMBE

serves 4

1 recipe quantity vanilla ice
    cream
1 oz. finely chopped blanched
    almonds
7½-oz. can apricots
2 tbsps. brandy

Allow the ice cream to soften a little, stir in the almonds.
Spoon two-thirds into a chilled ½-pint pudding basin and press it against the sides to form a shell. Pile the drained apricots with a tablespoon juice and the brandy into the centre and top with a lid of the remaining ice cream. Cover with foil and freeze until firm. Unmould to serve.

Gâteaux and Pâtisserie

Continental gâteaux and pâtisserie are made from traditional basic mixtures. Many of the decorations are also traditional. If you long for the lovely things that fill the windows of French and Viennese pastry shops, try your hand at some of these.

BASIC GENOESE SPONGE
this sponge is used as a base for many gâteaux

1½ oz. butter
2½ oz. (⅝ cup) plain flour
½ oz. cornflour
3 large eggs
3 oz. (⅜ cup) caster sugar

Grease and line a 9-in. straight sided sandwich tin or a 7-in. square cake tin.

Heat the butter gently until it is melted, remove it from the heat and let it stand for a few minutes. Sift together the flour and cornflour. Place the eggs in a large deep basin over a saucepan of hot water, whisk for a few seconds, add the sugar and continue whisking over the heat until the mixture is very pale in colour and a trail forms when the whisk is lifted.

Remove from the heat and whisk for a few seconds longer. Resift half the flour over the egg and carefully fold it in, using a metal spoon. Then pour in the melted butter (cooled until it just flows) round the side, folding it in alternately with the remaining flour. Turn the mixture into the prepared tin and bake near the top of the oven at 375°F. (mark 5) for about 30 minutes, or until well risen and just firm to the touch. Turn out carefully and leave to cool on a wire rack.

CREME AU BEURRE

3 oz. (⅜ cup) caster sugar
4 tbsps. water
2 egg yolks, beaten
4–6 oz. unsalted butter

Place the sugar in a heavy based saucepan; add the water and leave over a very low heat to dissolve the sugar, without boiling. When the sugar is completely dissolved, bring to boiling point and boil steadily for 2–3 minutes, to 225°F. Pour the syrup in a thin stream on to the egg yolks, whisking all the time. Continue to mix until the mixture is thick and cold.

Gradually beat the egg yolk mixture into the creamed butter and flavour as desired.

Chocolate: Put 2 oz. chocolate dots in a small bowl with 1 tablespoon water. Leave to stand over hot water until the mixture is smooth and the chocolate melted. Cool slightly and beat into the basic crème au beurre.

Coffee: Beat in 1–2 tablespoons coffee essence to taste.

GATEAU CENDRILLON

9-in. Genoese sponge
1 tbsp. coffee essence
coffee crème au beurre
apricot glaze
coffee fondant icing or glacé icing
12 hazel nuts, lightly toasted

To the basic recipe for Genoese add the coffee essence at the whisking stage. Bake in the usual way and cool.
Split the cold sponge in half and sandwich the halves together with two-thirds of the crème au beurre. Brush the top with apricot glaze, coat with icing and leave to set.
To decorate, pipe with whirls of crème au beurre and top each whirl with a hazel nut.

GATEAU MONT BLANC

for sponge base :

2 oz. (¼ cup) caster sugar
2 large eggs
2 oz. (½ cup) plain flour

For filling :

8½-oz. can sweetened chestnut purée
½ pint (1¼ cups) double cream, lightly whipped
icing sugar

Grease and line the raised base of an 8½-in. sponge flan tin. Whisk together the sugar and eggs until thick and creamy – the whisk should leave a trail when lifted. Sift the flour over the surface and lightly fold it in with a metal spoon. Turn the mixture into the prepared tin, level with a palette knife and tap the tin once or twice on the table top.
Bake the sponge flan above the centre of the oven at 425°F. (mark 7) for about 15 minutes. Turn out carefully on to a wire rack to cool.
To finish, place the chestnut purée in a forcing bag fitted with a large plain icing nozzle. Lightly whip the cream until it just holds its shape.
Spread a little of the whipped cream over the base of the flan and pipe the chestnut purée in a net over the cream, gradually working it into a dome shape. Using a large star vegetable nozzle, pipe the remainder of the whipped cream in a shell pattern round the edge. Lightly dust the whole with icing sugar.

Gâteau Mont Blanc, with piped chestnut purée

GATEAU ROXALANNE

5 oz. (1¼ cups) self-raising flour
1 oz. (¼ cup) cornflour
4 oz. (½ cup) caster sugar
1 level tsp. baking powder
½ level tsp. salt
2 fl. oz. (¼ cup) corn oil
¼ pint (⅝ cup) cold water
1 level tsp. grated lemon rind
1 tsp. lemon juice
2 egg yolks
4 egg whites
¼ level tsp. cream of tartar

For icing and decoration :

8 oz. plain (dark) chocolate
6 oz. butter
12 oz. (2⅝ cups) icing sugar
2 egg yolks
flaked almonds

Grease a 7-in. tube cake tin. Sift all the dry ingredients into a mixing bowl. Whisk together the corn oil, water, lemon rind, lemon juice and egg yolks. Add to the dry ingredients and beat to form a smooth, slack batter.
Whisk the egg whites and cream of tartar until stiff and dry, then fold into the batter mixture. Turn into the prepared tin and bake in the centre of the oven at 350°F. (mark 4) for about 1 hour. When the cake is cooked, invert it on to a wire rack until the cake slips out of the tin.
Melt the chocolate in a basin over hot, not boiling, water. Cream the butter and sugar together until light and creamy. Beat in the egg yolks and melted chocolate. When the cake is cold, spread the sides with this chocolate icing. Coat the edges in flaked almonds. Cover the top with more icing and pipe on a decoration.

GATEAU CARAQUE

4 oz. (½ cup) caster sugar
4 large eggs
4 oz. (1 cup) plain flour

For filling and decoration :

apricot glaze
chocolate crème au beurre
grated plain (dark) chocolate
chocolate caraque (see below)
icing sugar

Grease and base-line 2 oblong shallow tins 12 in. by 4½ in. In a deep bowl whisk together the sugar and eggs until really thick and creamy – the whisk should leave a trail when lifted from the mixture. Sift the flour over the surface and lightly fold in, using a metal spoon. Divide between the 2 prepared tins. Level the surface with a palette knife and bake just above the centre of the oven at 425°F. (mark 7) for about 25 minutes, until well risen, golden and spongy to the touch. Turn out and cool on a wire rack.
Sandwich the sponges together with apricot glaze and brush the top with the same glaze. Spread the chocolate crème au beurre round the sides and coat with coarsely grated chocolate. Arrange the chocolate caraque pieces side by side over the apricot glaze. Dust the centre with sifted icing sugar.

Chocolate caraque: Shred or grate 4 oz. plain (dark) cooking chocolate on to a plate and place over a pan of hot (not boiling) water. When melted, spread thinly over a marble slab or other cool surface. When just on the point of setting, run the edge of a sharp knife across the surface of the chocolate, so that it forms curls.

LINZER TORTE

6 oz. (1½ cups) plain flour
1 level tsp. ground cinnamon
a pinch of ground cloves
1½ level tsps. cocoa
½ level tsp. baking powder
3 oz. blanched almonds, finely chopped, or use nibbed almonds
6 oz. butter
5 oz. (⅝ cup) granulated sugar
2 eggs, beaten
raspberry jam
icing sugar
whipped cream (optional)

Grease a 9-in. spring-release cake tin.
Sift together the flour, spices, cocoa and baking powder. Put the almonds in a bowl, add the butter (straight from the refrigerator and coarsely grated). Stir in the sugar, eggs and flour mixture, in that order. Work together and shape into a roll. Wrap in greaseproof paper and chill for about 1 hour.
Roll out about two-thirds of the dough to line the base of the tin; press the dough up the sides to form a ½-in. wall. Fill with a thick layer of jam. Roll out the remainder of the dough, cut into strips and use to cover the jam in an open lattice. Bake in the centre of the oven at 350°F. (mark 4) for about 1 hour.
Leave the torte to cool in the tin, then remove the sides of the tin. Mature for 1–2 days before cutting. Fill in the lattice with fresh jam and serve dusted with icing sugar.

GATEAU NOUGATINE

For Genoese sponge :

3-4 oz. butter, melted
4 oz. (1 cup) plain flour
2 oz. (½ cup) cornflour
6 large eggs
6 oz. (¾ cup) caster sugar

For nougat :

5½ oz. caster sugar
4 oz. blanched almonds, finely chopped
a whole lemon

For filling and topping :

crème au beurre
2 tsps. Tia Maria
2 tbsps. apricot glaze
6 oz. plain (dark) chocolate cake covering

Grease and base-line 2 9-in. round sandwich tins.
Make up the Genoese mixture, divide it between the 2 tins and bake 1 above the other in the oven at 425°F. (mark 7) for 10 minutes. Reduce the temperature to 375°F. (mark 5) and bake for about a

further 15 minutes. Turn out and cool on a wire rack.

For the nougat, put the sugar in a heavy based pan and dissolve over a very low heat. When it is caramel coloured, add the almonds a little at a time, stirring gently with a metal spoon. Turn quickly on to an oiled surface then use a whole lemon to roll out the nougat thinly. Using a warmed cutter, quickly stamp out 12–14 leaf shapes. Leave the remainder of the nougat to set, then roughly crush it. (Should the nougat become too set before all the leaf shapes are cut, put it in a warm oven for a few minutes.)

To finish the cake, make up the crème au beurre, adding the Tia Maria, and sandwich the layers of Genoese together with it. Spread the remainder round the edges and coat evenly with the crushed nougat. Brush the cake top with apricot glaze.

Make up the chocolate covering and spread over the glazed surface, easing it to the edge with a knife. When it is nearly set, mark the chocolate into serving portions with a warmed knife. Arrange the nougat leaves in position before the chocolate completely sets, or fix with a little crème au beurre.

DOBOS TORTE

4 eggs
6 oz. (¾ cup) caster sugar
5 oz. (1¼ cups) plain flour
4 oz. (½ cup) caster sugar for caramel
a few toasted hazel nuts

For chocolate butter cream :
5 oz. butter or margarine
8 oz. (1¾ cups) icing sugar, sifted
2 oz. cooking chocolate, melted

Draw 5–6 rectangles, 10 in. by 4½ in., on non-stick paper. Place the papers on baking sheets.

Whisk the eggs and sugar together in a basin over a pan of hot water until very thick and fluffy. Sift the flour over the top and carefully fold it in with a metal spoon. Divide the mixture between the rectangles in thin, even layers. Bake towards the top of the oven at 375°F. (mark 5) for about 10 minutes, until golden brown.

Peel off the papers and if necessary trim the edges of the rectangles with a sharp knife to neaten them. Cool on wire racks.

Select the layer with the best surface and lay it on an oiled baking sheet or on non-stick paper. Put the caster sugar for the caramel in

Profiteroles, filled with cream and served with chocolate sauce

a wide based saucepan and place it over a low heat to dissolve, without stirring. Shake the pan occasionally. When it is completely dissolved, cook gently to a golden brown. Pour the caramel evenly over the selected cake layer, so that the surface is completely covered. Quickly mark it into 8 sections with the back of an oiled knife.

To make the butter cream, cream the butter and gradually beat in the icing sugar. Beat in the cool but still soft chocolate. Sandwich together the layers of cake with butter cream and place the caramel covered layer on top.

Cover the sides of the Torte with butter cream and mark decoratively with a fork. Pipe the remainder in whirls on the caramel surface and top each whirl with a toasted hazel nut.

GATEAU AMANDINE

4½ oz. (⅝ cup) caster sugar
3 large eggs
3 oz. (¾ cup) plain flour

For filling and decoration :
apricot glaze
4 oz. whole blanched almonds
½ pint (1¼ cups) double cream or coffee crème au beurre
icing sugar

Grease and base-line a 9½-in. (top measurement) moule à manqué cake tin.

Whisk together the sugar and eggs until thick and creamy – the whisk should leave a trail when lifted. Sift the flour over the surface and lightly fold in with a metal spoon. Turn the mixture into the prepared tin and bake just above the centre of the oven at 375°F. (mark 5) for about 30 minutes, until well risen and golden brown. Turn out and cool on a wire rack.

When the cake is cold, split and sandwich with apricot glaze. Using a sharp knife, split the nuts in half and cut in thin slices. Whip the cream and lightly sweeten with icing sugar. Completely mask the cake with the cream and cover with sliced nuts. Dust lightly with icing sugar and chill. Eat the same day.

BELGIAN TORTE

8 oz. butter
2 oz. (¼ cup) caster sugar
2 tbsps. corn oil
vanilla essence
1 large egg, beaten
1 lb. (4 cups) plain flour
2 level tsps. baking powder
a pinch of salt
½ lb. stiff apricot jam
icing sugar

Grease an 8-in. round cake tin. Beat the butter until creamy, add the sugar and beat again. Add the oil, a few drops of vanilla essence and the egg. Beat well. Sift the flour with the baking powder and salt and gradually work it into the mixture. Then, using the fingertips, knit the mixture together as for a shortbread dough.

Divide the dough into 2 pieces and knead lightly until smooth. Coarsely grate half the dough into the cake tin in an even layer. Cover with warm jam nearly to the edge. Coarsely grate the remainder of the dough over the top.

Bake the cake just above the centre of the oven at 300°F. (mark 1–2) for about 1½ hours, until the surface is lightly browned. While hot, dredge heavily with icing sugar. Cool in the tin and when cold, turn out carefully.

PROFITEROLES

makes about 20

2½ oz. choux pastry–i.e. made with 2½ oz. (⅝ cup) flour etc.
¼ pint (⅝ cup) double cream
1 egg white
icing sugar

For chocolate sauce :
4 oz. chocolate dots
½ oz. butter
2 tbsps. water
2 level tbsps. golden syrup
vanilla essence

Lightly grease 2 baking sheets. Spoon the choux pastry into a fabric forcing bag fitted with a ½-in. plain vegetable nozzle. Pipe out about 20 small bun shapes on the baking sheets; hold the nozzle upright while piping and lift it away with a sharp pull to release the mixture.

Bake the choux buns just above the centre of the oven at 425°F. (mark 7) for about 25 minutes until well risen and golden brown. If correctly cooked, the insides should be hollow and fairly dry. Make a hole in the base of each bun with a skewer or knife and cool them on a wire rack.

Shortly before the profiteroles are required, make the chocolate sauce. Melt the chocolate dots with the butter in a small pan over a very low heat. Add the water, syrup and 2–3 drops of vanilla essence; stir well until smooth and well blended.

Put the double cream and egg white into a bowl and whip them together until thick and standing in peaks. Spoon into a fabric forcing bag fitted with a small plain nozzle and pipe into the centre of each bun, through the hole in the bottom.

Dust with icing sugar and serve with the chocolate sauce spooned over or served separately.

CREAM PUFFS
makes about 16

2½ oz. choux pastry – i.e. made
   with 2½ oz. (⅝ cup) flour etc.
¼ pint (⅝ cup) double cream
2½ fl. oz. single cream
icing sugar

The characteristic light, crisp texture and crazy-paving tops of cream puffs are achieved by baking the pastry in its own steam. For this you will need large, shallow tins with tightly fitting lids, or heavy, flat baking sheets with roasting tins inverted over them, sealing the joint with a flour and water paste if necessary.

Spoon the choux pastry into a forcing bag fitted with a ½-in. plain vegetable nozzle and pipe into small rounds on the tins or baking sheets. Leave plenty of space between them.

Cover the piped choux with the lids or roasting tins and bake just above the centre of the oven at 400°F. (mark 6) for 40–50 minutes. It is important that the puffs are left undisturbed during cooking, or the steam will escape and cause the buns to collapse. Estimate the end of the cooking time by giving the tin a gentle shake – if the buns are cooked they will rattle on the base. Cool on a wire rack.

Just before the puffs are required, make a hole in the base of each. Whip the 2 creams together and fill the puffs, piping with a small plain vegetable nozzle. Dust with icing sugar.

PETITES FEUILLETEES

puff or flaky pastry
1 egg white, lightly broken
   with a fork
apricot jam
double cream, whipped
chopped nuts

Roll out the pastry thinly and cut into 3-in. squares. Fold the corners of each square to the centre and join them with a tiny cut-out shape of pastry. Brush with egg white and bake in the centre of the oven at 450°F. (mark 8) for 10–15 minutes.

Cool on wire racks. Sieve the apricot jam and brush it over each pastry to glaze. Decorate with piped whipped cream and chopped nuts.

BASIC PATE SUCREE
This French flan pastry is traditionally used in pâtisserie and larger gâteaux

4 oz. (1 cup) plain flour
a pinch of salt
2 oz. (¼ cup) caster sugar
2 oz. butter at normal room
   temperature
2 egg yolks

Sift together the flour and salt on to a pastry board or, better still, a marble slab. Make a well in the centre and into it put the sugar, butter and egg yolks.

Using the fingertips of 1 hand, pinch and work the sugar, butter and egg yolks together until well blended.

Gradually work in all the flour and knead lightly until smooth. Put the paste in a cool place for at least 1 hour to relax, then roll out and use according to the recipe.

BATEAUX AUX FRUITS
makes 6 ; for this and the following recipes, make up the basic quantity of pâte sucrée given above and use a third of the dough for each variation

⅓ quantity pâte sucrée recipe
apricot glaze
11-oz. can mandarin oranges,
   drained
6 glacé cherries

Roll out the pastry thinly and use to line 6 4½-in. boat shaped patty tins, pressing it lightly into shape. Bake blind, without baking beans, towards the top of the oven at 375°F. (mark 5) for 5–7 minutes, until just tinged brown. Cool on a wire rack.

Warm the apricot glaze slightly and brush it over the insides of the pastry boats.

Arrange the fruit neatly in the boats and brush with more warm apricot glaze.

BATEAUX SAINT ANDRE
makes 6

⅓ quantity pâte sucrée recipe
½ lb. cooking apples, peeled
   and cored
1 oz. sugar
1 tbsp. water
½ egg white
4 oz. (⅞ cup) icing sugar

Roll out the pastry and use to line 6 4½-in. boat shaped patty tins, pressing it lightly into shape.

Slice the apples into a pan and stew with the sugar and water until pulpy; then continue to cook until the purée is thick enough to hold its shape; leave until cold.

Make petites feuilletées from flaky pastry

Divide the purée between the uncooked pastry boats and spread it evenly.

Make up an icing, using the egg white and icing sugar and spread a thin layer over each boat. Roll out the pastry trimmings and cut into short strips; place 2 across each boat. Bake in the centre of the oven at 375°F. (mark 5) for about 10 minutes, until the pastry has set and the topping is tinged brown. Leave to cool in the moulds for a few minutes, then turn out carefully and cool on a wire rack.

BATEAUX DE MIEL
makes 6

⅓ quantity pâte sucrée recipe
4 oz. butter
4 oz. (½ cup) caster sugar
4 oz. ground almonds

3 tsps. thick honey
coffee essence
coffee glacé icing

Roll out the pastry thinly and use to line 6 4½-in. boat shaped patty tins, pressing it lightly into shape. Bake blind, without baking beans, towards the top of the oven at 375°F. (mark 5) for 5–7 minutes, until just tinged brown. Turn out and cool on a wire rack.

Cream the butter and sugar until light and fluffy. Beat in the almonds, honey and 2 teaspoons coffee essence.

Divide the creamed mixture between the boats, piling the mixture up to a ridge and smoothing the surface on either side. Chill.

When firm, coat with icing and decorate with a wavy line of stiffer piped icing.

Bateaux aux fruits, on a base of pâte sucrée

PERFECT PASTRY

Many people consider good pastry the mark of a good cook—so make sure of your results by checking a few general rules before you start. The first requirements for success are cool working conditions and a hot oven—and the richer the pastry, the hotter the oven. To help keep the pastry cool, handle it as little as possible and use only your fingertips for rubbing in the fat. Always use cold water for mixing (except for choux pastry and hot water crust). The rich pastries—flaky and puff—will be improved if you leave them in a cool place between rollings and again before baking.

The proportion of ingredients is vital to the texture of the finished pastry, so add the water cautiously, using only enough to make the mixture bind without becoming sticky—sticky dough leads to hard pastry. Use the barest minimum of flour on the rolling pin and working surface, or you will alter the proportions, giving you dry pastry.

Always roll pastry lightly and as little as possible. Avoid stretching it when you are lining a flan case or covering a pie, or it will shrink back during cooking and spoil the finished shape.

INGREDIENTS

Pastry ingredients are simple, basic foodstuffs, so make sure you use good quality brands for the best results.

Flour Plain flour is best, though for shortcrust pastry you can use self-raising with quite good results.

Fat Butter, margarine and lard are generally used, though nowadays proprietary vegetable shortenings (both blended and whipped) and pure vegetable oils are often used as well, with excellent results. If you are using one of these, remember to follow the directions on the packet, as the proportion of fat to flour may vary slightly.

Liquid As a rule, allow 1 teaspoon of liquid per ounce of flour for shortcrust pastry and 1 tablespoon per ounce to bind suet or flaky pastries to an elastic dough.

BAKING BLIND

Flans and tarts are often 'baked blind' when they are to be filled with a cold or soft uncooked filling, as with lemon meringue pie. To do this, line the pie dish or flan ring with the pastry. Cut out a round of greased greaseproof paper slightly larger than the pastry case and fit this, greased side down, inside the pastry. Half-fill the paper with uncooked haricot beans or rice or with stale bread crusts. Bake the pastry as directed in the recipe for 10–15 minutes, until it has set. Remove the paper and beans, rice or crusts from the pastry case and return it to the oven for another 5 minutes or so to dry out. It is now ready to use. Alternatively, line the pastry case with kitchen foil, which does not need filling with beans.

Small tartlet cases can be baked blind without lining. Line the tartlet tins with pastry, prick well with a fork and bake as directed in the recipe.

SHORTCRUST PASTRY

Quick and simple, using the 'rubbing-in' method. Forms the basis of a wide range of sweet and savoury dishes.

**6 oz. (1½ cups) plain flour
pinch of salt
1½ oz. lard
1½ oz. margarine
6 tsps. water (approx.)**

Sift the flour and salt together into a wide, shallow bowl. Cut the fat into small knobs and add it. Using both hands, rub the fat into the flour between finger and thumb tips. After 2–3 minutes there will be no lumps of fat left and the mixture will look like fresh bread-crumbs.

Add the water, stirring with a round-bladed knife until the mixture begins to stick together. With one hand, collect it together and knead lightly for a few seconds, to give a firm, smooth dough. The pastry can be used straight away, but is better allowed to 'rest' for 15 minutes. It can also be wrapped in polythene and kept in the refrigerator for a day or two. Alternatively store at the rubbed in stage. Allow dough to return to room temperature before rolling out.

When pastry is required, sprinkle a very little flour on a board or table and roll out the dough evenly, turning it occasionally. The usual thickness is about ⅛ in.; do not pull or stretch it. Use as required. The usual oven temperature is 400–425°F. (mark 6–7). This quantity of shortcrust pastry will line a 6–7-in. flan ring or top a 1½–2 pint fruit pie.

FLAN PASTRY

Slightly richer than shortcrust, made in the same way. It is usually sweetened and ideal for flan cases, tartlets and other sweet pastries. For savoury dishes, omit the sugar.

**5 oz. (1¼ cups) plain flour
3 oz. butter or margarine and lard, mixed
1½ level tsps. caster sugar
1 egg, beaten
4 tsps. water**

Sift the flour and salt together into a bowl and rub in the fat with the finger tips, as for shortcrust pastry, until the mixture resembles fine breadcrumbs. Mix in the sugar. Add the egg and water, stirring until the ingredients begin to bind, then with one hand collect the mixture together and knead very lightly to give a firm, smooth

dough. Roll out as for shortcrust pastry and use as required.
This pastry should be cooked in a fairly hot oven–400°F. (mark 6). This quantity of pastry will line a 7–8-in. flan ring.

CHEESE PASTRY

A savoury pastry, suitable for pies, tarts and flans. This is a simple version, not so rich as that given below.

**4 oz. (1 cup) plain flour
pinch of salt
2 oz. butter or margarine and lard (mixed)
2 oz. (½ cup) Cheddar cheese, finely grated
a little beaten egg or water**

Sift the flour and salt together into a bowl and rub in the fat, as for shortcrust pastry, until the mixture resembles fine crumbs in texture. Mix in the cheese. Add the egg or water, stirring until the ingredients begin to stick together, then with one hand collect the dough together and knead very lightly to give a smooth dough. Roll out as for shortcrust pastry and use as required.
The usual temperature for cooking cheese pastry is fairly hot–400°F. (mark 6).
This quantity of pastry will fill 8 boat moulds, 12 patty tins or a 7-in. flan ring.

RICH CHEESE PASTRY

Requires rather more care in making than the simpler version. Suitable for party and cocktail 'nibblers'–not suitable for flan cases.

**3 oz. butter or margarine and lard (mixed)
3 oz. (¾ cup) Cheddar cheese, finely grated
4 oz. (1 cup) plain flour
pinch of salt**

Cream the fat and cheese together until soft. Gradually work in the flour and salt with a wooden spoon or a palette knife until the mixture sticks together; with one hand collect it together and knead very lightly until smooth. Cover with greaseproof or waxed paper and leave in a cool place. Use as required.
Cook at 400°F. (mark 6).

SUETCRUST PASTRY

A traditional pastry, quick and easy to make and can be used for both sweet and savoury dishes. It can be baked, but steaming and boiling give much more satisfactory results.

Almonds and fruit for a frangipan flan

**8 oz. (2 cups) self-raising flour
½ level tsp. salt
4 oz. shredded suet
8 tbsps. cold water (approx.)**

Sift together the flour and salt into a bowl. Add suet and enough cold water to give a light elastic dough and knead very lightly until smooth. Roll out to ¼-in. thickness and use as required.
This quantity of pastry will be sufficient for a 1½-pint steak and kidney pudding.

FORK-MIX PASTRY

Made with oil, this is more suitable for savoury dishes than sweet.

**2½ tbsps. corn oil
1 tbsp. cold water
4 oz. (1 cup) plain flour
pinch of salt**

Put the oil and water into a basin and beat well with a fork to form an emulsion. Add the sifted flour and salt gradually to the mixture to make a dough. Roll this out on a floured board or between grease-proof paper.
Bake in a fairly hot oven–400°F. (mark 6). This quantity of pastry is sufficient to line a plate pie.

CORNISH PASTIES

makes 4

**12 oz. chuck or blade steak
4 oz. raw potato, peeled and diced
1 small onion, skinned and chopped
salt and pepper
12 oz. shortcrust pastry–i.e.
12 oz. (3 cups) flour, etc.**

Cut the steak into small pieces,

To line pastry into small moulds, ease the pastry to the shape of the moulds and then roll the rolling pin over the top

add the potato and onion and season well. Divide the pastry into four and roll each piece into a round about 8 in. in diameter. Divide the meat mixture between the pastry rounds, damp the edges, draw the edges of the pastry together to form a seam across the top and flute the edges with the fingers.

Place on a baking tray and bake in the oven at 425°F. (mark 7) for 15 minutes to start browning the pastry, then reduce the heat to 325°F. (mark 3) and cook for about 1 hour. Serve hot or cold.

FRANGIPAN FLAN

serves 4

6 oz. shortcrust pastry – i.e. made with 6 oz. (1½ cups) flour, etc.

For frangipan cream :

¾ oz. cornflour
¾ pint (2 cups) milk
4 egg yolks
1 oz. caster sugar
3 oz. (¾ cup) ground almonds
vanilla essence

For fruit layer :

¼ lb. white grapes, skinned and halved
2 oranges, peeled
1 banana, peeled and sliced

For topping :

caster sugar
2 oz. (½ cup) flaked almonds, toasted

Roll out the pastry and use to line a 7½-in. plain flan case. Bake blind at 425°F. (mark 7) for 20 minutes. Cool.

Mix the cornflour with a little of the cold milk, blend in remaining milk and bring slowly to the boil, stirring all the time.

Remove from the heat and beat in the egg yolks one at a time. Add the caster sugar, ground almonds and a few drops of vanilla essence. Cook for about 1 minute until the sauce thickens. Stir well, cover and leave until cold.

Meanwhile, remove the pips from the grape halves and cut the oranges into segments. Arrange the grapes, oranges and banana slices in the pastry case. Spread the frangipan cream over the fruit, piling it into a pyramid shape. Dust thickly with caster sugar.

Stand the flan on a serving plate. With a red-hot skewer (held in a cloth) brand the sugar until it caramellizes. Reheat skewer between brandings. Sprinkle the sugar with almonds. Use within a few hours of making.

Place the butter on the dough in small pieces, using a round bladed knife

CREAM CHEESE BOATS

makes 16

4 oz. cheese pastry – i.e. 4 oz. (1 cup) flour, etc.
3 oz. cream cheese
1 oz. lean ham, finely chopped
2 tsps. top of the milk
salt and pepper
4 slices processed cheese

Line 16 3½-in. boat shaped moulds with the pastry. Prick the bottom of the pastry well and bake blind just above the centre of the oven at 400°F. (mark 6) for about 10 minutes or until golden brown. When cool, remove from the moulds. Beat the cream cheese until smooth, add the ham and top of the milk. Season well. Pipe the cheese into the pastry boats and decorate with triangular 'sails' cut from the sliced processed cheese. Use within a few hours of making.

STEAK AND KIDNEY PUDDING

serves 4

8 oz. suetcrust pastry – i.e. 8 oz. (2 cups) flour, etc.
½–¾ lb. stewing steak, cut into ½-in. cubes
¼ lb. kidney, skinned and cored
2 level tbsps. seasoned flour
1 onion, skinned and chopped

Half-fill a steamer or large saucepan with water and put it on to boil. Grease a 1½-pint pudding basin. Cut off a quarter of the pastry to make the lid. Roll out the remainder and use to line the basin.

Slice the kidney and coat both the steak and the kidney with seasoned flour. Fill the basin with the meat, onion and 2–3 tablespoons of water. Roll out the remainder of the pastry to a round the size of the basin top and damp the edge of it. Place on top of the

meat and seal the edges of the pastry well.

Cover with greased greaseproof paper or foil and steam over rapidly boiling water for about 4 hours, refilling the pan as necessary with boiling water.

The meat can be prepared and stewed with the onion for about 2 hours earlier in the day or the previous night before being used for the filling. In this case, reduce the steaming time to 1½–2 hours.

RICH PASTRIES

Always handle flaked pastries lightly and as little as possible.

The fat to be used should be worked on a plate with a knife before you start to make the pastry. This softens it, as it needs to be about the same consistency as the dough with which it is going to be combined.

Remember to allow these richer pastries to 'rest' during the making as well as after shaping and before baking. Cover the pastry and leave in a cool place for 15 minutes or so. This prevents the fat becoming oily and spoiling the flaked texture of the finished pastry.

Roll out the pastry lightly, evenly and as quickly as possible.

FLAKY PASTRY

The commonest of the flaked pastries, used for both savoury and sweet dishes.

8 oz. (2 cups) plain flour
pinch of salt
6 oz. butter or butter and lard
8 tbsps. cold water to mix (approx.)
squeeze of lemon juice
beaten egg to glaze

Mix together the flour and salt. Soften the fat by working it with a knife on a plate; divide it into 4 equal parts. Rub one quarter of the softened fat into the flour with the fingertips and mix to a soft,

elastic dough with the water and lemon juice. On a floured board, roll the pastry into an oblong 3 times as long as it is wide.

Put another quarter of the fat over the top two-thirds of the dough in small flakes, so that it looks like buttons on a card. Fold the bottom third up and the top third down and give the pastry half a turn, so that the folds are now at the sides. Seal the edges of the pastry by pressing with the rolling pin. (On a warm day, allow to rest at this stage before continuing.) Re-roll into the same oblong shape as before.

Continue with the remaining two quarters of fat in the same way. When all the fat is used, wrap the pastry loosely in greaseproof paper or a polythene bag and leave it to rest in a refrigerator or a cool place for at least ½ hour before using. Sprinkle a board or working surface with a very little flour. Roll out the pastry ¼–⅛ in. thick and use as required.

The usual oven temperature for flaky pastry is hot – 425°F. (mark 7).

This quantity of pastry will line 2 8-in. pie plates or will make 16 Eccles cakes or cream horns.

ROUGH PUFF PASTRY

Similar in appearance and texture to flaky pastry, though generally not so even. Quicker and easier to make, and can be used as an alternative for flaky in most recipes.

8 oz. (2 cups) plain flour
pinch of salt
6 oz. butter or margarine and lard mixed
8 tbsps. cold water to mix (approx.)
squeeze of lemon juice
beaten egg to glaze

Sift the flour and salt into a bowl; cut the fat (which should be quite firm but not hard) into cubes about ¾ in. across. Stir the fat into the flour without breaking up the pieces and mix to a fairly stiff dough with the water and lemon juice. Turn on to a floured board and roll into a strip 3 times as long as it is wide, using firm, sharp movements. Fold the bottom third up and the top third down, then give the pastry a half-turn so that the folds are at the sides. Seal the edges of the pastry by pressing lightly with the rolling pin.

Continue to roll and fold in this way 4 times altogether. Leave to rest in a cool place wrapped in greaseproof paper or polythene bag for about 30 minutes before using. Roll out and use as for flaky pastry.

The usual oven temperature for cooking rough puff pastry is 425°F. (mark 7).

PUFF PASTRY

The richest of all pastries, giving the most even rising, the most flaky effect and the crispest texture. Requires very careful handling, allowing plenty of time to rest before the final rolling and shaping.

Although most cooks will want to be able to make it, the standard of bought puff pastry is very high. In our recipes we refer to the finished weight of pastry so that ready-made pastry may be used as an alternative.

8 oz. (2 cups) plain flour
pinch of salt
8 oz. butter (preferably unsalted)
8 tbsps. cold water to mix (approx.)
squeeze of lemon juice
beaten egg to glaze

Sift the flour and salt into a bowl. Work the fat with a knife on a plate until it is soft, then rub about ½ oz. of it into the flour.

Mix to a fairly soft, elastic dough with the water and lemon juice and knead lightly on a floured board until smooth.

Form the rest of the fat into an oblong and roll the pastry out into a square.

Place the fat on one half of the pastry and enclose it by folding the remaining pastry over and sealing the edges firmly with the rolling pin.

Turn the pastry so that the fold is to the side, then roll out into a strip 3 times as long as it is wide. Fold the bottom third up and the top third down and seal the edges with the rolling pin. Cover the pastry and leave it to rest in a cool place (preferably the refrigerator) for about 20 minutes.

Turn the pastry so that the folds are to the side and continue rolling, folding and resting until the sequence has been completed 6 times altogether.

After the final resting, shape the pastry as required. Always brush the top surfaces with beaten egg before cooking, to give the characteristic glaze of puff pastry – add a pinch of salt if a really rich glaze is required.

The usual oven temperature for cooking puff pastry is 450°F. (mark 8).

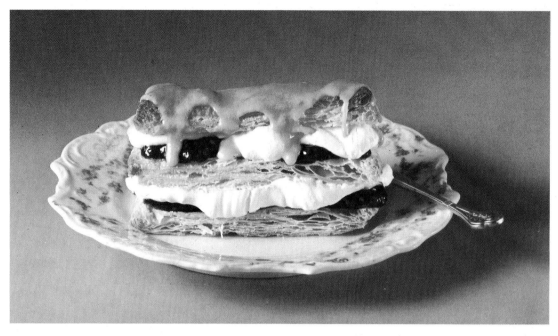

Puff pastry, cream, jam and glacé icing for a mille-feuilles slice

This quantity of pastry will make 12 cream slices or a flan case 12 in. by 6 in.

BAKEWELL TART
serves 4

4 oz. flaky or rough puff pastry – i.e. 4 oz. (1 cup) flour, etc. (or 8 oz. frozen puff pastry, thawed)
1–2 tbsps. raspberry jam
2 oz. butter or margarine
2 oz. (¼ cup) caster sugar
grated rind and juice of ½ lemon
1 egg, beaten
3 oz. (1 cup) cake crumbs, sieved
3 oz. (¾ cup) ground almonds

Roll out the pastry thinly and line a deep 7-in. or 8-in. pie plate. Spread the bottom of the pastry case with the jam.

Cream the fat and sugar with the lemon rind until pale and fluffy. Add the eggs a little at a time and beat after each addition. Mix together the cake crumbs and ground almonds, fold half into the mixture with a tablespoon, then fold in the rest, with a little lemon juice if necessary to give a dropping consistency.

Put the mixture into the pastry case and smooth the surface with a knife. Bake near the top of the oven at 425°F. (mark 7) for about 15 minutes, until the tart begins to brown; transfer to the centre of the oven and reduce the temperature to 350°F. (mark 4) and cook for a further 20–30 minutes, until the filling is firm to the touch.

Serve hot or cold.

HOT CHICKEN PIE
serves 6

4 lb. oven-ready chicken
1 small onion, skinned and halved
1 carrot, peeled
1 leek, washed and trimmed or 1 stick of celery, scrubbed
6 peppercorns
salt

For the sauce :
2 oz. butter
6 oz. (¾ cup) onion, skinned and chopped
½ lb. sweet red peppers, seeded and finely chopped
2 oz. green chillies, halved and seeded
4 level tbsps. flour
1 pint (2½ cups) chicken stock
4 oz. (1 cup) mature Cheddar cheese, grated
salt and freshly ground black pepper

6 oz. puff pastry (i.e. made with 6 oz. flour) or 13 oz. frozen puff pastry, thawed
1 egg, beaten

Simmer the chicken in sufficient water to cover with the vegetables – onion, carrot, leek or celery – peppercorns and salt, for about 2 hours. Remove chicken, reduce the liquor to 1 pint by rapid boiling and then strain. Melt the butter in a saucepan, fry the chopped onion, peppers and chillies for 10 minutes; if wished, the chillies may be removed at this stage.

Carve the chicken, cutting it into fork-size pieces, and discard the skin. Place the meat in a 3-pint pie dish with a funnel. Blend the flour into the fried vegetables and slowly add the strained stock, stirring continuously. Bring to the boil.

When the liquid has thickened, add the cheese and adjust the seasoning. Spoon over the chicken and allow to cool.

Roll out the puff pastry and use to cover the filled pie dish. Knock up and scallop the edge and score the top of the pastry into diamonds with a knife, glaze with beaten egg, place on a baking sheet and cook in the oven at 450°F. (mark 8) for 30 minutes. Reduce heat to 325°F. (mark 3) and cook for a further 30 minutes.

MILLE-FEUILLES SLICES
makes 6

4 oz. puff or rough puff pastry – i.e. 4 oz. (1 cup) flour, etc. (or 8 oz. frozen puff pastry, thawed)
raspberry jam
whipped cream
glacé icing
chopped nuts

Roll the pastry into a strip ½ in. thick, 4 in. wide and 12 in. long. Brush the baking tray with water, lay the pastry on it and cut it from side to side in strips 2 in. wide, but don't separate the slices. Bake near the top of the oven, at 450°F. (mark 8) for 10 minutes. Separate the strips and cool them. Split each into two and sandwich them together in threes or fours with jam and cream. Cover the tops with glacé icing and sprinkle a few chopped nuts at each end.

CHOUX PASTRY

A rich pastry that swells in cooking to a crisp, airy texture. It is traditionally used for sweet pastries such as éclairs and profiteroles, and occasionally for special savoury dishes.

1½ oz. butter or margarine
¼ pint (⅝ cup) water
2½ oz. (⅝ cup) plain flour, sifted
2 eggs, lightly beaten

Melt the fat in the water and bring to the boil. Remove from the heat and quickly tip in the flour all at once. Return the pan to the heat and beat the paste until it is smooth and forms a ball in the centre of the pan. (Take care not to over-beat or the mixture becomes fatty.) Allow to cool slightly. Beat in the eggs gradually, adding

long on to a baking tray. Keep the lengths even and cut the paste off with a wet knife against the edge of the nozzle. Bake the éclairs near the top of the oven at 400°F. (mark 6) for 30–35 minutes, until well risen, crisp and of a golden brown colour.

Remove from the tray, make a slit in the side to allow the steam to escape and leave on a wire rack to cool.

When the éclairs are cold, fill with the whipped cream or crème pâtissière, then ice the tops with a little chocolate glacé icing or dip them in melted chocolate.

HOT-WATER CRUST PASTRY

Used for raised pies, as the hot water used to mix the pastry makes it pliable enough to mould easily.

Fill each éclair with cream and dip in melted chocolate

just enough to give a smooth, glossy mixture of piping consistency. Use as required.

The usual oven temperature is 400°F. (mark 6).

This quantity will make 10–12 éclairs or 20 profiteroles.

CHOCOLATE ECLAIRS

makes 10–12

2½ oz. choux pastry–i.e.
    2½ oz. (⅝ cup) flour, etc.
whipped cream or crème
    pâtissière
chocolate glacé icing
    made with 4 oz. (⅞ cup) icing
    sugar etc., or 3–4 oz.
    melted chocolate

Make up the choux pastry and spoon into a fabric forcing bag fitted with a ½-in. diameter plain round nozzle; pipe fingers 3½–4 in.

1 lb. (4 cups) plain flour
2 level tsps. salt
4 oz. lard
¼ pint (⅝ cup) plus 4 tbsps.
    milk or milk and water

Sift the flour and salt together. Melt the lard in the liquid, then bring to the boil and pour into a well made in the dry ingredients. Working quickly, beat with a wooden spoon to form a fairly soft dough. Turn it out on to a lightly floured board and knead until smooth. Use as required, keeping the part of the dough not actually being used covered with a cloth or upturned bowl to prevent it hardening.

The usual oven temperature is 425°F. (mark 7) for the first 15 minutes, reduced to 365°F. (mark 4) for the remainder of the time.

SHAPING A RAISED PIE BY HAND

Roll out ⅔ of the prepared dough to a round 12 in. in diameter. Take a straight-sided container 4 in. in diameter (e.g. a large jam jar), dredge with flour and turn upside down. Lift the round of dough with the rolling pin and place over the base of the container. Mould dough round the container by pressing firmly to the sides, keeping the edge even.

Cut a double thickness of grease-proof paper or kitchen foil to fit round the pie. Wrap the paper round the pastry and tie with string. Leave in a cool place until the pastry is firm enough to stand in the 'raised' position without a mould.

Turn the container the right way up and gently ease it out of the pastry case, twisting it gently to loosen. Leave the paper in position. Place the pastry case on a baking sheet, and fill with the prepared meat mixture. Pack the filling well down at the sides to hold the shape of the pie. Brush the edge with water. Roll out the remaining pastry to make a lid. Place on top of the pie and press the edges together to seal. Trim away the surplus pastry and paper with scissors.

Make a hole in the centre of the lid and decorate the top with pastry leaves cut from the trimmings. Brush with beaten egg white or water and bake as directed.

MAKING A RAISED PIE IN A CAKE TIN OR MOULD

Grease a 6-in. round cake tin – preferably one with a loose bottom,

which makes it easier to remove the pie after baking. Roll out ⅔ of the dough and use to line the sides and bottom of the tin, making sure that the pastry is free of creases and splits. Add the filling, cover with the remaining dough, rolled out to form a lid, and decorate. Bake as directed in the recipe.

RICH RAISED PIE

serves 6–8

1 lb. hot-water crust pastry
    i.e. 1 lb. (4 cups) flour, etc.
veal bones
2½-lb. oven-ready chicken,
    boned
salt and pepper
½ lb. lean pork
½ lb. lean streaky bacon
    rashers, rinded
½ lb. shoulder veal
2 tbsps. chopped parsley
1 lb. pork sausage meat

Chop the veal bones and use them, together with the chicken bones, skin and giblets, to make a well-seasoned, concentrated jellied stock; leave to cool in the refrigerator.

Separate the chicken breasts and cut into pieces; mince the remainder of the flesh, together with the pork and half the bacon rashers. Dice the veal. Blend the parsley into the sausage meat. Cut the remaining bacon rashers in half, stretch each piece with the back of a knife, spread a thin layer of sausage meat on to each rasher and roll up.

Make the pastry and use two-thirds of it to line an 8-in. oval fancy pie mould, placed on a baking sheet. Press the pastry well into the base and the pattern. Use three-quarters of the remaining sausage meat to make a lining over the pastry. Fill the centre alternately with bacon rolls, minced pork mixture, veal and chicken breasts, piled well up. Season well and cover with the remaining sausage meat.

Damp the edges of the pastry, roll out the remaining piece and use for a lid. Trim the edges and seal. Decorate with pastry trimmings, and make a hole in the centre of the pie. Brush well with beaten egg.

Bake at 400°F. (mark 6) for 30 minutes, reduce the heat to 350°F. (mark 4) and cook for a further 2 hours. Cover with foil once the pastry is a good golden brown.

When the pie is quite cold, fill with cool but not cold liquid stock through the hole in the centre of the lid. Leave for several hours.

CAKES FOR THE FAMILY

Most cakes are straightforward to make if you follow the recipe carefully. Always use the ingredients specified, as substituting granulated sugar for caster, or self-raising flour for plain, will alter the texture considerably and could be disastrous. Always make sure eggs are at room temperature when you use them and don't use butter or margarine straight from the refrigerator either; let them soften a little first, unless you are using one of the 'soft' margarines. Oven temperature is critical in cake baking, so always pre-heat the oven before you start and don't open the door until after two-thirds of the cooking time given in the recipe has elapsed. If the cake seems to be browning too quickly, lower the temperature towards the end of the time. To test whether a light textured cake is cooked, press it lightly with the tip of a finger – it should be spongy, give only very slightly to the pressure,

then rise again immediately. With a fruit cake, lift it gently from the oven and listen to it carefully; if there is a sizzling sound, the cake is not yet cooked through. Alternatively, insert a warm skewer (never a cold knife) into the centre of the cake. It should come out perfectly clean; if any mixture is sticking to it, the cake requires longer cooking.

WHISKED SPONGE

2 eggs
4 oz. (½ cup) caster sugar
4 oz. (1 cup) plain flour, sifted

Grease and base-line an 8-in. sandwich tin.
Whisk the eggs and sugar in a bowl over hot water until thick and leaving a trail. Remove from the heat. Sprinkle the sifted flour over the egg mixture and carefully fold in, using a metal spoon, until the flour is evenly distributed. Pour into the prepared tin and bake just above the centre of the

oven at 350°F. (mark 4) for 25–30 minutes
Turn out and cool on a wire rack and use as required.

VICTORIA SANDWICH CAKE

4 oz. butter or margarine
4 oz. (½ cup) caster sugar
2 large eggs
4 oz. (1 cup) self-raising flour
grated rind of 1 lemon (or other flavouring)

Grease and base-line 2 7-in. sandwich tins or line 1 8½-in. straight sided sandwich tin with paper to come a little above the rim.
In a bowl, cream together the butter and sugar until light and fluffy. Add the eggs one at a time, beating well after each addition. Add the lemon rind or other flavouring.
Lightly beat in the flour. When well mixed, divide the mixture evenly between the 2 tins and level off the surface of each. Bake

the cakes (side by side, if possible) at 350°F. (mark 4) for about 25 minutes (30 minutes for a single deeper cake).
Turn the cakes out on to a wire rack to cool. To prevent marking the top surface if the cakes are to be left un-iced, first cover the rack with a clean tea towel, or turn them on to the hand and quickly reverse on to the rack. Sandwich the cakes (or split and sandwich the large cake) with jam or butter cream; ice the top with glacé icing or dust with icing sugar.

COFFEE NUT CAKE

6 oz. butter or margarine
6 oz. (⅔ cup) caster sugar
3 large eggs
6 oz. (1½ cups) plain flour
¾ level tsp. baking powder
pinch of salt
coffee butter cream
chopped and whole walnuts to decorate
coffee glacé icing

Grease and line 2 7-in. sandwich tins.

Cream the butter and sugar until light and fluffy, then beat in the eggs one at a time. Sift the flour, baking powder and salt and fold in a little at a time.

Divide the mixture equally between the prepared tins and bake in the centre of the oven at 350°F. (mark 4) for about 30 minutes, until golden brown and firm to the touch. Turn out the cakes and cool on a wire rack.

Make some butter cream with 3 oz. butter and 6 oz. (1 cup) sifted icing sugar and add sufficient coffee essence to give a good flavour.

Sandwich the layers together with the butter cream and use the remainder to coat the sides of the cake. Roll the sides in chopped walnuts and coat the top with glace icing flavoured with coffee essence; decorate with the whole walnuts.

GRASMERE CAKE

12 oz. (3 cups) plain flour
1 level tsp. mixed spice
1½ level tsps. bicarbonate of soda
6 oz. butter or margarine
½ pint (1¼ cups) milk plus 1 tbsp.
1 tbsp. lemon juice
6 oz. (1 cup) Demerara sugar
6 oz. currants, cleaned
3 oz. sultanas, cleaned

Line a 9¾-in. by 5¾-in. loaf tin (top measurement) with greased greaseproof paper.

Sift the flour, spice and bicarbonate of soda into a wide bowl; cut the fat into small pieces and add to the bowl. Using the tips of the fingers, rub the fat into the flour until the mixture resembles fine breadcrumbs.

Add the lemon juice to the milk (the milk will clot and turn sour). Add the sugar, currants and sultanas to the dry ingredients and mix well. Gradually add the soured milk, stirring with a wooden spoon, until a dropping consistency is reached.

Leave the mixture covered for several hours or overnight.

Turn the mixture into the prepared tin. Level off the surface of the mixture with a spatula or knife. Place the tin on a baking sheet and bake in the centre of the oven at 325°F. (mark 3) for about 2 hours.

The Grasmere cake should be evenly risen and have a smooth surface. Leave it for a few minutes

Grasmere cake to cut and keep

in the tin before lifting it out on to a wire rack to cool. Carefully remove the paper.

Grasmere cake can be stored satisfactorily for about 1 week. Wrap it in kitchen foil when cold, or else wrap it in greaseproof paper and store in an airtight tin.

Note: If you prefer, omit the milk and lemon juice and use an equivalent quantity of buttermilk.

FROSTED APPLE CAKE

4 oz. butter or margarine
4 oz. (½ cup) caster sugar
2 large eggs
4 oz. (1 cup) self-raising flour
vanilla essence

For topping:
1 level tbsp. caster sugar
2 level tsps. powdered cinnamon
2 oz. flaked almonds
1 large cooking apple
icing sugar

Grease and line an 8-in. double sandwich tin.

Cream together the butter and sugar and beat in the eggs one at a time. Lightly beat in the flour, with a few drops of vanilla essence. Turn the mixture into the prepared cake tin.

Toss together the sugar, cinnamon and nuts. Cover the surface of the cake evenly with peeled, cored and very thinly sliced apple, and sprinkle with the nut mixture. Bake in the centre of the oven at 350°F. (mark 4) for about 30 minutes.

Cool slightly, then turn out carefully on to a wire rack covered with a clean tea towel. Reverse with the apple side uppermost and cool.

DATE SCONE BAR
makes 8

8 oz. (2 cups) plain flour
½ level tsp. bicarbonate of soda
1 level tsp. cream of tartar
pinch of salt
2 oz. butter or margarine
1 oz. (⅛ cup) sugar
3 oz. (⅝ cup) dates, stoned
¼ pint (⅝ cup) milk approx.

Sift together the dry ingredients. Rub in the fat to resemble fine breadcrumbs and add the sugar. Using kitchen scissors, snip the dates into small pieces and add to the mixture. Mix to a light dough with the milk. Roll out into an oblong approximately 12 in. by 4 in. Brush with milk and place on a greased baking sheet. Mark through into 8 bars, using the back of a knife. Bake near the top of the oven at 450°F. (mark 8) for about 15 minutes. Break apart, and cool on a wire rack. Serve the bars plain or buttered.

SPICY DATE AND NUT CAKE

12 oz. (3 cups) plain flour
6 oz. butter or margarine
6 oz. (¾ cup) caster sugar
2 level tsps. ground cinnamon
6 oz. nuts, chopped
6 oz. stoned dates, chopped
14½-oz. can apple purée
1½ level tsps. bicarbonate of soda
1 tbsp. milk (approx.)

For topping:
2 tbsps. chopped dates and nuts
2 level tsps. caster sugar
½ level tsp. ground cinnamon

Grease and line a 9¾-in. by 5¾-in. loaf tin (top measurement).

Sift the flour into a bowl and rub in the fat; add the sugar, cinnamon, nuts and dates. Make a well in the centre and add the apple purée. Dissolve the bicarbonate of soda in the milk and add to the mixture; mix well and put into the prepared tin.

Mix together the ingredients for the topping, sprinkle over the surface of the cake and bake in the centre of the oven at 375°F. (mark 5) for about 1¼ hours. Carefully remove and cool on a wire rack.

RICH FRUIT CAKE
suitable for Christmas and celebration birthday cakes

8 oz. (2 cups) plain flour
½ level tsp. ground ginger
½ level tsp. ground mace
8 oz. butter
8 oz. (1⅓ cups) soft dark brown sugar
4 large eggs, beaten
1-2 tbsps. brandy
grated rind of 1 lemon
8 oz. currants, cleaned
8 oz. stoned raisins, cleaned and roughly chopped
8 oz. sultanas, cleaned
4 oz. small glacé cherries, halved
4 oz. mixed chopped peel
2 oz. nibbed almonds

Choose either a 7-in. square or an 8-in. round cake tin. Cut a double strip of greaseproof paper long enough to line the sides of the tin and 2 in. deep. Make a 1-in. fold lengthwise and snip at intervals. Cut 2 paper squares or rounds for the base.

Grease the tin. Fit 1 paper square or round into the bottom of the tin, line the sides, fitting the snipped edges into the corners and overlapping them smoothly at the base.

Fit in the other square or round and grease the lining. Either tie a band of brown paper round the outside of the tin, or place it inside a slightly larger tin.

Sift the flour with the spices. Cream the butter and sugar together in a bowl using a wooden spoon; beat well until the mixture is pale in colour, light and fluffy in texture and about twice its original volume. Add 1 tablespoon egg at a time, beating well. If the mixture shows signs of curdling, beat in 1-2 tablespoons sifted flour.

Using a metal spoon, lightly fold in the flour, alternately with the brandy and followed by the lemon rind, fruit and nuts. Mix thoroughly to distribute the fruit evenly. Then spoon all the mixture into the prepared tin, pushing it well into the corners. Use a rubber spatula to get all the mixture from the bowl.

With the back of a spoon, make a slight hollow in the centre of the mixture to prevent uneven rising. Put the tin on a newspaper-lined baking sheet. Bake below the centre of the oven at 300°F. (mark 2) for about 3¾ hours. If the cake shows signs of browning too quickly, cover the top with a sheet of greaseproof paper and reduce the heat to 275°F. (mark ½) for the last hour of the cooking time. Test by sticking a warmed skewer into the centre of the cake. If no uncooked mixture adheres to it, remove the cake from the oven. Allow it to cool for a few minutes in the tin, then turn it out on to a wire rack. When it is cold, remove the papers.

DEVIL'S FOOD CAKE

10 oz. (2½ cups) plain flour
2 level tsps. bicarbonate of
**   soda**
½ level tsp. salt
3 oz. butter or margarine
9 oz. (1½ cups) soft light
**   brown sugar**
2 large eggs
4 oz. unsweetened chocolate,
**   melted**
8 fl. oz. (1 cup) milk
1 tsp. vanilla essence

For butter filling:
3 oz. butter
5 oz. (1 cup) icing sugar
1 tbsp. top of the milk

For frosting:
6 oz. chocolate dots
1 lb. (3½ cups) icing sugar
2 tbsps. hot water
2 egg yolks
3 oz. butter, melted

Grease and line 2 8½-in. sandwich tins, keeping the greaseproof paper round the sides above the rims.

Sift together the flour, bicarbonate of soda and salt. Cream together the fat and sugar until pale and fluffy, then gradually add the eggs, one at a time, beating well after each addition. Add the melted chocolate and beat well. Then add the flour alternately with the milk and vanilla essence. Turn the mixture into the tins and bake at 350°F. (mark 4) for about 40 minutes. Cool on a wire rack. To finish, sandwich the cakes together with butter filling and coat with the frosting; finish in swirls

A light, fluffy gâteau for tea-time

using a round-bladed knife. Leave to set, preferably until the next day, before slicing.

Butter filling:
Cream the butter until soft then gradually beat in the sifted icing sugar with the milk.

Frosting:
Melt the chocolate dots in a bowl over warm, not boiling, water. Off the heat, stir in the sifted icing sugar and hot water. Gradually beat in the egg yolks, one at a time, followed by the melted butter, a little at a time, Continue to beat until of a spreading consistency.

GATEAU A L'ORANGE

4 eggs, separated
4 oz. (½ cup) caster sugar
grated rind of 1 orange
4 tbsps. orange juice
3½ oz. (⅞ cup) plain flour

For filling and decoration:
4½ oz. butter
5 oz. (⅝ cup) caster sugar
1 egg
1 egg yolk
grated rind of 1 orange
4 tbsps. orange juice
1 tbsp. orange liqueur
2 oz. almonds, flaked and
**   toasted**
1 whole orange

Grease and base-line a 9-in. straight sided sandwich tin.

Place the egg yolks and sugar in a basin and whisk until pale and thick. Beat in the orange rind and juice. Fold in the flour. Beat the egg whites stiffly and fold into the mixture. Turn it into the prepared tin and bake above the centre of the oven at 350°F. for about 30 minutes.

Turn out and cool on a wire rack. Meanwhile prepare the filling. Put 1½ oz. butter in a bowl with the caster sugar, egg, egg yolk, orange rind and juice and liqueur. Place over a pan of hot water and

whisk until smooth and thick. Leave until completely cold. Split the cake in 2 and sandwich together with a little of the butter cream. Cream the remaining butter and beat it into the rest of the filling. Use this thickened butter cream to cover the top and sides of the cake. Press the toasted almonds into the cream round the sides of the cake. Peel remaining orange free of all white pith; divide into segments to decorate the top.

FRUIT AND ALMOND SLICES

makes 12

3 oz. (¾ cup) plain flour
1 oz. (2 tbsps.) caster sugar
2 oz. butter
1 oz. currants
12 glacé cherries, halved

For topping:
2 oz. butter
2 oz. (¼ cup) caster sugar
1 large egg, beaten
2 oz. (½ cup) ground almonds
almond essence
icing sugar

Grease a shallow oblong tin measuring 12 in. by 4 in. and line the base with greased greaseproof paper.

In a bowl, mix together the flour and 1 oz. caster sugar. Lightly work in the butter, using the fingertips, until the mixture begins to bind together. Spoon it into the tin and press into an even layer over the base, using a round-bladed knife. Scatter the currants over, then arrange the cherries at intervals in between.

For the topping, cream the butter and sugar together until light and fluffy. Add the egg gradually and beat thoroughly. Stir in the ground almonds and 1–2 drops almond essence. Spread carefully over the fruit layer and bake the cake just below the oven centre at 375°F. (mark 5) for about 40 minutes,

until just set and golden brown. Loosen the edges, turn out and cool on a wire rack. Dredge with icing sugar and cut into bars.

MADEIRA CAKE

6 oz. butter
6 oz. (¾ cup) caster sugar
3 large eggs
5 oz. (1¼ cups) self-raising
**   flour**
4 oz. (1 cup) plain flour
juice and grated rind of
**   ½ lemon**
citron peel to decorate

Grease a 7-in. round cake tin. Cream the butter and beat in the sugar until light and fluffy. Add the eggs one at a time, beating well after each addition.

Sift the flour and fold it in alternately with the lemon juice and rind. Turn the mixture into the prepared tin, add a few slices of thinly cut citron peel on top. Bake in the centre of the oven at 325°F. (mark 3) for about 1 hour and 10 minutes.

Cool for a short time in the tin, then turn it out on to a wire rack to cool thoroughly.

UNCOOKED CHOCOLATE CAKE

4 oz. sweet biscuits
2 oz. digestive biscuits
2 oz. shelled walnuts or
**   seedless raisins**
3½ oz. butter or margarine
1 oz. (2 tbsps.) caster sugar
3 oz. golden syrup
2 oz. (½ cup) cocoa

For icing:
2 oz. cooking chocolate
1 tbsp. hot water
2½ oz. (½ cup) icing sugar
knob of butter

Place a 7½- or 8-in. flan ring on a flat serving plate.

Roughly crush the biscuits with a rolling pin. Coarsely chop the walnuts or raisins and mix with the biscuits. Cream together the butter, sugar and syrup. Beat in the sifted cocoa and work in the biscuits and walnuts or raisins. When the ingredients are well mixed, press evenly into the flan ring and leave to refrigerate overnight. The next day remove the flan ring, spread the icing over the top of the cake and leave to set.

To make the icing, put all the ingredients in a small saucepan and stir together over a very low heat until the chocolate has melted. Spread over the cake when of a coating consistency.

QUICK CAKES AND COOKIES

CHOCOLATE CRACKLES
makes 12

8 oz. chocolate dots
1 oz. golden syrup
2 oz. butter
2 oz. cornflakes or rice crispies

Melt the chocolate dots with the golden syrup and butter over a very low heat, or put in a basin set over a pan of hot water. Fold in the cornflakes or crispies.
When well mixed, divide between 12 paper cases and leave to set.

TRUFFLE CAKES
makes 16–18

4 oz. stale cake or cake trimmings
4 oz. (½ cup) caster sugar
4 oz. (1 cup) ground almonds
apricot jam
sherry or rum to flavour
chocolate vermicelli to decorate

Rub the stale cake or cake trimmings through a fairly coarse sieve and add the caster sugar, ground almonds and enough apricot jam to bind. Flavour as liked with sherry or rum.
Shape the mixture into small balls and leave to become firm. Sieve some apricot jam. Dip each ball into the jam and roll in chocolate vermicelli. When firm, put into small paper cases.

SHELL CAKES
makes 12–14

3 oz. butter
3 oz. (⅓ cup) caster sugar
½–1 egg, beaten
5 oz. (1¼ cups) plain flour
jam for filling
icing sugar for dredging

Grease 2 baking sheets.
Cream the butter and sugar until really light and fluffy. Beat in the egg (if the egg is small, use all of it). Fold in the flour and mix well. Place the mixture in a forcing bag fitted with a large star nozzle and pipe in small shell shapes on to the baking sheets.
Bake in the centre of the oven at 400°F. (mark 6) for 10–15 minutes, until just coloured. Cool on a wire rack.
To serve, sandwich together in pairs with jam and dredge with icing sugar.

TUTTI FRUTTI CUPS
makes 20

4 oz. butter or margarine
4 oz. (½ cup) caster sugar
2 eggs, beaten
4 oz. (1 cup) self-raising flour
grated rind of ½ lemon
1 oz. glacé cherries, chopped
1 oz. flaked or chopped almonds
2 oz. currants
2 oz. (⅓ cup) Demerara sugar

Cream the butter and sugar until light and fluffy. Beat in the eggs, one at a time. Gently beat in the flour and lemon rind. Divide between 20 paper bun cases (for a better shape, place the cases inside patty pans). Mix together the glacé cherries, almonds, currants and Demerara sugar and top each bun with a spoonful. Bake at 375°F. (mark 5) for 15–20 minutes and leave to cool on a wire rack.

STRAWBERRY SHORTCAKES
makes 12

8 oz. (2 cups) plain flour
2 level tsps. baking powder
2 oz. butter
1 oz. (2 tbsps.) caster sugar
1 egg, beaten
milk to mix
¾ lb. strawberries, hulled
caster sugar for berries
¼ pint (⅝ cup) double cream, whipped

Lightly grease a baking sheet.
Sift together the flour and baking powder. Rub in the butter, add the sugar and mix to a stiff scone dough with the egg and a little milk. Roll out to ½–¾ in. thick and cut out 12 rounds, using a 3-in. plain cutter. Place on the baking sheet and bake near the top of the oven at 450°F. (mark 8) for 7–10 minutes, until well risen and golden brown.
Crush ½ lb. strawberries very

lightly, adding a little sugar if desired. Beat the cream until light and fluffy. While the shortcakes are still warm, split each in half and spread with crushed berries. Top with whole berries and whipped cream.

ONE-TWO-THREE BISCUITS
makes about 9

2 oz. butter
1 oz. (2 tbsps.) caster sugar
3 oz. ($\frac{3}{4}$ cup) plain flour
sugar to dredge

Grease a baking sheet.
Cream together the butter and sugar. Work in the flour and knead lightly to form a ball. Roll out carefully on a lightly floured surface – the mixture will be crumbly and needs knitting together between rollings.
Stamp out rounds, using a $2\frac{1}{4}$-in. fluted cutter, or cut into fingers and mark in lines with a fork. Bake in the centre of the oven or just below at 300°F. (mark 1–2) for about 25 minutes, until just lightly tinged with colour. Cool on a wire rack.
To serve, dredge with caster sugar.

MACAROON STICKS
makes about 12

1 egg white
2 oz. ($\frac{1}{2}$ cup) ground almonds
3 oz. ($\frac{3}{8}$ cup) caster sugar
$\frac{1}{4}$ oz. ground rice
2 oz. plain (dark) chocolate, melted

Ground hazelnuts can be used to replace the almonds, if liked.

Lightly whisk together the egg white, ground almonds, caster sugar and ground rice. Pipe in 2-in. lengths through a $\frac{1}{4}$-in. plain vegetable nozzle on to rice paper. Bake at 375°F. (mark 5) for 7–10 minutes, until tinged with brown. Allow to cool. When cold tear off the rice paper and drizzle with the melted chocolate.

GINGER NUTS
makes about 24

4 oz. (1 cup) self-raising flour
$\frac{1}{2}$ level tsp. bicarbonate of soda
1–2 level tsps. ground ginger
1 level tsp. ground cinnamon
2 level tsps. caster sugar
2 oz. butter
3 oz. golden syrup

Grease 2 baking sheets.
Sift together the flour, bicarbonate of soda, ginger, cinnamon and sugar. Melt the butter and stir in the syrup. Stir this mixture into the dry ingredients and mix well. Roll the mixture into small balls, place well apart on the baking sheets and flatten slightly.
Bake just above the centre of the oven at 375°F. (mark 5) for 15–20 minutes. Cool for a few minutes before lifting carefully from baking sheets on to a wire rack. Finish cooling, and store in an airtight tin.

1-2-3 biscuits, ginger nuts, shell cakes and florentines

FLORENTINES
makes about 24

$3\frac{1}{2}$ oz. butter
4 oz. ($\frac{1}{2}$ cup) caster sugar
4 oz. almonds, chopped
1 oz. sultanas, chopped
1 tbsp. cream
1 oz. glacé cherries, chopped
1 oz. mixed peel, chopped
cooking chocolate

Line baking sheets with non-stick paper.
Melt the butter, add the sugar and boil together for 1 minute. Stir in all the other ingredients except the chocolate. When beginning to cool, drop in small, well-shaped heaps on the baking sheets, keeping them well apart to allow for spreading – about 4 per tray. Bake near the centre of the oven at 350°F. (mark 4) for about 10 minutes, until golden brown.
Remove from the oven and press the edges to a neat shape with a knife. Lift each florentine carefully from the tray and cool on a wire rack.
To finish, spread the smooth underside of each with melted chocolate. When this is beginning to set, mark it in wavy lines with a fork. Leave to harden, then serve.
The biscuits may be stored without the chocolate coating for up to 1 week. Place in an airtight container between sheets of non-stick paper.

OVEN SCONES
makes 10–12

8 oz. (2 cups) self-raising flour
1 level tsp. baking powder
$\frac{1}{4}$ level tsp. salt
$1\frac{1}{2}$ oz. butter or margarine
$1\frac{1}{2}$ oz. (3 tbsps.) sugar
2 oz. sultanas or currants
$\frac{1}{4}$ pint ($\frac{5}{8}$ cup) milk

Sift the flour, baking powder and salt into a mixing bowl. Cut the fat into small pieces and add to the flour. Rub in the fat with the fingertips until no lumps are left and the mixture looks like fine breadcrumbs. Stir in the sugar and the cleaned fruit, then add the milk 1 tablespoon at a time, stirring well with a round-bladed knife until the mixture begins to bind, making a light dough.
Using one hand, collect the mixture together and knead it lightly to form a smooth, fairly soft dough. Turn it out on to a lightly floured board, form into a flat, round shape and roll out 1 in. thick. Cut into 2-in. rounds, put on a baking sheet and brush the tops with a little milk. Bake towards the top of the oven at 450°F. (mark 8) for about 10 minutes, until well risen and golden. Cool on a wire rack. Serve split and buttered on the same day.

DROP SCONES (SCOTCH PANCAKES)
makes 15–18

4 oz. (1 cup) self-raising flour, or 4 oz. plain flour sifted with a pinch each of bicarbonate of soda and cream of tartar
$\frac{1}{2}$–1 oz. (1–2 tbsps.) sugar
1 egg
$\frac{1}{4}$ pint ($\frac{5}{8}$ cup) milk

Prepare a special griddle, a heavy frying pan, or the solid hot plate of an electric cooker, by rubbing the surface with salt on a pad of kitchen paper, wiping clean and then greasing it very lightly. Just before cooking the scones, heat the griddle until the fat is 'hazing'; wipe the surface with paper.
Put the flour and sugar in a bowl, add the egg and half the milk and beat until smooth. Add the remaining milk and beat until bubbles rise to the surface. Spoon the batter on to the heated griddle, spacing well.
When the bubbles rise to the surface, turn the scones with a palette knife and cook for a further $\frac{1}{2}$–1 minute, or until golden brown. Place on a cooling rack and cover with a clean tea towel until the rest are cooked. Serve buttered.

GINGER AND DATE CAKES
makes 15–18

6 oz. ($1\frac{1}{2}$ cups) self-raising flour
pinch of salt
3 oz. butter or margarine
3 oz. ($\frac{3}{8}$ cup) caster sugar
2–3 oz. dates, chopped
1 oz. crystallized ginger, chopped
1 egg, beaten
milk to mix

Grease 18 patty tins.
Sift the flour and salt into a bowl and rub in the fat lightly. Stir in the sugar, dates and ginger, then mix in the egg and milk to form a stiff dropping consistency.
Place in spoonfuls in the patty tins and bake just above the centre of the oven at 375°F. (mark 5) for 15 minutes. Cool on a rack.

ROCK CAKES
makes 12

8 oz. (2 cups) plain flour
pinch of salt
2 level tsps. baking powder
$\frac{1}{2}$ level tsp. mixed spice
$\frac{1}{2}$ level tsp. ground nutmeg
2 oz. butter or margarine
2 oz. lard or cooking fat
4 oz. mixed dried fruit
4 oz. ($\frac{2}{3}$ cup) Demerara sugar
1 large egg, beaten
grated rind of $\frac{1}{2}$ lemon
milk to mix

Grease 2 baking trays.
Sift together the flour, salt, baking powder and spice. Rub in the fat. Add the fruit and sugar, mix well. Add the egg and sufficient milk to give a stiff dough. Using 2 forks, place the mixture in small rough piles on the greased trays and bake towards the top of the oven at 400°F. (mark 6) for 15–20 minutes. Cool on a wire rack.

Devil's food cake

CAKE DECORATING

Many of the nicest cakes are also the simplest to make, but they often require a little filling or decoration with a simple icing to turn them into something special. A sponge or Victoria sandwich would be nothing without its touch of glacé icing, jam filling or butter cream. None of these is a specialist decoration, anyone can make an attractive finish with a very little practice, and even beginners' mistakes are not too expensive!

Icings are not merely decoration, of course. They add moisture and a contrast of texture and flavour to the cake itself. So ring the changes and add to your repertoire. There is very little special equipment you need. For piped decorations you will want a forcing bag and a few nozzles, but even if you don't possess a piping set, that needn't deter you. Butter cream,

glacé icing and fondant icing can all be poured over the top of the cake or spread on with a palette knife. There are just a few simple rules to follow in order to achieve a perfect result.

First, allow the cake to cool thoroughly before you start. While it is cooling, prepare any decorations you plan to use – chop walnuts, cut glacé cherries or angelica into small pieces, grate chocolate, cut up crystallized fruit, etc. When you are ready to start, brush any crumbs off the top of the cake. If you are planning to ice the top, it must be level, so if necessary level the top, turn the cake over and use the flat underside. Most cakes can be left on the wire cooling rack while you are icing, but a soft sponge should be placed on a flat plate, as moving it would crack a soft icing. Do the filling

first, then decorate the sides and finally the top.

If you are going to pipe some icing on to the cake, you may find the large fabric forcing bags are rather large for icing nozzles – so here's how to make your own paper icing bag.

Fold a 10-in. square of greaseproof paper in half to form a triangle and then roll it up along the longest edge, so that it looks like an ice cream cone. Snip off the tip of the bag, drop in the icing nozzle (preferably one without a screw band) and fill with the required amount of icing. Be careful to avoid overfilling. Fold the top flap down, enclosing the front edge until the bag is sealed and quite firm.

To decorate the sides of a cake with jam, coconut, nuts and so on, first brush apricot glaze round

the sides of the prepared cake, or spread it on with a knife. Either put the chosen decoration on greaseproof paper and, holding the cake carefully on its side, roll it through the decoration, or press the nuts etc. a little at a time on to the cake with a round-bladed knife. Continue until the sides are evenly and completely coated. Do this before icing the top.

BUTTER CREAM OR ICING
This amount will coat the sides and top of a 7-in. cake or give a topping and a filling

4 oz. butter
6–8 oz. (1½–1¾ cups) icing sugar, sifted
a few drops of vanilla essence or other flavouring
1–2 tbsps. milk

Cream the butter until soft and

Many attractive decorations can be made using only a palette knife

gradually beat in the sugar, adding a few drops of essence and the milk.

As a filling Spread the butter cream evenly over the lower half of the cake with a round-bladed knife, taking it right to the edges, then put the top half of the cake neatly in place.

As a side covering Spread the butter cream evenly round the sides of the cake, using a round-bladed knife and making sure all the cake is coated. Then, using the flat blade of the knife, pat chopped nuts or chocolate vermicelli on to the sides.

As a topping Pile the butter cream on top of the cake and spread it out smoothly and evenly to the edges until it completely covers the surface. To give a more interesting effect, the surface of the butter cream can be patterned by using a fork or knife before being decorated with crystallized fruits, nuts, glacé cherries, chocolate drops, or extra butter cream piped in whirls, etc.

ALMOND BUTTER CREAM

Substitute almond essence for vanilla and add 2 tbsps. very finely chopped toasted almonds; mix well. This is not suitable for piping.

APRICOT BUTTER CREAM

Omit the vanilla essence and milk. Add 3 tbsps. sieved apricot jam and a squeeze of lemon juice.

BUTTERSCOTCH BUTTER CREAM

Omit the vanilla essence. Melt 1 level tbsp. soft brown sugar and 1 oz. butter together and heat for a few minutes. Cool slightly and beat well into the basic butter cream.

CHOCOLATE BUTTER CREAM

Add either 1–1½ oz. melted but not hot chocolate or chocolate dots, or 1 level tbsp. cocoa blended to a paste with a little hot water.

COFFEE BUTTER CREAM

Omit the vanilla essence and flavour instead with 2 level tsps. instant coffee powder or 1 tbsp. coffee essence.

COFFEE AND WALNUT BUTTER CREAM

Omit the vanilla essence. Add 1–2 tsps. coffee essence and 1 level tbsp. chopped walnuts. This is not suitable for piping as the nuts will block the nozzle.

GINGER BUTTER CREAM

Omit the vanilla essence. Add 3 oz. preserved ginger, very finely chopped. This is not suitable for piping.

LIQUEUR BUTTER CREAM

Omit the vanilla essence and milk. Add 1–2 tsps. liqueur, and colouring according to the flavour of the liqueur.

MOCHA BUTTER CREAM

Omit vanilla essence and milk. Blend 1 level tsp. cocoa and 2 level tsps. instant coffee powder with a little warm water; cool before adding to the mixture.

ORANGE BUTTER CREAM

Omit vanilla essence and milk. Beat in 2 tbsps. orange juice, the grated rind of 1 orange and 1 tsp. Angostura bitters.

RASPBERRY BUTTER CREAM

Omit the milk. Beat in 2 tbsps. raspberry purée or sieved jam.

WALNUT BUTTER CREAM

Add 2–3 level tbsps. very finely chopped walnuts. This is not suitable for piping.

GLACE ICING

This amount is sufficient to cover the top of a 7-in. cake or 18 small buns. If the sides are also to be iced, make twice the amount

4 oz. (⅞ cup) icing sugar, sifted
1–2 tbsps. warm water
colouring and flavouring (see below)

Put the icing sugar in a basin and gradually add the warm water. The icing should be thick enough to coat the back of a spoon quite thickly. Add a few drops of colouring or flavouring essence as required and use immediately. For icing of a finer texture, put the sugar, water and flavouring into a small pan and heat, stirring, until the mixture is warm—don't make it too hot. The icing should coat the back of a wooden spoon and look smooth and glossy.
If the sides of the cake are to be decorated, other than with glacé icing, do this before icing the top. To coat the whole cake, place the filled or plain cake on a wire cooling rack over a large sheet of greaseproof paper. Pour the icing evenly from the bowl on to the centre of the cake and allow it to run down the sides, guiding the flow with a palette knife. Keep a little of the

Feather icing – simple but pretty

icing in reserve in the bowl to fill any gaps.
If only the top of the cake is to be coated, pour the icing on to the centre of the cake and spread it, using a round-bladed knife and stopping just inside the actual edge to prevent the icing dripping down the sides. Decorate with cherries, angelica and so on and leave to set, or leave the plain icing to set and add piped decoration later.

Adding decorations Put these in place quickly before the icing sets – this holds them firmly and prevents the icing from cracking, as it would do if they were added later. Allow the icing to set firmly before attempting to do any piped decoration.

Small cakes These can be iced either by pouring the icing over

them as above, or by holding them lightly in the fingers and dipping them into it.
Note: Glacé icing should not be runny, but should coat the back of a spoon quite thickly.

CHOCOLATE GLACE ICING

Dissolve 2 level tsps. cocoa in the measured water.

COFFEE GLACE ICING

Blend 1 tsp. coffee essence or 2 level tsps. instant coffee in a little water.

LEMON GLACE ICING

Substitute 1–2 tbsps. strained lemon juice for the water.

LIQUEUR GLACE ICING

Replace 2–3 tsps. of the water by the required liqueur.

Butter cream and chopped walnuts turn a plain cake into a glorious gâteau

MOCHA GLACE ICING

Add 1 level tsp. cocoa and 2 level tsps. instant coffee to a little water.

FEATHER ICING

Before you start, make up a small amount of icing in a contrasting colour (e.g. chocolate on plain or lemon glacé icing); it should be of a slightly thicker consistency than the basic icing. Ice the cake with glacé icing in the usual way. Immediately, while the original icing is still wet, using a writing nozzle or a paper piping bag with the tip cut off, pipe parallel lines $\frac{1}{2}-\frac{3}{4}$ in. apart across the cake. Quickly draw a skewer or the sharp point of a knife through the icing at right angles to the piping, in alternate directions. Wipe the point clean after drawing each line.

FONDANT ICING

Makes sufficient icing to give a thick coating to a 7-in. cake

$\frac{1}{4}$ **pint ($\frac{5}{8}$ cup) water**
1 lb. lump or granulated sugar
1 oz. glucose or a good pinch of cream of tartar

Choose a strong, heavy pan large enough to avoid the syrup boiling over. Put the water into the pan, add the sugar and let it dissolve slowly without stirring. When the sugar has dissolved, bring the syrup to the boil, add the glucose or cream of tartar and boil to 240°F. Pour into a heat-resistant bowl and leave to cool until a skin forms on top.

Beat the icing until it thickens, then work the fondant with a knife and finally knead with the hands until it is smooth. Colouring and/or flavouring (e.g. lemon, coffee, chocolate) may be worked in at this stage. The icing may now be used at once, or stored.

To use Place the icing in a basin over hot water and heat until it is the consistency of thick cream (don't over-heat or the texture will be spoilt). If necessary, dilute with sugar syrup or water.

To ice small cakes or pastries Spear them on a fork or skewer and dip them in the prepared fondant.

To ice a large cake Put the cake on a wire rack with a plate below and pour the icing quickly all over the cake. Don't touch the icing with a knife, or the gloss finish will be spoilt. Add any decoration and leave the icing to set.

To give a thick topping Pin a band of double greaseproof paper

Marzipan shapes like these teddy bears are favourites with the children

closely round the cake so that it comes 1 in. above the top. Prepare the fondant from 8 oz. sugar and the thinning syrup from 4 oz. sugar. Pour the fondant over the top of the cake. When the icing has set, ease off the paper collar, using the back of a knife blade dipped frequently in hot water. This method can also be used with glacé icing. *Note :* Cakes to be coated with fondant icing should first be coated completely with apricot glaze and then covered with almond paste.

APRICOT GLAZE

Place $\frac{1}{2}$ lb. apricot jam and 2 tbsps. water in a saucepan over a low heat and stir until the jam softens. Sieve the mixture, return it to the pan, bring to the boil and boil gently until the glaze is of a suitable coating consistency. This glaze can be potted, as for jam, and kept for future use.

ALMOND PASTE
(Marzipan)
yield : 1 lb.

4 oz. ($\frac{7}{8}$ cup) icing sugar, sifted
4 oz. ($\frac{1}{2}$ cup) caster sugar
8 oz. (2 cups) ground almonds
1 tsp. lemon juice
almond essence
beaten egg to mix

Blend together the sugars and ground almonds, add the lemon juice, a few drops of almond essence and enough beaten egg to bind the mixture together to give a firm but manageable dough. Turn it out on to a sugared board and knead lightly until smooth. Almond paste can be used to make many simple yet attractive decor-

ations for a cake. There are two basic methods to achieve this.

1 For flat decorations, roll out the paste on a sugared board and cut out the required shapes. This can be done either with a pastry cutter, if this will give the shape you want; or with a sharp knife drawn carefully round a template of stiff card. Don't choose anything too complicated to begin with – stars, candles, engines or boats all have straight sides and clear, simple outlines.

2 For animal figures, roll the paste in the hands to form small balls or sausage shapes and use these to make up the animal. It is a good idea to draw the figure first to give you an idea of the proportions. Make the body first, then stick on the arms, head, legs, etc. Paint on a face with food colouring, using a very fine brush. Simple shapes to start with are cats, teddy bears, Santa Claus (coloured red where appropriate) and snails (made from one long 'sausage' wound round and round).

To give more variety, almond paste may be coloured if wished – Santa Claus, as we've already suggested, can be a nice bright red and holly or ivy leaves to decorate a Christmas cake could be a good, strong green. But be careful to colour only as much paste as you need, or the rest will be wasted. As you gain more confidence, you will find the ideas are almost inexhaustible. Almond paste shapes and figures are particularly good for children's party cakes – a clown, rocket ships, a 'magic roundabout', trains and houses can all be made from a basic cake shape and imaginative use of almond paste. Colour some paste

with a very little black treacle or caramel colouring and cut out witches and broom sticks for a Hallowe'en cake.

Leaves – particularly good for decorating a Christmas cake – can be made by drawing round a real leaf on to a piece of white card and using that as a template for cutting the shape from the almond paste. Draw in the veins with the point of a skewer and leave the paste to dry lying over a piece of crumpled foil, to give it a naturalistic curve. To make holly leaves, cut strips of thinly rolled green almond paste, $\frac{1}{2}$ in. wide and $1-1\frac{3}{4}$ in. long. Using a tiny round cutter (the reverse end of a piping nozzle may be suitable) cut curves out of the sides to make the holly leaf shape. And, of course, almond paste is the traditional decoration for an Easter-time simnel cake. You can make miniature coloured Easter eggs for the top of the cake and cut out little chick shapes to go round the edge.

AMERICAN FROSTING

Makes sufficient frosting for a 7-in. cake. This is the traditional finish for a walnut cake

8 oz. (1 cup) sugar
4 tbsps. water
1 egg white

Gently heat the sugar in the water, stirring until dissolved. Then, without stirring, heat to 240°F. Beat the egg white stiffly in a deep bowl. Remove the sugar syrup from the heat and when the bubbles subside, pour it on to the egg white, whisking continuously. When the mixture thickens, is almost cold and starts to look opaque, pour it quickly over the cake. With a palette knife, quickly swirl the frosting into peaks. Add any required decorations.

Note : To make this frosting properly, it is necessary to use a sugar-boiling thermometer.

CARAMEL FROSTING

Substitute Demerara sugar for the white sugar.

COFFEE FROSTING

Add 1 tsp. coffee essence to the mixture while beating.

LEMON FROSTING

Add a little lemon juice while beating the mixture.

ORANGE FROSTING

Add a few drops of orange essence and a little orange colouring to the mixture while it is being beaten.

MORE ADVANCED CAKE DECORATING

Most rich fruit cakes for celebration occasions are decorated with almond paste and royal icing. Royal icing is not so easy to handle as glacé or fondant, but the results can be so delightful that it is well worth a little practice. It makes economic sense too, since most confectioners charge quite highly to ice even a birthday cake. Practice on family birthday cakes, before you tackle something for a big party; or try out one or two designs on paper (it's cheaper than cake!).

QUANTITIES OF ICINGS FOR A FORMAL CAKE

Cake size		Almond Paste	Royal Icing
	6 in. ●	¾ lb.	1 lb.
6 in. ■	7 in. ●	1 lb.	1¼ lb.
7 in. ■	8 in. ●	1¼ lb.	1½ lb.
8 in. ■	9 in. ●	1¾ lb.	2 lb.
9 in. ■	10 in. ●	2 lb.	2¼ lb.
10 in. ■	11 in. ●	2¼ lb.	2¾ lb.
11 in. ■	12 in. ●	2½ lb.	3 lb.
12 in. ■	13 in. ●	3 lb.	3½ lb.

ALMOND PASTE

Make up a quantity of paste, according to the size of your cake. With a piece of string, measure round the outside of the cake. Take two-thirds of the almond paste and roll it out on a surface dredged with icing sugar to a rectangle half the length of the string and in width twice the depth of the cake. Trim with a knife and cut in half lengthwise. Knead the trimmings into the remaining paste and roll out to fit the top of the cake. Check at this stage that the surface of the cake is absolutely level.

Brush the sides of the cake with apricot glaze. Put the 2 strips of almond paste round the cake and smooth the joins with a round-bladed knife, keeping the top and bottom edges square. Brush the top with apricot glaze, place the rolled-out top paste in position and roll lightly with a sugar-dusted rolling pin. Make sure the joins adhere well. Run a straight-sided jam jar round the edge to smooth the paste and stick it firmly to the cake. Leave the

Break up a spray of artificial flowers to make a delicate decoration

almond paste for a week before icing, loosely covered.

ROYAL ICING

4 egg whites
2 lb. (7 cups) icing sugar, sifted
1 tbsp. lemon juice
2 tsps. glycerine

Whisk the egg whites until slightly frothy. Stir in the sugar a spoonful at a time with a wooden spoon. When half the sugar is incorporated, add the lemon juice. Continue adding more sugar, beating well after each addition until you reach the right consistency.

It is this initial beating that gives it a light texture; skip it and the result will be disappointing, often heavy and difficult to use. The mixture is right for coating if it forms soft peaks when pulled up with a wooden spoon; it should be a little stiffer for piping and thinner for flooding.

Lastly stir in the glycerine, which prevents the icing becoming too hard. If you use an electric mixer, take care not to overbeat. If royal icing becomes too fluffy, it gives a rough surface and breaks when piped. It helps to allow it to stand for 24 hours in a covered container before using. Gently beat by hand and if necessary adjust the consistency before using.

Note : powdered albumen is available commercially and avoids the problem of large quantities of left over egg yolks.

EQUIPMENT

Before starting to decorate with icing you will need the following equipment:

1. A turntable – this enables you to get a smooth finish all over and round the sides of the cake. It is possible to work without a turntable, using an upturned basin instead, but it makes it much more difficult to obtain a good finish.

2. An icing ruler, or a long, straight bladed knife longer than the diameter of the cake – this is for flat icing.

3. An icing nail or a cork fixed to a skewer. This serves the same function as a turntable, in miniature, for piping flowers and other small designs.

4. Plain writing nozzles in 3 sizes, to make lines, dots or words.

5. Star nozzles for rosettes, zig-zags and ropes.

6. Shell nozzles.

7. Petal and leaf nozzles.

8. A forcing bag. Preferably make one yourself from greaseproof paper and use with icing nozzles without a screw band. If you use a fabric bag, attach a screw adjustment and use nozzles with a screw band.

FLAT ICING

To ice the cake, place it on a silver cake board 2–3 in. larger than the cake. With the cake and board on a turntable, spoon on an ample quantity of icing then use a palette knife to work it evenly over the top, using a paddling motion to remove any air bubbles. Roughly level the surface.

Draw an icing ruler (or a knife longer than the width of the cake) steadily across the cake top at an angle of 30° to smooth the surface. Be careful not to press too heavily. Neaten the edges, removing surplus icing by holding the knife

parallel with the side of the cake. Leave to dry for about 24 hours. Cover the sides the same way, still using a paddling motion. Hold a small palette knife or plain edged icing comb in one hand to the side of the cake and at a slight angle towards it. Pass the other hand under and round the turntable so that a little more than a complete revolution can be made. Keeping the knife quite still in one hand, revolve the turntable with the other, smoothly and fairly quickly. Towards the end, draw the knife or comb away without leaving a mark. Remove any surplus from the edge with a knife. If you prefer, ice the sides before the top.

To achieve a really professional looking finish (and this is a must with a tiered wedding cake), give the cake a second coating with slightly thinner icing, about 2 days after the first. Trim off any rough edges from the first coat with a sharp knife or fine clean sandpaper and brush off the loose icing before starting the second coat.

PIPING TECHNIQUES

When using a forcing bag, avoid over filling. Small sized bags are easier to handle especially when using a writing nozzle – it is much better to refill frequently. Insert the appropriate nozzle in the end of the bag, spoon the icing in and fold the top flap down, enclosing the front edge, until the bag is sealed and quite firm. Hold the bag in one hand with the thumb on top, the first finger resting down on the side of the bag and the second finger curved underneath. Use your other hand to steady the bag while you are piping.

To pipe lines use a writing nozzle. Make contact with the surface of the iced cake and squeeze out just enough icing to stick to the surface. Continue squeezing and at the same time raise the bag and pull towards you; hold the bag at an angle of about 45°. Lift the nozzle and the line of piped icing from the surface, to keep a sagging line. The icing can then be guided and lowered into the required design.

To pipe stars and scrolls use a star nozzle. For stars, hold the nozzle almost upright to the flat iced surface, pipe out a blob of icing and withdraw nozzle with a quick up and down movement. For scrolls, hold the bag at an

Piping random lacework to fill in the scallops

angle, as for a straight line. With the nozzle almost on the iced surface, pipe out a good head and then gradually release the pressure on the bag and pull away with a double or single curve; the whole operation is one movement.

Trellis work can be very effective. Use a writing nozzle to pipe parallel lines across the space to be covered; when these are dry pipe more lines on top of them in the opposite direction. For a really good finish, pipe a third layer, using a very fine nozzle. If

any 'tails' are left at the ends of lines, trim them off while still soft.

Flowers and leaves Leaves are piped with a special leaf nozzle directly on to the surface of the cake. Flowers are made up in advance on paper and fixed to the cake after they have dried out. Stick a 2-in. square of non-stick paper to an icing nail with a small blob of icing (or to a cork fixed to a skewer). Work on this surface and leave the flowers to dry on the paper. When dry, peel away the paper and fix the flowers to the cake with a small blob of icing.

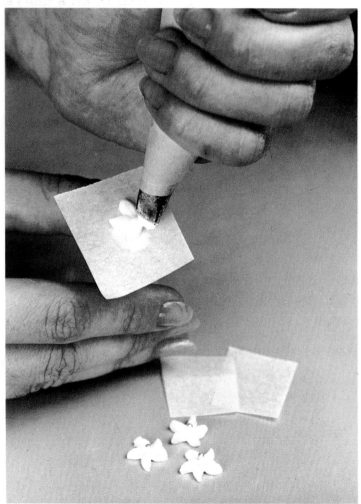

Making daisies separately to be fixed on the cake later

'Run out' designs, may either be piped directly on to the cake and flooded, or on to non-stick paper and fixed on the cake when dry. For separate 'run outs', draw out the design first on card, quite clearly. Cut a piece of non-stick paper to cover it and fix it with a spot of icing at each corner. Trace the outline of the design with a medium-fine writing nozzle; thin the icing to a 'just-flowing' consistency with unwhisked egg white and pour it into a small paper forcing bag. Cut the tip off the bag and flood the icing into the outline; if it is the correct consistency it will run smoothly into place. Leave flat for several days before peeling off the paper.

To pipe a 'run-out' directly on to the cake, prick the design out first with a fine pin and work as above.

TO DECORATE OUR WEDDING CAKE

Before starting any piping, place the pillars in position and prick round them with a pin. This will ensure that there is still room for them when everything else is done!

SCALLOPS

For each cake in turn, cut a circle of greaseproof paper the diameter of the cake. Fold the large one into 8, the middle one into 8 and the small one into 6, then for each cake proceed as follows.

Either free-hand or with compasses mark in the scallops (about 1 in. deep at the widest point) between the folds in the paper. Place the paper on the cake and secure with pins. Prick the outline of the scallops on to the flat iced surface. Remove and, using the prick marks as a guide, pipe the scallops in with a No. 2 writing nozzle. Pipe a second scallop ¼ in. outside the first, using a No. 3 writing nozzle, and a third line using the No. 2 nozzle again.

To make the scallops on the side of the cake, measure the depth of the cake and cut a band of greaseproof paper to size. Place it round the cake and secure with a pin at a point where one of the top scallops comes to the edge of the cake. Mark the points of the scallops right round the cake, remove the paper and draw in the scallops as for the top. At the same time draw corresponding scallops ½ in. deep at the base. Secure the paper round the cake and prick out the design. Tilt the cake slightly and rest it on a firmly wedged, shallow tin, so that you can work on the sides. A

damp cloth under the tin helps to prevent movement. Pipe in the scallops round the top and base, as for the flat surface.

LACE

Fill in the scallops – top, sides and base – with 'lace'. This is done with a No. 2 writing nozzle, almost resting on the surface. Pipe a wriggly line with no obvious set pattern, but keep it looking neat.

FLOWERS

The easiest flowers to pipe are daisies. Fix a square of paper to an icing nail or cork and use a medium petal nozzle. Pipe one petal at a time by squeezing out a small amount of icing, withdrawing the nozzle with a quick down and up movement. Pipe 5 petals, almost touching in the centre. Fill in the centre of each daisy either with a silver ball or with a small dot or several tiny dots from a No. 2 nozzle.

FERN SHAPED LINES

The fern shaped lines have to be piped on the side of the cake freehand. Tilt the cake as for the scallops and pipe the lines ¼ in. from the side scallop, using a No. 3 nozzle. Repeat with a No. 2 nozzle ¼ in. below the first line. The vertical line is done with a No. 2 nozzle. Finish with a bold dot from a No. 3 nozzle at the apex of the lines. This pattern may be piped as a fine line or as a series of small dots, which are easier to control.

FINISHING

Neaten the base of each cake with a series of dots in the angle between the cake and the board; for the large cake using a No. 3 nozzle, for the smaller cakes a No. 2 nozzle. Where the scallops meet at the base, bring a line of 3 dots up the side of the cake, with a No. 2 nozzle, using varying degrees of pressure to obtain different sizes. Position the pillars within the guide lines previously pricked out. Check that they are level, to ensure that the tiers stand level when positioned. Ideally use a spirit level for this. Fix each pillar in position with icing, using a little extra if the height needs adjusting at all. Ensure that none of the icing creeps out from under the base of the pillars. Allow to dry.

Mount the tiers carefully on the pillars to make sure that everything fits together properly, and decide on the decoration for the top. Then dismantle the cake again and keep the tiers separately until the day.

BREAD MAKING AT HOME

For centuries bread has been a symbol of all that is good in life. Even today, when commercially baked bread is so readily available, there is something peculiarly satisfying about baking your own. Perhaps it is the special flavour and smell of bread that has just come out of the oven, perhaps it is working with live yeast that causes it – either way it is a joy not to be missed.

There is nothing unduly difficult about yeast cookery, provided you realise that yeast, unlike other raising agents, is a living plant, requiring gentle warmth in order to grow. Like any other plant, yeast also requires food and water; it obtains these from the flour itself and from the moisture used in mixing the dough. Given these conditions, yeast grows rapidly and as it grows carbon dioxide is formed. The bubbles of this gas are responsible for the spongy texture of the bread. The growing yeast also gives the characteristic smell of bread.

Not all breads use yeast as the raising agent; baking powder and bicarbonate of soda are also used. Breads made with these raising agents, except for soda bread, are usually slightly sweetened and are used as tea breads rather than as general purpose breads.

YEAST

Dried yeast can be stored for up to 6 months if kept in a tightly sealed container. It comes in the form of small, hard, light brown granules and instructions for activating it are usually given on the package.

Fresh baker's yeast looks rather like putty and has faint 'winey' smell. To keep it fresh, store it in a loosely tied polythene bag in a cold place – it will keep for 4–5 days in a larder, up to a month in the refrigerator; it can also be

Cheese loaf, floury Scotch bap and morning rolls

frozen, in which case it will keep for up to a year if tightly wrapped.

FLOUR

For the best results when making a basic white bread, use 'strong' plain flour. This has a higher gluten content than household plain flour, so it absorbs more water, giving a larger volume and a lighter texture. 'Soft' flour, which absorbs fat but less water, is suitable for some types of richer fancy breads.

BASIC WHITE LOAF

this quantity of flour makes about 2½ lb. dough, giving 1 large loaf or 2 small loaves, or about 18 rolls

1½ lb. (6 cups) strong plain white bread flour
2 level tsps. salt
½ oz. lard
½ oz. fresh baker's yeast (for dried yeast, see note below)
¾ pint (1⅞ cups) water

Grease a 2-lb. loaf tin or 2 1-lb. tins, or 2 baking sheets if making rolls.

Sift the flour and salt into a large bowl and rub in the lard. Blend the yeast with the water. Mix the dry ingredients with the yeast liquid, adding the liquid all at once. Stir in with a wooden fork or spoon. Work it to a firm dough, adding extra flour if needed, until it will leave the sides of the bowl clean.

Turn the dough on to a floured surface and knead thoroughly, to stretch and 'develop' it. To do this, fold the dough towards you, then push down and away with the palm of your hand. Continue kneading until the dough feels firm and elastic and no longer sticky – about 10 minutes. Shape it into a ball.

Put the dough in a lightly oiled polythene bag to prevent a skin forming (the bag must be large enough to allow the dough to rise), tie it loosely and allow to rise until it is doubled in size and will spring back when pressed with a floured finger.

Allow time for the rising of the dough to fit with your day's arrangements, but the best results are achieved with a slow rise. Allow ¾–1 hour in a warm place, 2 hours at average room temperature, up to 12 hours in a cold larder or up to 24 hours in the refrigerator. Refrigerated risen dough must be allowed to return to room temperature before it is shaped.

Turn the risen dough on to a lightly floured surface, flatten it firmly with the knuckles to knock out the air bubbles, then knead to make it firm and ready for shaping (do not use too much flour or the colour of the crust will be spoilt.) Stretch the dough into an oblong the same width as the tin, fold it into 3 and turn it over so that the 'seam' is underneath. Smooth over the top, tuck in the ends and place in a greased 2 lb. loaf tin. (For 2 small loaves, divide the dough into 2 and continue as above; for rolls, divide the dough into 2-oz. pieces and roll each into a ball, place on the baking sheets about 1 in. apart.)

Place the tin inside a lightly oiled polythene bag and leave to rise again until the dough comes to the top of the tin and springs back when pressed with a floured finger.

Leave for 1–1½ hours, or longer in a refrigerator. Leave rolls until doubled in size.

Remove the polythene bag, place the tin on a baking sheet and put in the centre of the oven. Put a pan of boiling water on the oven bottom. Bake at 450°F. (mark 8) for 30–40 minutes (15–20 minutes for rolls), until well risen and golden brown. Rolls will double in size. When the loaf is cooked it will shrink slightly from the sides of the tin, and will sound hollow if you tap the bottom of the tin. Turn out and cool on a wire rack.

Note: If dried yeast is used, dissolve 1 level teaspoon caster sugar in ¾ pint (1⅞ cups) water warmed to 110°F.; sprinkle on 2 level teaspoons dried yeast and leave in a warm place until frothy – about 10 minutes. Then continue as for fresh yeast.

WHOLEMEAL LOAF

makes 2 large or 4 small loaves; the detailed technique is the same as for a basic white loaf

2 oz. fresh baker's yeast (for dried yeast see note below)
1½ pints (3¾ cups) water
3 lb. (12 cups) plain wholemeal flour
2 level tbsps. caster sugar
4 level tsps. salt
1 oz. lard

Blend the yeast with ½ pint of the measured water.

Mix together the wholemeal flour, sugar and salt. Rub in the lard. Stir the yeast liquid into the dry ingredients, adding sufficient of the remaining water to make a firm dough that leaves the bowl clean.

Turn the dough on to a lightly floured surface and knead as for white bread. Shape it into a round ball, place in an oiled polythene bag and leave to rise. When risen, knock the dough down with the knuckles to knock out the air bubbles and shape to fit 2 2-lb. tins or 4 1-lb. tins, greased. Put aside to rise again, wrapped in oiled polythene bags.

Bake the loaves in the centre of the oven at 450°F. (mark 8) for 30–40 minutes. Cool on a wire rack.

Note: When using dried yeast, dissolve 1 level teaspoon caster sugar in ½ pint (1¼ cups) of the water warmed to 110°F. and sprinkle 2 level tablespoons dried yeast on top. Leave until frothy–about 10 minutes.

ORANGE TEABREAD
make 2

2 oz. butter
6 oz. (¾ cup) caster sugar
1 egg, beaten
grated rind of ½ orange
2 tbsps. orange juice
2 tbsps. milk
8 oz. (2 cups) plain flour
2½ level tsps. baking powder
pinch of salt

Grease and bottom-line an 8-in. by 4¼-in. loaf tin.

Beat the butter, add the sugar and beat again until well mixed. Gradually beat in the egg until smooth and creamy. Slowly add the orange rind and juice. Lightly beat in the milk alternately with sifted flour, baking powder and salt.

Turn the mixture into the tin. Bake in the centre of the oven at 375°F. (mark 5) for 40–50 minutes. Turn out and cool on a wire rack. Make 1–2 days before required and wrap in foil to store. Slice and spread with honey and cream cheese spread or butter.

EASTER BREAD

1 oz. yeast
½ pint (1¼ cups) warm milk
1 lb. (4 cups) plain strong bread flour
6 egg yolks
6 oz. (¾ cup) sugar
2 oz. butter, melted
4½ oz. candied fruit, chopped

Dissolve the yeast in the milk, mix with half the flour and leave in a warm place to start to work.

Beat the egg yolks and sugar together and when the dough has risen, mix them in, with the melted

Sally Lunn is a traditional tea bread from Bath

butter. Add the remaining flour and the candied fruit.

Beat the mixture well, leave to rise again and form it into plaited loaves. Place on a baking sheet, prove for 20–30 minutes and bake at 450°F. (mark 8) until well risen and browned – about 30–40 minutes.

CHEESE LOAF
makes 2 1-lb. loaves

1 lb. (4 cups) strong plain white flour
2 level tsps. salt
1 level tsp. dry mustard and pepper, mixed
4-6 oz. Cheddar cheese, grated
½ oz. fresh baker's yeast (for dried yeast see note below)
½ pint (1¼ cups) water

In a large bowl, sift together the flour, salt, mustard and pepper. Add nearly all the cheese, reserving a little for the tops of the loaves.

Blend the baker's yeast in the water until smooth. Add to the dry ingredients and work to a firm dough, adding extra flour if needed, until the dough leaves the bowl clean. Turn the dough out

on to a lightly floured surface and knead until elastic and no longer sticky–about 10 minutes. Put into a lightly oiled polythene bag, tie loosely and leave to rise until the dough doubles in size (see basic white loaf).

Turn the dough on to a board and flatten firmly with the knuckles to knock out the air bubbles, then knead to make a firm dough. Halve the dough and shape to fit 2 greased 1-lb. loaf tins (shape as for basic white loaf).

Place the tins in an oiled polythene bag and put in a warm place to rise until the dough reaches the top of the tin and springs back when lightly pressed with a floured finger–about 45 minutes. Remove the bag.

Sprinkle the remaining cheese on top of the loaves. Place the tins on a baking sheet and bake in the centre of the oven at 375°F. (mark 5) for about 45 minutes – take care not to over-bake. Cool on a wire rack.

Note: If dried yeast is used, dissolve 1 level teaspoon sugar in ½ pint (1¼ cups) water warmed to 110°F. and sprinkle 2 level teaspoons dried yeast on top. Leave in a warm place until frothy – about 10 minutes.

SALLY LUNN
makes 2

2 oz. butter
¼ pint (⅝ cup) milk plus 4 tbsps.
1 level tsp. caster sugar
2 eggs, beaten
½ oz. fresh yeast or 2 level tsps. dried yeast
1 lb. (4 cups) strong plain white flour
1 level tsp. salt
sugar glaze, made by boiling 1 tbsp. water with 1 tbsp. sugar for 2 minutes

Melt the butter slowly in a pan, remove from the heat and add the milk and sugar. Add the warm milk mixture and the eggs to the yeast; blend well. Sift together the flour and salt, add the liquid, mix well and knead lightly. Divide the dough between 2 well greased 5-in. round cake tins and leave to rise in a warm place for about ¾–1 hour until the dough fills the tins. Bake just above the centre of the oven at 450°F. (mark 8) for 15–20 minutes.

Turn the loaves out on to a wire rack. Make up the sugar glaze and glaze the loaves while they are hot.

CROISSANTS
makes 12

1 oz. fresh baker's yeast (for dried yeast see note below)
½ pint (1¼ cups) water, less 4 tbsps.
1 lb. (4 cups) strong plain white flour
2 level tsps. salt
1 oz. lard
1 egg, beaten
4-6 oz. hard margarine

For glaze:
1 egg, beaten with a little water
½ level tsp. caster sugar

Blend the yeast with the water. Sift together the flour and salt and rub in the lard. Add the yeast liquid and the egg and mix well together. Turn the dough on to a lightly floured surface and knead until the dough is smooth – 10–15 minutes. Roll the dough into a strip about 20 in. by 8 in. and ¼ in. thick, taking care to keep the edges straight and the corners square. Soften the margarine with a knife, then divide it into 3. Use 1 portion to dot over the top two-thirds of the dough, leaving a small border clear. Fold the dough in 3 by bringing up the plain (bottom) third first, then folding the top third over. Turn the dough so that the fold is on the

Keep the malt fruit bread for a few days before cutting it

right-hand side and seal the edges with a rolling pin.

Reshape the dough to a long strip by gently pressing at intervals with a rolling pin. Repeat with the other 2 portions of margarine.

Place the dough in an oiled polythene bag and allow to rest in the refrigerator for 30 minutes. Then roll out as before and repeat the folding and rolling (but without fat) 3 more times. Place in the refrigerator for at least 1 hour. Roll the dough out to an oblong about 23 in. by 14 in. Cover with lightly oiled polythene and leave for 10 minutes. Trim with a sharp knife to 21 in. by 12 in. and divide in half lengthwise. Cut each strip into 6 triangles, each 6 in. high and with a 6 in. base.

Mix together the egg and caster sugar for an egg glaze and brush this over the dough. Roll up each triangle loosely from the base, finishing with the tip underneath. Curve into a crescent shape. Put the shaped croissants on to ungreased baking sheets. Brush the tops with more egg glaze and put each baking sheet inside a lightly oiled polythene bag. Leave at room temperature for about 30 minutes, until light and puffy.

Brush the croissants again with egg glaze before baking in the centre of the oven at 425°F. (mark 7) for about 20 minutes. Eat while warm.

Note : If you are using dried yeast, warm the water to 110°F. and add 1 level teaspoon caster sugar, then sprinkle 1 level tablespoon dried yeast over it. Leave in a warm place until frothy – about 10 minutes.

Swedish tea ring – try it with coffee

APRICOT AND WALNUT LOAF

4 oz. (1 cup) brown flour
4 oz. (1 cup) strong white
  flour
1 level tsp. salt
1 level tsp. caster sugar
good knob of lard
1 oz. (⅛ cup) caster sugar
4 oz. dried apricots, chopped
2 oz. walnut halves, broken
¼ oz. fresh baker's yeast
¼ pint (⅝ cup) water

For topping :
1 oz. butter
1 oz. (⅛ cup) caster sugar
1½ oz. plain flour

Line the base and grease a 1-lb. loaf tin.

Mix together the flours, salt and sugar, into a large bowl. Rub in the lard, add the sugar, apricots and walnuts. Blend the yeast with the water and add all at once to the flour. Mix to a soft, scone-like dough that leaves the bowl clean (adding more flour if necessary). Two-thirds fill the prepared tin and put it inside a polythene bag until the dough rises to within ½ in. of the top of the tin.

Lightly rub together the butter, sugar and flour until the mixture resembles coarse breadcrumbs and cover the loaf with this mixture. Bake in the centre of the oven at 400°F. (mark 6) for 40–45 minutes. Cool in the tin for 10 minutes before turning out.

MALT FRUIT BREAD

12 oz. (3 cups) plain flour
½ level tsp. bicarbonate of
  soda
1 level tsp. baking powder
2 level tbsps. Demerara sugar
4 level tbsps. golden syrup
4 level tbsps. malt extract
¼ pint (⅝ cup) milk
2 eggs
9 oz. sultanas, seedless raisins
  or chopped dates

Grease a loaf tin measuring 9 in. by 5 in. by 2⅝ in. (top measurements).

In a large bowl, sift together the flour, bicarbonate of soda and baking powder. Add the sugar. In a small pan, warm together the syrup, malt and milk. Cool.

Beat the milk, eggs and fruit into the flour until evenly mixed. Turn into the prepared tin. Bake just below the centre of the oven at 325°F. (mark 3) for 1 hour. Reduce oven temperature to 300°F. (mark 2) and bake for a further 30 minutes.

Turn out and cool on a wire rack. Store, wrapped in kitchen foil, for several days before serving sliced and buttered.

SWEDISH TEA RING

For dough :
8 oz. (2 cups) strong plain
  white flour
½ level tsp. caster sugar
1 level tsp. dried yeast
4 oz. warm milk
½ level tsp. salt
1 oz. margarine
½ egg, beaten
½ oz. butter, melted
2 oz. (⅓ cup) brown sugar
2 level tsps. powdered
  cinnamon

For decoration :
4 oz. icing sugar, sifted
water
lemon juice
4 glacé cherries
angelica
½ oz. almonds, blanched

In a large bowl, blend together 2½ oz. of the flour, the sugar, yeast and milk. Set aside in a warm place until frothy – about 20 minutes. Sift the remaining flour with the salt and rub in the margarine. Add the egg and the flour mixture to the yeast batter and mix well to give a fairly soft dough that will leave the sides of the bowl clean. Turn the dough out on to a lightly floured surface and knead until it is smooth and no longer sticky – about 10 minutes. Place the dough in a lightly oiled polythene bag, tie loosely and leave as for a basic white loaf.

When risen, turn out the dough on to a lightly floured surface and roll to an oblong 12 in. by 9 in. Brush with melted butter then mix together the brown sugar and the cinnamon and sprinkle it over the dough. Roll up tightly from the long edge and seal the ends together, to form a ring. Place the ring on a greased baking sheet.

Using scissors, cut slashes at an angle, 1 in. apart and to within ½ in. of the centre. Twist each section slightly so that it lies at an angle. Cover with a lightly oiled polythene bag and put to rise in a warm place for about 30 minutes. Bake just above the centre of the oven at 375°F. (mark 5) for 30–35 minutes.

Blend the icing sugar with a squeeze of lemon juice and just enough water to give a thick coating consistency. While the ring is still warm, coat it with the icing. Decorate with halved cherries, angelica and flaked almonds.

93

LOBSTER THERMIDOR

Lobster is the most delicious of shellfish, and is popular even in parts of the world where it is comparatively commonplace.' Lobster thermidor is a classic way of preparing it as a hot main dish for 2.

When buying lobster, choose one that weighs heavy in proportion to its size. If you are buying a live one, make sure it is lively, too, as one that seems tired may have been around for a day or two and grown thin inside its shell. A good 2-lb. lobster should yield about 12 oz. meat.

The smaller, hen lobsters are the more tender and delicate and the coral, or spawn, from the hen is an extra delicacy. If you are making a dish such as lobster thermidor, which does not require the coral, save it for a sauce or soup the next day. (You could add it to the thermidor sauce, but the subtle flavour would be lost with the cheese.)

Most people buy lobsters ready boiled, but if you have a live one, wash it, place in cold salted water, bring slowly to the boil and boil fairly quickly for 15–25 minutes, according to size. When the water is brought slowly to the boil like this, the warmth penetrates the central nervous system gradually and the lobster apparently experiences no discomfort.

Do not over-cook it as the flesh tends to become hard and thready. An alternative method of killing a lobster for this dish, so that you don't cook it twice, is to pierce the brain with the sharp point of a knife. To do this, lay the lobster out flat on a wooden board, hard shell uppermost. Have the head toward your right hand and cover the tail with a cloth. Hold it behind the head and pierce through the little cross marking on the head – this is the brain and the lobster will be killed instantly.

a 2 lb. lobster (cooked)
2 oz. butter
1 small onion, skinned and
   finely chopped
1 oz. (¼ cup) flour
¼ pint (⅝ cup) milk
1 oz. Cheddar cheese
1 tbsp. white wine
pinch of paprika pepper
salt and pepper
Parmesan cheese, grated
lettuce, watercress and lemon
   to garnish

serves 2

Cut the cooked lobster down the centre back, and open out

Crack the claws with a rolling pin and take out the flesh

Using a large, sharp-pointed knife cut the lobster carefully down the centre back; open out the two halves and take out all the flesh. Discard the intestine, which looks like a small vein running through the centre of the tail, the stomach, which lies near the head, and the spongy gills, which are not edible. Clean the shells thoroughly and rub them with oil to make them shine. Twist the large and small claws from the shells and, using a rolling pin, crack the large claws and carefully remove all the flesh using a small, pointed knife and a skewer.

Cut all the flesh into pieces about ½ in. long (you will find it easier if you cut the meat at an angle). Heat half the butter in a small frying pan and add the lobster meat. Sauté gently, turning occasionally.

Sauté the lobster and start to make the thermidor sauce

Meanwhile, in a small pan, heat the remaining butter. Add to it the onion and sauté until soft. Add the flour and blend thoroughly. Add the milk, stirring, and bring to the boil. Simmer for a few minutes. Grate the Cheddar cheese finely and add to the sauce. Mix thoroughly over a low heat, add the wine and paprika; season.

Pour the sauce over the lobster in the frying pan and mix well. Cook over a low heat for a few minutes. Place the cleaned lobster shells on a grill rack, then spoon the lobster mixture into them.

Add grated cheese, wine, paprika and seasoning to the sauce

Pour the sauce over the lobster and cook over gentle heat

Fill the mixture into the shells, sprinkle with Parmesan and grill

Sprinkle thickly with grated Parmesan cheese and place under a pre-heated grill. Cook until the sauce is bubbling and golden brown. Place on an oval platter on a bed of lettuce. Garnish with watercress and lemon slices.

serves 6-8

3½-4 lb. oven-ready chicken
1 onion, skinned
1 carrot, peeled
3 parsley stalks
1 bay leaf
6 peppercorns
½ lb. pork sausage meat
½ lb. lean pork, minced
2 shallots, skinned and chopped
salt and pepper
4 tbsps. Madeira
3 oz. cooked ham, sliced
3 oz. cooked tongue, sliced
2 oz. sliced bacon fat
½ oz. pistachio nuts, blanched
6 black olives, stoned

For finishing :
1 pint (2½ cups) aspic jelly,
  made from aspic jelly
  powder and chicken stock
¾ pint (1⅞ cups) béchamel
  sauce
salt and pepper
2-3 tbsps. double cream
¼ oz. powdered gelatine
cucumber, radishes and black
  olives for garnish

Lay the bird on a board, breast side up. Using a sharp boning knife, cut off the wings at the second joint and the legs at the first. Turn the bird over and make an incision down the centre of the back. Keeping the knife close to the carcass and slightly flattened, to avoid damaging the flesh, carefully work the flesh off the rib cage – scrape just enough to expose both of the wing joints.

Take hold of the severed end of 1 wing joint. Scrape the knife over the bone backwards and forwards, working the flesh away from the bone. Continue until both wing and socket are exposed. Sever all the ligaments and draw out the bone. Repeat for second wing.

Carry on working the flesh off the carcass until the leg and socket are reached. Sever the ligaments attaching the bone to the body flesh and break the leg joint by twisting it firmly in a cloth. Hold the exposed joint firmly in 1 hand and scrape away all the flesh down to

the broken leg joint. Working from the opposite end of the leg, eas out the bone, scraping off th flesh until the bone is completel exposed. Pull the leg bone free repeat for the other leg. Continu working the flesh cleanly off th body and breast, being careful no to break the skin.

Lay the boned chicken, skin sid down, on the board and turn th legs and wings inside out. Mak a stock using the chicken bones giblets, onion, carrot, parsley, ba leaf, peppercorns and enoug water just to cover.

Work together the sausage meat pork, shallots, salt and pepper i a bowl. Moisten with the Madeir wine. Slice the ham, tongue and bacon fat into long strips abou ¼ in. wide.

Spread half the farce over th boned out chicken. Lay along th bird, in alternate lines, strips o ham, tongue and bacon fat, pist achio nuts and the olives. Cove with the remaining farce. Drav the sides of the chicken togethe

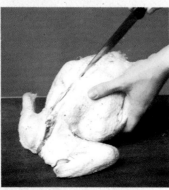

Turn the chicken on its breast and cut down the centre back

Scrape the flesh off the leg bone, down to the broken joint

Chicken Galantine

and sew up, using a trussing needle and fine string.

Wrap the galantine in a double thickness of muslin and tie the ends to make a neat shape. Strain the stock, pour it into a large pan and immerse the galantine in it. Cover well and simmer for about $2\frac{1}{4}$ hours. Drain, reserving the stock.

Place the galantine, still wrapped in muslin, on a plate; cover with another plate and top with a weight. When nearly cold, remove

Work the flesh cleanly off the carcass without breaking the skin

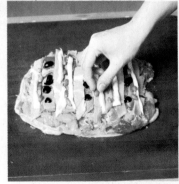

Flatten the bird and arrange the stuffing ingredients on it

the muslin, and when thoroughly cold carefully remove the trussing string.

Make up 1 pint aspic jelly using some of the strained chicken stock. To make a chaudfroid sauce, make up $\frac{3}{4}$ pint ($1\frac{7}{8}$ cups) béchamel sauce, cover with damp grease-

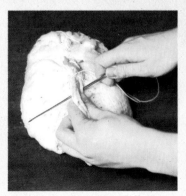

Sew up the chicken carefully, using a trussing needle

proof paper to prevent a scum forming and allow to cool. Dissolve the gelatine in 4 fl. oz. ($\frac{1}{2}$ cup) of the prepared aspic and stir into the cold béchamel sauce. Strain the sauce and beat well. Place the chicken on a wire rack with a board or baking sheet

underneath. When the chaudfroid sauce is on the point of setting, pour it over the chicken to coat it thoroughly.

When the chaudfroid sauce is set, decorate the galantine with cucumber, radishes and olives and spoon over the remaining aspic jelly. Put in a cool place to set.

Coat the cooked galantine in a rich chaudfroid sauce

Creamy white chicken breasts, filled with rich garlic butter, coated in breadcrumbs and crisp fried in deep fat—chicken Kiev is another perfect choice for a special dinner for two, and relatively easy for four, as it can be kept hot for a short while. Warn your guests what is in the middle of the golden ball on their plates—if they attack it too ferociously the butter will spurt! As you want the breasts only of two chickens for this dish, why not use packaged chicken portions? Or if you prefer to use whole birds, save the legs for a delicious casserole for the family. Make your breadcrumbs freshly to give a real soft-and-crispy outside to the chicken. If you use ready-made crumbs (your own or bought) you will find that they brown long before the chicken is cooked and in the full cooking time will become unpleasantly brown and hard. For the best results, use a day-old sandwich loaf and either grate it or crumb in a blender. A frying thermometer is essential for chicken Kiev, as the temperature of the oil is critical. If it is too hot, the outside will brown before the inside is cooked. If it is not hot enough, the oil will soak right through coating and chicken before the outside is brown, making it soggy and oily.

Good Housekeeping Classic
CHICKEN KIEV

Beat out the chicken breasts with a heavy knife or meat bat

4 chicken breasts (about 8 oz. each with bone)
4 oz. butter
grated rind of ½ a lemon
4 tsps. lemon juice
salt and pepper
1 large clove of garlic
2 tbsps. chopped parsley
1 oz. (¼ cup) seasoned flour
4 eggs, beaten
12 oz. fresh white breadcrumbs
oil for frying

serves 4

If the chicken breasts are frozen allow to thaw completely. Using a small, sharp knife, carefully work the flesh off the bone. Be very careful not to split the flesh. Place each piece of chicken flesh between 2 sheets of silicone (non stick) kitchen paper and beat out with a heavy knife or meat bat until quite thin. Put aside in a cool place.

In a bowl, beat together the butter and lemon rind. When the butter is soft, add the lemon juice slowly, beating all the time. Add the sa...

Cream the butter with lemon juice

and pepper and mix well in. Skin and crush the garlic and add to the butter with the parsley and mix well together. Turn the butter out on to a sheet of non-stick paper, roll up and chill.

When the butter is firm, divide it into 4, placing 1 piece in the centre of each piece of chicken. Fold the chicken round and secure with cocktail sticks. Dip each piece of chicken in seasoned flour, brush with beaten egg and then with breadcrumbs. Brush with

Coat well with egg and fresh white breadcrumbs

Fry the chicken Kiev 2 at a time in deep fat, and keep hot

Crush the garlic before adding it

Roll a portion of butter in each

egg and roll in the crumbs a second time, to give a thorough coating. Chill for 1–2 hours. (The chicken *may* be fried immediately, but a short time in the refrigerator helps to make the breadcrumb coating firm.)

In a large saucepan or deep fat fryer, heat the oil to 325–350°F. Place 2 pieces of chicken in the frying basket and lower into the oil. Fry for 12–15 minutes, de-

pending on size, until golden brown. Take out of the fat, remove cocktail sticks, drain on absorbent kitchen paper and keep warm in the oven at 350°F. (mark 4) while you fry the remaining portions.

Serve with new potatoes and tomato and chicory or celery salad.

Good Housekeeping Classic

Veal à la Crème Flambé

This is a dinner party dish using a choice cut of veal. With a delicious creamy flavour, and a light hint of herbs, you'll find it a treat by any standard.

Serve it with a white Burgundy and your guests will remember your cooking with pleasure.

Just a hint before you start – you will need a really sharp knife to skin the veal neatly and economically; if you don't have one that you think will be up to the job, it is better to ask the butcher to do it for you.

2 lb. leg of veal, boned
4 oz. butter
1 onion, skinned
bouquet garni
1 clove of garlic, skinned and crushed
½ pint (1¼ cups) veal stock
½ pint (1¼ cups) white wine
salt and pepper
8 oz. button mushrooms
1 tbsp. lemon juice
8 oz. button onions
1 tsp. sugar
beurre manié (made from 1½ oz. flour and 2 oz. butter)
4 tbsps. double cream
2–3 tbsps. brandy
watercress

serves 6

To trim the meat, loosen the skin with a knife. Take hold of the skin with a cloth in one hand and work in towards the meat with the blade close against the fatty tissue. Cut

Cut the skin and fatty tissue away from the meat

Fry the cubes of veal a little at a time to brown them all over

the meat into 1-in. cubes.

Melt 2 oz. butter in a pan, allow it to sizzle, then fry the meat quickly on all sides to seal. Fry the meat in 2 lots, so that all the meat in the pan can rest on the bottom. When it is well sealed, remove the meat from the pan and place in a casserole.

Add the whole onion, the bouquet garni and the crushed garlic.

Make a bouquet garni by tying the herbs in a piece of muslin

Bring the stock and wine to the boil together and pour over the meat. Season well.

Cover and cook in the oven at 325°F. (mark 3) for about 1 hour, until tender.

Meanwhile, wipe the mushrooms but do not peel. Using a small knife, 'turn' the mushrooms by removing tapering fillets from the caps, all the way round; insert the blade into the dome of the caps and draw the knife in a spiral,

Pour boiling stock over the meat and seasoning in the casserole

turning the mushrooms towards you until the knife rests horizontally.

Put the mushrooms in a small pan and just cover them with water. Add the lemon juice and 1 oz. butter and cook until the water has evaporated. Keep warm.

Soak the button onions for 5 minutes in warm water, then peel them quickly.

Place in a small pan, just cover with water, add a pinch of salt, sugar and 1 oz. butter. Cook for 5 minutes, raise the heat and quickly

evaporate all the water. Add to the cooked mushrooms and keep warm.

When the veal is cooked, remove the bouquet garni and onion from the casserole and strain off the liquid. Keep the veal warm.

Reduce the liquid to ¾ pint (2 cups) by boiling fast. Whisk in the beurre manié little by little, bring to the boil and simmer for 5

'Turn' the button mushrooms to make an attractive garnish

Button onions soaked in warm water are easy to peel

minutes. Stir a spoonful of sauce into the cream and return all the cream to the pan. Reheat carefully, without boiling, and adjust seasoning.

Warm the brandy in a soup ladle or small pan, ignite and pour over the meat. Add the meat to the sauce.

Serve on a pre-heated dish, with the glacé onions, mushrooms and a watercress garnish.

Add beurre manié a little at a time and whisk into the liquid

Good Housekeeping Classic

COLONIAL GOOSE

Colonial goose is a New Zealand classic, stemming presumably from a time when goose was hard to come by, but lamb was plentiful. The apricot and honey stuffing is delicious and the flavour of the meat itself is enhanced by marinading.

Of course, you don't have to bone the meat yourself if you order it from the butcher in advance. If you do attempt it yourself, use a really sharp knife and keep the blade close to the bone. That way it is comparatively easy. For the marinade, a polythene bag is not essential but it is a convenient way of keeping the wine and vegetables close to the meat so that the flavour penetrates thoroughly.

4½ lb. leg of lamb

For stuffing :
1 oz. butter
1 tbsp. clear honey
4 oz. dried apricots
2 oz. onion, skinned and quartered
4 oz. fresh white breadcrumbs
¼ level tsp. dried thyme
1 egg, beaten
¼ level tsp. salt
freshly ground black pepper

For marinade :
½ lb. carrots, peeled and sliced
6 oz. onion, skinned and sliced

Start to work the meat away from the bone with a sharp knife

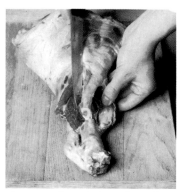

Next, cut along the bone from the opposite end of the leg

1 bay leaf
3 parsley stalks, crushed
¼ pint (⅝ cup) red wine

serves 6–8

Place the meat on a wooden board. Using a small, sharp knife, work

Draw out the bone, carefully severing all the ligaments

the meat away from the bone, from the top of the leg down to the first joint. Now cut along the line of the bone from the opposite end of the leg, just enough to release the bone. Work the flesh away from the bone, being careful not to puncture the skin in any other place. Sever the bone from all the flesh and ligaments. Draw out the bone, working from the top of the leg.

Put the butter and honey in a small pan, melt over a low heat. Grate the onion and add to the breadcrumbs in a basin with the melted butter, honey, thyme and egg.

Apricots and honey make this stuffing pleasantly unusual

Snip the apricots with scissors into the basin and season well. Bind all the stuffing ingredients together. Wipe the lamb with a clean, damp cloth, trim off the excess fat from the top of the leg and spoon the stuffing into the cavity from which the bone was removed. Force the stuffing well down into the leg with the back of the spoon. Sew up with a trussing needle and fine string. Do not sew it too tightly, or the skin may split while the meat is roasting.

Lift the meat into a polythene

bag placed inside a large deep bowl. Add the marinade ingredients and leave in a cool place for about 6 hours, turning the meat occasionally in the juices. Remove from the marinade and weigh the stuffed joint. Roast at 350°F. (mark 4) for 25 minutes per lb. If

Fill the lamb with as much stuffing as it will hold

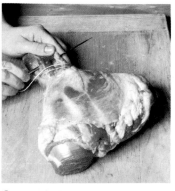

Sew up the joint with a trussing needle, but not too tightly

the meat starts to over-brown, cover it with foil. Remove the string and place the joint on a serving dish. Keep hot.

Pour off the fat from the roasting tin and stir a little flour into the juices. Cook for a few minutes. Add 2–3 tablespoons of the strained marinade and a little water. Adjust seasoning. Bring to the boil, stirring, and simmer for a further 5 minutes. Serve the gravy separately.

A large polythene bag helps when marinading the joint

These delicious steaks are served on slices of fried aubergine and accompanied by a rich sauce of tomatoes, onions and herbs. Serve them with creamed potato and sauté mushrooms.

Tournedos are thick slices of beef cut from the heart of the

Cut strips of pork fat and flatten with a knife

fillet and tied into rounds. In England they are lean, but in France the butchers make them up with a small piece of fat tied round each steak. We show you how to add the fat for this classic dish from southern France.

For a more economical recipe you could substitute noisettes of lamb, in which case there is no need to wrap the meat in fat.

serves 4

6 oz. pork fat in a piece
4 6-oz. tournedos, 1½ in. thick
2 medium-sized aubergines
salt
1 lb. ripe tomatoes
4 oz. onion
1½ oz. butter
¼ pint (⅝ cup) water
bay leaf
¼ level tsp. dried basil
1 clove of garlic
1 tbsp. cooking oil
freshly ground black pepper

Cut the pork fat through the skin into strips as wide as the tournedos are thick. Now slice thinly along each strip and flatten by drawing the blade of a knife along each

Wrap a strip round each steak and tie with string

slice. Trim the edges. Wrap a strip of fat round each steak; press the steaks down slightly and secure the fat with string. Do not tie too tightly.

Slice the aubergines thickly and at an angle. Each slice should be roughly the same diameter as the tournedos, so that each steak will sit comfortably on a slice of aubergine. Place in a single layer on a plate and sprinkle with salt. Insert the point of a small knife into the stem of each tomato; give 1–2 sharp twists. Bring a small pan of water to the boil and blanch 1 tomato at a time for 10 seconds, then place it immediately in cold water. Skin the tomatoes, reserving the skins, and halve them. Scoop out the seeds with a spoon and roughly dice the flesh. Melt ½ oz. butter in a pan with a tightly fitting lid. Skin the

Skin the tomatoes and scoop out the seeds with a spoon

Tie the tomato seeds and skin in muslin and add to the pan

onions, slice them finely and sauté in the butter until tender. Tie the tomato seeds and skin in a double thickness of muslin and add to the pan with the tomatoes, water, bay leaf and basil. Bring to the boil, cover and simmer for about 15 minutes until reduced to a thick pulp. Season and keep hot. Meanwhile, skin the garlic, cut off 1 end and push it on to the prongs of a fork to rub the cut edge over the surface of a frying pan. Heat the oil in this pan. Add the remaining butter and when it

is on the point of turning brown add the tournedos, using tongs. Cook over medium heat for about 14 minutes (see chart below), turning the meat half way through. When the meat is turned, dry the aubergine slices on absorbent paper and fry on both sides in the

Cook the provençal sauce until it is thick and pulpy

same pan for the remaining time. Arrange the aubergine on a hot serving plate, snip the string from the tournedos and sit each on a slice of aubergine. Garnish with sauté mushrooms and watercress. Remove the muslin bag, squeeze it to extract all the juice and serve the sauce separately.

Cooking times in minutes

Thick-ness	Rare	Medium	Well-done
¾ in.	5	9–10	12–15
1 in.	6–7	10	15
1½ in.	10	12–14	18–20

Rub the frying pan with a cut clove of garlic

Fry the steaks in oil and butter, handling them with tongs

FILET DE BOEUF EN CROUTE

This succulent, rich French way with fillet of beef is a delectable main course for a special occasion dinner party. The finest, tenderest cut of beef is coated with a rich pâté de foie and encased in crisp puff pastry. The contrasting textures and flavours will delight any palate. Be sure to choose your best Burgundy to go with it! When buying the beef for this dish it is essential to ask for the best quality. Ask the butcher to cut a 2-lb. fillet about 8–9 inches long – this will be the right thickness for the cooking times given in this recipe. The pâté used must also be a good one – firm and fine textured. Beat it well with a wooden spoon to make it soft and easy to spread.

We start by tying the fillet with string to keep its shape – fillet tends to shrink and curl when cooked and this is the only way to keep it in a long narrow roll – so whatever you do, don't try to take short cuts. Filet de boeuf en croûte is at its best served piping hot straight from the oven. Make sure the vegetables match the standard of the meat – asparagus and broccoli are a suitable choice in season, and creamed potatoes offer a better contrast of texture with the pastry than roast. Any leftover beef will still be good served cold, with a tossed green salad and new potatoes.

2 lb. fillet of beef
salt and pepper
2 oz. butter
1 tbsp. cooking oil
8 oz. liver pâté
11-oz. pkt. frozen puff pastry, thawed
1 egg, beaten
watercress and 1 tomato for garnish

serves 6

Place the meat on a board and, using a sharp knife, trim off all excess fat and sinewy parts from the meat. Sprinkle all over with salt and pepper.

Tie some fine string round the meat at intervals to form it into a neat shape. Carry the string round the ends and across to the other side as for a parcel. Tie firmly.

Heat half the butter with the oil in a frying pan and fry the meat until browned all over, turning frequently. Put the meat in a roasting tin and dot with the remaining butter. Cook at the top of the oven at 400°F. (mark 6) for 10 minutes. Remove, leave until cold and then untie the string.

Mix the pâté well in a small basin until smooth. Season to taste. Using a small palette knife, spread pâté over the top and sides of the meat. Roll out the pastry about $\frac{1}{8}$ in. thick, to a rectangle large enough to cover the meat completely. Place the meat pâté side down in the centre of the pastry. Spread pâté over the rest of the

Brown the fillet in hot oil and butter to seal

Soften the pâté and spread it all over the meat

Brush the edge of the pastry with egg to help it seal

Trim the ends at an angle and cut off close to the meat

Brush the trimmed ends with egg and fold diagonally across

Decorate the croûte with leaves cut from pastry trimmings

meat. Brush one long side of the pastry with egg.

Fold the unbrushed side over the meat, fold up the second side and press together. Trim the ends of the pastry at an angle, cutting it straight off close to the meat. Reserve these trimmings for decoration. Brush the upper surfaces of the trimmed ends with beaten egg and fold diagonally across the ends of the parcel. Raise the oven tem-perature to 425°F. (mark 7). Roll out the pastry trimmings and cut into leaf shapes. Brush the pastry surface with beaten egg, arrange the leaves in the centre and brush those with egg. Bake in the centre of the oven for 40 minutes until the pastry is golden.

Serve on a flat platter with a garnish of watercress and tomato.

Crème Caramel

Rich and creamy, smooth and delicately flavoured – that is our vanilla flavoured custard. Topped with the burnt flavour of caramel it becomes the most delicious sweet ever, a favourite from nursery to adult dinner parties.

The recipe is basically simple, but it is not always easy to turn out successfully, so follow our step by step instructions and pictures for perfect results every time.

The traditional moulds to use are individual dariole moulds, for which you can substitute tea cups so long as they will withstand the heat of the caramel (boiling sugar is much hotter than boiling water). Alternatively you can make it in a single 2-pint capacity mould (in this case, extend the cooking time to about 1 hour).

This is one of the best examples of the use of a bain marie for cooking; it is vital that the custards should not get too hot in the oven, or they will curdle, so a bain marie is used to ensure an even, low temperature.

Crème caramel is an ideal recipe for the busy hostess to prepare – it can be made well in advance and kept in a cool place.

For caramel :
2 tbsps. cold water
5 oz. ($\frac{5}{8}$ cup) caster sugar
3 tbsps. boiling water
For custard :
1 pint (2$\frac{1}{2}$ cups) milk
1 vanilla pod
4 large eggs
2 egg yolks
1$\frac{1}{2}$ oz. caster sugar

serves 8

Pour the cold water into a small, thick based frying pan. Stir in the sugar, using a wooden spoon.

Dissolve the sugar in the water, then bring to the boil

Place over a low heat to dissolve the sugar, stirring occasionally. When the sugar has dissolved, bring to the boil and boil without stirring until the sugar turns a dark, golden brown. Remove at once from the heat and slowly spoon in the boiling water, stirring to loosen the caramel. Lightly oil

The caramel is ready when it is a rich, golden brown

8 $\frac{1}{4}$-pint ($\frac{5}{8}$ cup) capacity dariole moulds. Spoon some of the caramel into each mould and leave in a cool place until set.

Meanwhile, make the custard. Pour the milk into a saucepan, add the vanilla pod and bring slowly to the boil. Leave to infuse for about

Pour the milk on to the eggs, stirring, and strain into a measuring jug. Skim off the froth from the top, or leave it to subside. Divide the custard between the caramel based moulds. Place in a large roasting tin, in $\frac{1}{2}$ in. cold water. Cover with a double sheet of kitchen foil, to prevent a skin forming on the surface of the custards.

Cook in the centre of the oven at 325°F. (mark 3) for about 45 minutes until set. To test whether the custards are cooked, insert a fine skewer two-thirds of the way through each one; if it comes out clean the custard is cooked. Re-

Strain the custard before pouring into the moulds

Ease the custard away from the mould with a knife

o minutes. Crack the 4 eggs into a deep bowl and add the extra egg yolks. Add the caster sugar and whisk with a rotary whisk until well blended and pale in colour. Remove the vanilla pod from the milk, rinse and dry it and store in a ar of caster sugar for further use.

Spoon a little caramel into each mould before filling with custard

Cook the cremes caramels au bain marie to prevent them boiling

move the moulds from the water and, while still warm, ease the custard away from the side of the mould with a small, sharp knife. Shake once and invert into an individual glass dish. Ease the mould away and allow to cool completely before serving.

Cool, rich bavarois is the smoothest dessert you can offer. Make it in an old-fashioned mould like the copper one we have used to make it even more interesting.

A bavarois (or Bavarian cream as it is sometimes called) is a rich egg custard mixture set with gelatine and flavoured either with chocolate, as here, or with coffee, or just vanilla.

Don't try to hurry the making, or you are likely to curdle the custard or to get a stringy gelatine mixture. Work at it gently and slowly, stirring all the time when necessary, until it is setting.

As a change from this moulded dessert, make the cream in small individual soufflé dishes and flavour individual portions differently, say 2 chocolate, 2 coffee and 2 vanilla.

serves 6–8

3 large eggs, separated
¾ pint (1⅞ cups) milk
1 vanilla pod
3 oz. (⅜ cup) caster sugar
5 tbsps. water
1½ level tbsps. powdered gelatine
3 oz. chocolate dots, or plain (dark) block chocolate, grated
½ pint (1¼ cups) double cream

Make sure the egg whites are at room temperature; this makes whisking easier.

Ladle some of the warmed milk on to the creamy yolks and sugar

Stir custard over gentle heat, without boiling, until it thickens

Put the milk in a pan with the vanilla pod and heat gently until it just reaches boiling point. Whisk together the egg yolks and sugar in a bowl until the mixture is pale and fluffy.

Ladle about one-third of the warm milk on to the creamy yolks and

Dissolve the gelatine in a small basin over a pan of warm water

Pour the gelatine steadily into the custard, stirring constantly

sugar, scrape down the sides of the bowl with a spatula and blend in well.

Remove the vanilla pod (if this is rinsed under running water and dried thoroughly it may be stored in a jar of caster sugar for future use).

Blend the egg custard with the remaining milk in the saucepan and stir over gentle heat to thicken. This will take 15–20 minutes. Do not allow it to boil or the mixture will curdle. If you find it difficult to control the heat sufficiently, put the custard in a basin over a pan of hot water to thicken it.

Stir the chocolate dots or grated block chocolate into the hot custard until completely dissolved and evenly mixed.

Measure the water into a bowl and sprinkle in the gelatine. Place it over a pan of hot water and dissolve the gelatine slowly. Allow to cool for 1–2 minutes.

Stir 1–2 tablespoons of the chocolate custard into the dissolved gelatine and pour this blend in a thin stream into the remainder of the custard, stirring continuously

with a spoon.

Turn the custard into a bowl and place it in a larger basin of ice cubes and water and stir continuously until thick but still flowing.

Lightly whip three-quarters of the cream and whisk the egg whites until stiff but not dry. Spoon a little of the chocolate custard into the cream, then add all the cream to the custard, blending thoroughly.

The chocolate mixture should now be on the point of setting. Pour it on to the whisked egg whites and fold it in quickly and lightly with a tablespoon, until no pockets of egg white are visible. Do not fold in too much as this will beat out some of the air in the mixture, and the bavarois will be small and solid.

Pour into a lightly oiled 2½-pint

In a bowl over ice, stir cream and custard together until blended

capacity mould and put in the refrigerator to set.

To serve, remove the moulded bavarois from the refrigerator and allow it to stand for 15 minutes. Then ease the bavarois away from the side of the mould by tilting at a slight angle and rotating the mould. Unmould it on to a wet serving plate and slide it into the centre of the plate.

Whip the remaining cream and pipe rosettes round the base of the bavarois with a large star vegetable nozzle. Decorate with caraque chocolate.

When almost setting, pour the mixture into a mould and leave to set

CREPES SUZETTE

If you have a chafing dish, let your guests enjoy watching you finish this delicious flambé dish of pancakes in orange butter sauce. If you don't have a pan pretty enough for public scrutiny (or if you're not sufficiently extrovert to want to display your skills), simply heat the pancakes and sauce in the oven and pour the flaming brandy over when you take it to the table. Either way you can do the main preparation the day before if you wish.

For pancake batter :
4 oz. (1 cup) plain flour
pinch of salt
grated rind of ½ a lemon
1 egg
½ pint (1¼ cups) milk or milk and water
½ oz. butter, melted
butter for frying
For orange butter sauce :
5–6 lumps of sugar
2 large oranges
3 oz. butter
2 oz. (¼ cup) caster sugar
1 tbsp. orange juice
1 tbsp. cointreau
2–3 tbsps. brandy
serves 4

Beat in the liquid gradually to obtain a smooth batter

Sift the flour and salt together and mix in the grated lemon rind. Make a well in the centre and break in the egg. Gradually add half the liquid, beating well until the batter is smooth. Add the remaining liquid and the melted butter and beat until well mixed. Heat a little butter in a 7-in., thick-based frying pan. When it is really hot, tilt the pan so that the butter runs round and completely coats the sides of the pan; pour off any surplus. Pour in just enough batter to cover the base of the pan thinly and cook quickly until golden brown underneath. Turn with a palette knife or by tossing and cook the second side until golden. The pancakes for this dish should be really thin and lacy. As the pancakes are cooked, stack

flat on a plate with a sheet of greaseproof paper between each one. Cover and, if you are cooking ahead, keep in a cool place until required; if using straight away, keep warm.

Remove the zest from the oranges by rubbing the lumps of sugar over the rind until they are soaked in oil. Crush the sugar lumps and add them to the butter with the caster sugar. Beat the butter and sugar until soft and creamy and then add the orange juice and cointreau.

The pancakes should be thin and lacy for this dish

Remove the zest from the oranges by rubbing with lump sugar

Work again until thoroughly mixed. Keep in the refrigerator until required.

If you have a chafing dish, put it ready on a trolley or sideboard before the meal. Have ready also the brandy, some matches, a table-spoon and fork. Half an hour before serving, put the stack of pancakes, covered with a second plate or foil, in the oven at 300°F. (mark

Work the butter and sugar with a wooden spoon until soft

2). Melt the orange butter over a gentle heat and leave in a warm place. To serve, pour half the orange butter sauce into the chafing dish and light the flame underneath. Take one pancake at a time and place it in the dish, spoon over the sauce, fold the pancake in half and in half again. Push to one side of the dish while you repeat with more pancakes until the pan is full. You will have to do this in two batches. Make sure that all the pancakes are well soaked with sauce. Pour brandy into the table-spoon, heat the bowl of the spoon

Add orange juice and cointreau to the orange butter

Fold the pancakes and soak in the warm butter sauce

with a lighted match, pour over the pancakes in the chafing dish and ignite. Serve at once. Repeat with remaining sauce and pancakes.

To prepare without using a chafing dish, place a little of the orange butter in the middle of each pancake, fold the pancakes into four and arrange them in a shallow ovenproof serving dish. Melt the remaining orange butter in a pan on top of the stove and pour over the pancakes. Put the dish in the oven at 300°F. (mark 2) and leave while the first course is eaten (about ½ hour).

To serve, uncover the dish and take it to the table. By this time the orange butter will have melted and thoroughly soaked the pancakes. Warm the brandy gently as above, pour it over the pancakes and ignite.

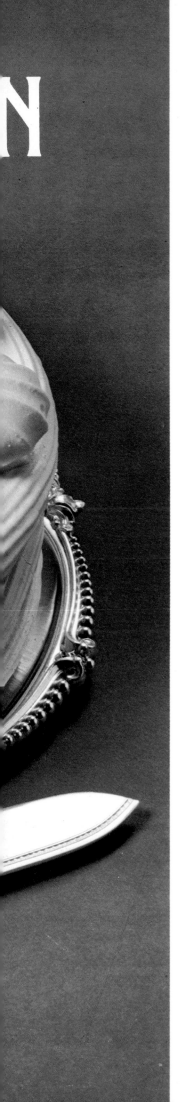

N

This is a classic French sweet made of mouth-watering meringues and cream flavoured with chestnut purée. Although it looks and tastes so luscious it is quite easy to make and because of its exotic appearance it is sure to gain you many compliments from your guests at a dinner party or buffet.

For a party, make the meringue rounds and shells well in advance and store them in airtight tins until you require them.

To whip the maximum amount of air into meringues, the egg whites must be at room temperature and they should be whisked by hand with a balloon or rotary whisk. It will help if you use a really large, deep bowl.

An electric mixer works too fast and tends to produce a flat, close-textured meringue.

serves 8–10

6 large egg whites
12 oz. (1½ cups) caster sugar
½ pint (1¼ cups) double cream
2 tbsps. milk
8¾-oz. can sweetened chestnut purée
1 tbsp. dry sherry
3 marrons glacés
1 oz. chocolate dots

Cover 3 baking sheets with non-stick paper. Invert a 9-in. sandwich tin on to each one and draw a

Pipe out 3 9-in. circles of meringue on to non-stick paper

whisked egg white. Whisk well, drawing all the meringue into the centre of the bowl.

Using a forcing bag fitted with a large vegetable star nozzle, fill the meringue into the bag. Pipe

When the meringue is cooked the paper should peel off easily

Whisk the egg whites in a large bowl until stiff and frothy

line round the tin. Ensure that the eggs are at room temperature by taking them out of the refrigerator at least 1 hour before you start.

Place a large mixing bowl (6-pint capacity) on a damp cloth to stop it slipping and use a rotary whisk to whisk the whites. (A balloon whisk is even better.) Draw the whites continually from the sides of the bowl into the centre and whisk until they stand stiffly in peaks and cling around the whisk, looking dry like cotton wool.

Gradually whisk in all the sugar a spoonful at a time, sprinkling it over the whole surface of the

meringue circles to fill the pencil circles on the non-stick paper, starting from the centre and working out. Use slightly less than a third of the meringue for each circle. With the remaining meringue pipe 6 shell shapes on to the paper in the corners of the baking sheets.

Dry the meringues in the oven set at its lowest for about 4 hours. Half way through the cooking time, reverse the top and bottom baking sheets in the oven so that one meringue does not colour more than either of the others When they are dry, remove from the oven

and cool slightly. Then turn the meringue discs over on to the palm of your hand and peel away the paper.

Cool on wire racks. Place 1 meringue disc on a flat serving plate. Whip the cream with the milk until it just holds its shape and put 7 dessertspoons cream to one side. Fold the chestnut purée and sherry into the remaining cream.

Spoon half the chestnut cream around the meringue base. Spread to the edges with a palette knife. Place the second meringue disc on top. Repeat this process with the remaining cream and the third disc. Position the meringue shells evenly round the top of the vacherin.

Removing one shell at a time, dab

Fix the meringue shells in position with plain whipped cream

a little of the reserved plain cream under each with a palette knife and press back into position. Drop more reserved cream from a dessertspoon between the meringue shells. Place the marrons glacés directly on the meringue in the centre.

Melt the chocolate dots in a bowl over a pan of hot water. Spoon into a small greaseproof paper piping bag and snip off the tip

Spoon cream between the shells and drizzle with melted chocolate

with scissors. Press the bag firmly and evenly and drizzle the chocolate over each spoonful of cream, drawing the bag from side to side. Chill 1–2 hours before serving.

au
noré

For pastry base:
4 oz. (1 cup) plain flour
salt
2 oz. butter
1 oz. (⅛ cup) caster sugar
1 egg yolk
¼ tsp. vanilla essence

For choux pastry:
2 oz. butter
¼ pint (⅝ cup) water
2½ oz. (⅝ cup) plain flour
pinch of salt
2 eggs, beaten

For filling:
¼ pint (⅝ cup) double cream,
   whipped, optional

For glaze:
8 oz. (1 cup) granulated sugar
8 tbsps. water

For pastry cream:
1 pint (2½ cups) milk
4 oz. (½ cup) caster sugar
2 oz. (½ cup) plain flour
½ oz. cornflour
2 large eggs
2 oz. butter

For decoration:
1-lb. 13-oz. can apricot
   halves, drained
angelica

serves 8

For the pastry base, sift the flour and salt on to a working surface. Make a well in the centre, add the butter and sugar and work them together with the fingertips of 1 hand. Add the egg yolk and

Mix the pastry on a flat surface with the fingers of one hand

vanilla essence and mix to a soft dough with the heel of 1 hand. Wrap in greaseproof paper or polythene and chill for ½ hour. Roll out to a round 8½ in. in diameter. Place the round on a baking sheet, prick with a fork and crimp the edge with the fingers. Bake in the oven at 350°F. (mark 4) for about 20 minutes. Cool on the baking sheet until beginning to firm, then lift carefully on to a wire rack.
Meanwhile, place the butter and water in a pan and melt over a

low heat. Sift the flour and salt on to a piece of greaseproof paper. Bring the butter and water to the boil, remove from the heat and tip the flour quickly into the pan. Beat the mixture to a paste until it starts to leave the sides of the pan. (Take care not to over-beat or the

Crimp the edge of the pastry base with the fingers

mixture become fatty). Add the eggs slowly, beating hard between each addition until it is a smooth piping consistency.
Grease a baking sheet. Press the rim of an 8½-in. diameter flan ring in flour and place the ring on the baking sheet, to make a floured imprint. Spoon the choux paste into a forcing bag fitted with a large plain nozzle. Using the floured ring as a guide, pipe two-thirds of the paste in a circle.
With the remaining choux, pipe out 16 small buns on to another greased baking sheet. Bake buns

Pipe out a choux ring, using the flour circle as a guide

Pipe 16 small buns, taking care to keep them all the same size

and ring in the oven at 450°F. (mark 8) for 15 minutes. Reduce the heat to 375°F. (mark 5) and cook for about a further 20 minutes. When cooked, pierce the bases of buns and ring to release the steam, and cool on a wire rack. If you wish, split the buns when cold and pipe in whipped cream. For the glaze, dissolve the sugar with the water over gentle heat, then bring to the boil and boil rapidly to 260°F. (when a drop of syrup will harden in cold water). Dip the tops and sides of the buns into the syrup, using tongs to hold them. Place the pastry base on a flat plate, position the ring on top and arrange the glazed buns round the ring, dipping your fingers in iced water as you do so, so that the hot syrup does not stick.
To make the pastry cream, heat the milk in a pan. Mix together the

Use tongs to dip the choux buns in hot sugar glaze

sugar, flour, cornflour and eggs and stir in a little of the hot milk. Pour all the mixture into the saucepan of milk and stir over gentle heat until it thickens and just comes to the boil. Add the butter and beat well.
Arrange all but 6 apricot halves in the centre of the gâteau. Spoon over the warm (not hot) pastry cream, brush with apricot juice and decorate with the remaining apricot halves and the angelica. Serve cold on the same day.

Arrange the choux ring and buns on the flat pastry base

Baba au Rhum

Rum babas are favourites both at tea time and as a dessert. Traditional French pâtisserie, the dough is light and fluffy because of the yeast used to raise it. Spoon over it the warm honey and rum syrup and the result is delicious indeed. French pastry shops sell them heavily glazed with apricot to give a really rich, glowing appearance.

Babas are difficult to serve if you pour over too much syrup initially,

Leave the yeast mixture in a warm place until frothy

Half fill the baba moulds and cover with oiled polythene

Blend together yeast, milk and 2 oz. flour until smooth

Add all the ingredients to the original dough

Spoon honey and rum syrup over the babas while they are hot

as they become wet while standing, but if you serve a small jug of syrup separately, the extra syrup is good added just before eating. Alternatively, some people will appreciate an extra spoonful of rum spooned over at the last minute.

makes 8–10

1 oz. fresh baker's yeast (or 1 level tbsp. dried yeast)
6 tbsps. warm milk
8 oz. (2 cups) plain strong flour
½ level tsp. salt
1 oz. (⅛ cup) caster sugar
4 eggs, beaten
4 oz. butter, soft but not melted
4 oz. currants
For honey and rum syrup:
4 tbsps. clear honey
4 tbsps. water
rum
For apricot glaze and decoration:
3 tbsps. apricot jam
2 tbsps. water
whipped cream
glacé cherries

Grease 8–10 3½-in. ring moulds with lard.

In a bowl, blend together the yeast, milk and 2 oz. (½ cup) of the flour, until smooth. Allow to stand in a warm place until frothy – about 20 minutes for fresh yeast, 30 minutes for dried. During this period the yeast is growing and as it does so it forms carbon

Beat thoroughly with a wooden spoon for 3–4 minutes

dioxide. The bubbles of this gas are responsible for the spongy texture of the finished cake.

Add the remaining flour, the salt, sugar, eggs, butter and currants, and beat thoroughly for 3–4 minutes. This develops the dough so that it will rise well.

Half fill the tins with the baba dough, cover with oiled polythene to prevent a skin forming and allow to rise until the moulds are two-thirds full.

Bake near the top of the oven at

400°F. (mark 6) for 15–20 minutes. Cool for a few minutes and turn out on to a wire rack, placed over a plastic tray to catch the drips of syrup.

Warm the honey and water together and add rum to taste. While the babas are still hot, spoon over them sufficient warm honey and rum syrup to soak each baba well.

Heat the jam and water together, sieve it, brush the babas with the apricot glaze and leave to cool.

Pipe a whirl of whipped cream into each baba with a large star vegetable nozzle, and top with a cherry. Transfer to serving plates and serve extra syrup and/or whipped cream separately if you wish.

When cold, fill the centre of each with piped cream

Information

COOK AHEAD – WITH A FREEZER

Freezing is fast superseding bottling, canning and drying as the most important means of preserving food. Unlike other forms of preserving, freezing does not destroy or alter anything contained in the food. The natural cycle of life is not destroyed, but held in 'suspended animation'; equally, enzymes and micro-organisms in the food (which cause normal deterioration) are not destroyed.

The food will therefore come out of the freezer as good (or as bad) as it went in. There is only one proviso – that it is wrapped and sealed correctly.

Frozen food, then, is as fresh as fruit and vegetables from the greengrocer. Indeed, it is often fresher and in better condition, as stock at the shop has probably been in transit for several days, whereas fruit and vegetables from your own garden (and commercially frozen) are frozen within hours of picking – with the result that they will have lost far fewer vitamins.

Almost any food can be frozen, but whatever it is, it should, of course, be in first class condition. Fruit and vegetables should be ripe, firm and freshly picked; meat and poultry must be good quality and suitably hung. Cooked foods need to be cooled as rapidly as possible before going into the freezer. Everything should be clean and done as quickly as possible – food deteriorates quickly if it is left

lying around and may become contaminated.

USING THE FREEZER

To freeze food successfully, retaining its appearance, taste and food value, it must be frozen quickly so that the ice particles that form are tiny. If you freeze slowly, the ice particles are large and damage the cell structure of the food. This means choosing a freezer with a special low freezing temperature and freezing in smallish quantities so that the fresh food going in doesn't raise the temperature in the cabinet too much and slow the freezing process (a maximum of $\frac{1}{10}$ the freezer's capacity in any 24 hours is recommended by most manufacturers). Once the food is frozen, raise the temperature to the normal 0°F. (−18°C.) for storage.

PACKAGING

Packaging food for your freezer is all-important. Solids should be packed as tightly as possible, excluding all the air. Aluminium foil is best for moulding difficult shaped objects, like chickens or joints, but it tears easily on jagged bones, so it is safest to overwrap with polythene (again squeezing out as much air as you can) afterwards.

Fruit and vegetables can either be packed in rigid containers (imperative for delicate whole fruits) or simply in sealed polythene bags. In this case, if you are having problems removing the air, dip the bag into a bowl of water – this pushes all the air out and moulds the bag snugly round the vegetables. Alternatively, suck the air out through a straw. Seal the bag immediately, and don't forget to dry the outside before putting it into your freezer.

If you can't fill a rigid container completely, use crumpled greaseproof or waxed paper to fill up the remaining space. Liquids expand when frozen, so always allow at

Frozen fruit salad in a solid block

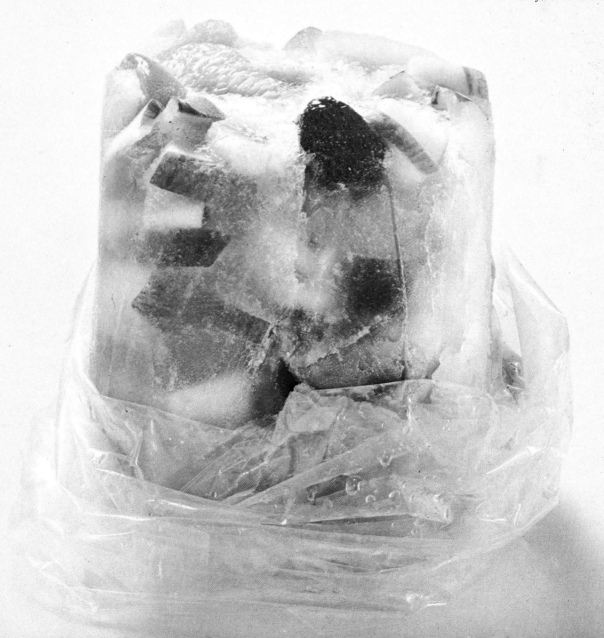

least ½ in. headspace when sealing a polythene bag or a container with a lid. Alternatively, leave the container open until the liquid is frozen – but don't forget to seal it when it *is* frozen, or it will dehydrate rapidly. If you are using a polythene bag for liquids, it helps to fit the bag into a pre-former – any straight-sided carton or plastic box – before pouring in the liquid. Freeze the liquid in the pre-former and when it is solid just slip it out and pack it away – and your carton is ready to be used again.

If you're freezing a combination of solids and liquid – such as fruit in syrup, or a casserole – do be sure the solid pieces are all below the level of the liquid. A piece of crumpled greaseproof paper over the top will generally be sufficient to keep the pieces down. Aluminium foil is the best material in which to freeze casseroles, again because it moulds so closely; you can freeze them in a casserole dish, but this slows the freezing and thawing processes and also puts one of your dishes out of action. The best way is to cook and cool the casserole; line an ovenproof dish with foil and spoon the meat and sauce into it, making sure the meat is completely covered. Put it in the freezer and when it is solid lift the foil out of the dish, wrap it over the top and overwrap in polythene. To use the casserole, simply remove the polythene and foil and pop the food into the same ovenproof dish to reheat.

There are available foil dishes in various shapes and sizes which are invaluable for use in freezing, as they can go straight from the freezer to the oven. With care they can be used more than once, which needn't make them an extravagance. Many small containers used for commercial products, such as ice cream and yoghourt, can be re-used in home freezing and are a great help for freezing small quantities of sauces, herbs and breadcrumbs.

Remember to package food in the quantities you will want to use. It's no good freezing a pâté for 10 if you are going to need only 4 slices from it; so slice it *before* you freeze it, put a sheet of waxed paper or polythene between each piece and then wrap the whole thing in foil. The same applies to cakes, meat, or anything that you freeze in quantity but use only in small amounts. If you make up a sauce, freeze it in ½-pint or pint containers, not in 1 solid block.

Another idea is to freeze stock and sauces in an ice-cube tray. When solid, turn out the cubes and put them in a polythene bag. A little soda water squirted into the bag will prevent the cubes sticking together. This is also an ideal way to freeze a variety of foods used in small quantities – concentrated mint sauce, tomato sauce, chopped herbs in a little water and so on. Finally, do label everything you put in the freezer. You may think that you'll remember what each package is, but after a while you may find it a problem – especially if you have a number of packages all much the same shape. Serving a dish of mashed potato instead of shepherd's pie, or a second course of chicken pie instead of blackberry and apple could be embarrassing! So tie or stick a label on to each package as it goes into your freezer and put on the date as well as the contents. A list of everything you freeze, kept handy inside the lid of the freezer, will ensure a steady rotation of stock.

PREPARING FOOD FOR THE FREEZER

FRUIT should be just ready for eating; over-ripe fruit can be puréed and frozen for use in fools, mousses, etc. Rinse all but soft fruits (such as raspberries) in ice-cold water and drain very thoroughly. To prevent discolouration, keep fruits such as apples and pears covered in water and lemon juice during preparation.

Fruit may be frozen in 3 ways – as a dry pack, in sugar, or in syrup.

Dry packing is suitable for fruit that is to be used for pies or preserves and for small whole fruit, so long as the skin is undamaged. Pick over, wash, dry on absorbent kitchen paper and use a rigid container to prevent damage during handling and storage.

Free-flow dry packing is suitable for small fruit or pieces of fruit such as strawberries or grapefruit segments. Pick the fruit over and prepare as necessary; spread it out on a baking sheet and freeze until firm. Then pack (preferably in a rigid container) for storage.

Dry sugar packing is particularly suitable for soft fruits. Pick over the fruit but don't wash it unless really necessary. The sugar and fruit can either be put into rigid containers in layers, or else mixed together before being packed. The fruit is more likely to retain its shape if layered, because when it is mixed with sugar the juice is

Freeze small quantities of stock or sauces in ice-cube trays

drawn out and leaves the fruit almost in purée form. Use caster sugar.

Syrup is best for non-juicy fruits or for those which discolour during preparation and storage. The strength of the syrup varies according to the particular fruit being frozen – refer to the chart for the correct strength.

20 % syrup is 4 oz. sugar dissolved in 1 pint water
30% syrup is 8 oz. sugar dissolved in 1 pint water
40% syrup is 10 oz. sugar dissolved in 1 pint water
50% syrup is 1 lb. sugar dissolved in 1 pint water.

Dissolve the sugar in the water by heating gently and bringing to the boil; cover and allow the syrup to become quite cold before using. Normally you will find ½ pint syrup is enough to cover 1 lb. fruit. Leave about ½ in. space at the top of the container to allow for expansion during freezing. If the fruit tends to float above the level of the syrup, hold it down with a piece of crumpled waxed or greaseproof paper.

VEGETABLES

Speed is particularly important when dealing with vegetables.

These should be frozen as soon as possible after picking. They need to be blanched before freezing, to kill some of the micro-organisms which cause discolouration and 'off' flavours. Of course, this also drives off some of the vitamins, but don't think it ruins the nutritional value of the vegetables – after all, when you cook them fresh, some of the vitamins are still lost.

For blanching you need a very large pan and a wire basket. Place the vegetables in the basket and immerse in boiling water (approximately 6 pints to 1 lb. of vegetables). When the water re-boils, cook for the recommended blanching time (see chart), then plunge the vegetables into ice-cold water. Drain and pack immediately. Don't try to do too large a quantity – 1 or 2 lb. at a time is about right, in successive batches. Pack the vegetables in rigid containers or polythene bags, allowing a little space for expansion for vegetables which pack tightly, such as peas.

MEAT

If you are going to home-freeze meat, do be absolutely sure the meat is fresh. Many butchers now

Extracting air from the package is essential for successful freezing

provide meat ready-packed for the home freezer and this is probably a better bet than trying to butcher half a carcass yourself. If you buy jointed fresh meat to freeze yourself there are 1 or 2 points to watch for. Very lean meat tends to dry out during freezing, so look for a good 'marbling' of fat, which helps to prevent this. On the other hand, too much fat tends to go rancid after a while, so trim some of it off if you think it's excessive.

It is generally better to freeze meat off the bone whenever possible – the bones slow down freezing and thawing and take up a lot of space in your freezer. If, however, you leave the bone in place – such as in a leg of lamb or pork chops – pad it well to avoid puncturing the wrapping. Separate steaks and chops with waxed paper or polythene so that you can remove just one or two.

POULTRY AND GAME

Truss the bird as for the table, but *do not* stuff it. Pad the protruding bones before you wrap it. Game must be hung before freezing, for the same length of time as if you were going to eat it immediately. Then proceed as for poultry.

FISH

Fish should be frozen only if you can get it to your freezer within 12 hours of the catch. Clean the fish as usual, leaving small fish whole but removing the heads and tails of larger ones. Skin and fillet flat fish. Salmon, trout and similar fish can be frozen whole in a sheet of ice; dip them in cold water, leave them in the freezer until frozen and then repeat the process several times until the ice glaze is about ⅛ in. thick. Wrap individual fish in polythene and pack in cartons or overwrap with heavy-duty polythene.

COOKED DISHES

One of the great advantages of a freezer is that you can cook when you feel like it and store whole meals for future use. You can make 3 or 4 pies at once (particularly useful if you have a glut of fruit in your garden), eat 1 now and freeze the rest; or make up a casserole using double your normal quantity – eat half and freeze the rest.

In general, the foods can be prepared and cooked as if they were to be served immediately,

A well stocked freezer, with each package clearly labelled

but it is wise to reduce the amount of seasoning. Take care not to over-cook the food, particularly if it is to be reheated for serving. Chill food quickly after cooking and wrap and freeze it carefully. When you are freezing stock or soups, remember that liquid expands when frozen, so allow some space for this.

THAWING AND REHEATING

Ideally, food should be thawed very gently in the refrigerator – but this can take up to 6 hours *per lb.*, and most people simply don't have that amount of time in hand. There are some foods, though, that *must* be thawed right through before they are cooked – in particular poultry. Whole fish retain their flavour and texture better if thawed out slowly and whole fruit that is to be eaten with no further preparation will retain its shape more readily. Leave the food in its original wrapping while thawing.

If you don't have quite so much time in hand, thaw at room temperature, but don't let it stand too long. Once food thaws out, the micro-organisms start working again and it will deteriorate much more quickly than if the food were fresh.

Luckily, a lot of the real standbys you keep in the freezer can be cooked straight from frozen. Stews, casseroles, cooked meat in gravy, fruit pies will all reheat appetizingly from frozen – but if the dish the food is in isn't one of the freezer-to-oven type, do allow it at least 30 minutes at room temperature. Anything in a foil

container, of course, can go straight into the oven.

Chops, steaks, small fish and other small items can be cooked without thawing. The only point to watch is that the food is thoroughly hot right through – and not burnt to a cinder on the outside at the same time. A joint of meat can equally well be thawed or cooked straight from the freezer – either way is quite satisfactory. Again, you must ensure that it is cooked through to the centre.

Soups and sauces are best thawed slowly, though if you're in a hurry you can turn the frozen lump into a saucepan and heat it very gently. Cakes, pâtés, sweets and so on also need slow, gentle thawing (though, of course, if you've followed our advice and sliced them before freezing they won't take more than an hour).

Finally, vegetables should never be thawed. Pop them straight into a little boiling water, or toss them gently in butter in a heavy lidded pan.

DO NOT FREEZE . . .

Eggs in their shells (they crack) or hardboiled (they turn rubbery). The solution is simple – freeze the whites and yolks separately.

Boiled old potatoes (they go leathery); mash them with butter – but not milk – and they will be fine.

Fully-cooked chips (they go soggy); the answer is to part-cook them, freeze, and just crisp them up in deep hot fat straight from the freezer.

Salad stuffs – lettuce, watercress, celery, chicory – all go limp, soggy and unattractive. If you have a

glut in the garden you can freeze a soup made from one of these ingredients.

Single cream – of less than 40 per cent butterfat (it separates). Double cream is fine.

Mayonnaise (it curdles).

Custards (they tend to separate) – so freeze them *before* cooking.

Moulds – anything containing a high proportion of gelatine.

Anything flavoured with garlic (it develops an unpleasant, musty flavour) – if possible, add garlic at point of reheating or use it very sparingly.

GOLDEN RULES

1. Always start with good-quality foods and freeze them at peak freshness.
2. Keep handling to a minimum and make sure everything is clean.
3. Pay special attention to packaging and sealing. Exposure to air and moisture damages frozen foods.
4. Cool food rapidly if it's been cooked or blanched; never put anything hot – or even warm – into your freezer.
5. Freeze as quickly as possible, and in small quantities.
6. Freeze in the coldest part of the freezer, and don't pack the food to be frozen too closely.
7. Transfer newly added items to the main part of the cabinet once they've been frozen.
8. Remember to return the switch from 'accelerated' to 'normal' once newly added foods have been frozen – i.e. after 24 hours.
9. Maintain a steady storage temperature of −18°C. (0°F.) and don't do anything that will cause temperature fluctuations within the freezer.
10. Label and date food to ensure a good rotation of stock.
11. Defrost the freezer at a time when stocks are low.
12. Be prepared for emergencies. Make sure you know what to do in case of breakdown or powercuts.

And for freezing cooked foods
1. Go lightly with the seasoning and preferably omit garlic entirely.
2. Use shallow rather than deep dishes.
3. Cool everything as rapidly as possible and freeze at once.
Note: Polythene bags or film *must* be removed before food is put into the oven.

Foods such as meat, fish, dairy produce, fruits and vegetables are all perishable and if they are kept too long the action of bacteria, mould and enzymes (called micro-organisms) will make changes in them so that milk will sour, fats go rancid, meat, fish and eggs decompose and fruits and vegetables discolour and go mouldy. The lower the temperature, the less micro-organism activity there will be, so that the best way to store perishable foods is in a refrigerator at a steady temperature of 35°F.–45°F. The next best thing is a cool larder where the temperature does not exceed 50°F.

Bacon, cheese, eggs and fats should really be bought at least once a week – or twice a week in hot weather if a refrigerator is not available. Meat, fish, poultry, soft fruits, green and salad vegetables should, ideally, be purchased as you need them – preferably not too much at a time.

In the store cupboard (in covered containers)

Flour

Plain, self-raising	Up to 6 months
Wheatmeal	2–3 months
Wholemeal	Up to 1 month
Cake mixes (unopened)	Up to 6 months

Raising agents

Baking powder, bicarbonate of soda, cream of tartar	2–3 months
Dried yeast	Up to 6 months

Cereals

Cornflour, custard powder	Up to 12 months
Dried vegetables – pearl barley, lentils, peas, etc.	Up to 12 months
Oatmeal	Up to 1 month
Rice, sago, tapioca	Up to 12 months

Nuts

Whole almonds, walnuts	Up to 1 month
Ground almonds, coconut	Up to 1 month

Jams and bottled goods

Gravy browning	Up to 12 months
Sauces	Up to 6 months
Salad oil	Up to 18 months
Pickles and chutneys	Up to 12 months
Lemon curd, bought home-made	2–3 months Up to 1 month
Jams and mincemeat	Up to 12 months
Mayonnaise, salad cream (bought)	Up to 12 months
Vinegar	At least 2 years

Cans

Fish, meat, fruit and juices	Up to 12 months
Ham	Up to 6 months

Sugars

Granulated, caster, cubes	Up to 12 months
Icing, brown	Up to 1 month

Syrups

Golden syrup, treacle	Up to 12 months
Honey	Up to 6 months

Dried fruit

Currants, sultanas, raisins	2–3 months
Prunes, figs, apricots	2–3 months
Candied peel, glacé cherries	2–3 months

Miscellaneous

Dried milk, whole skimmed	Up to 1 month 2–3 months
Jellies and gelatine	Up to 12 months
Breakfast cereals	Up to 1 month
Tea	Up to 1 year
Coffee (beans) (ground)	Up to 1 month 1 week
Soups (including condensed)	Up to 12 months
Vegetables (including tomato juice and purée)	Up to 12 months
Evaporated milk	6–8 months
Condensed milk	4–6 months
Cocoa, drinking chocolate	Up to 12 months
Packet soups	Up to 12 months

Herbs, spices and seasonings

Allspice, bay leaves, cloves, celery seeds, cinnamon, dried herbs, ginger, mace, mixed spice, curry powder	Up to 6 months
Curry paste, mustard, pepper	Up to 12 months
Salt	Up to 6 months (or longer if perfectly dry)

Colourings and flavourings

Flavouring essence	Up to 12 months
Block chocolate or polka dots	Up to 1 month
Colourings	Up to 12 months
Silver balls, vermicelli and other decorations	Up to 1 month

Note: Many of these items will keep for longer than the recommended times if the packaging is not disturbed. In particular, most canned goods will keep for years if the tin is not exposed to damp that will cause it to rust. However, it is advisable to turn out your storecupboard 3 or 4 times a year, so as to ensure a regular turnover of stock.

In the refrigerator	How to store	Time
Milk produce		
Fresh milk	In the bottle or carton. If in a jug, keep covered	3–4 days
Milk puddings, custards, etc.	In a covered dish	2 days
Yoghourt	Leave in the original container	7 days
Fats		
Butter, margarine, lard, etc.	Leave in original wrapping and store in the special door compartment	2–4 weeks
Cheese		
Hard and blue cheeses	Wrapped in the original pack, in polythene, or foil	1–2 weeks
Cream cheese	Keep in a covered container, or wrap in polythene or foil	5–7 days
Poultry		
Whole, fresh birds	Draw, wash, dry and wrap in polythene or foil. Remove wrappings from ready-to-cook poultry	2–3 days
Cooked birds	Cool and refrigerate straight away. Remove any stuffing and wrap or cover with polythene or foil	2–3 days
Frozen birds	Leave in the original wrapping and put while still frozen into the frozen food compartment	Depends on star rating (refer to manufacturer's instructions) 2–3 days in main cabinet
Cooked and made-up poultry dishes	Cool quickly and refrigerate in covered dish or container	1 day
Meat		
Joints	Rinse off any blood and wipe dry. Cover lightly with polythene or	3–5 days
Steaks, chops, stewing veal	foil (do not seal tightly) and refrigerate straight away	2–4 days
Smoked hams, sliced bacon		1 week
Offal and mince		1–2 days
Cooked meats		
Joints	Wrap in foil or polythene or leave, covered, in the dish they were	3–5 days
Casseroles, made-up dishes	cooked in. Alternatively, store in any covered container	2–3 days
Fish		
Raw	Cover loosely in polythene or foil	1–2 days
Cooked	Cover loosely in polythene or foil, or place in covered container	2 days
Eggs		
Fresh in shells	Small end down	About 2 weeks
Yolks	Covered with water if whole	2–3 days
Whites	In a covered container	3–4 days
Hard-boiled in shell	Leave uncovered	Up to 1 week
Fruit and vegetables		
Soft fruits	Clean and store in a covered container	1–3 days
Hard and stone fruits	Lightly wrapped, or in the crisper	3–7 days
Bananas	*Never refrigerate*	
Salad vegetables	Wash and dry; store in crisper, plastic container or wrap lightly in polythene	4–6 days
Greens	Prepare ready for use. Wrap lightly or place in the crisper	3–7 days

OPERATION RESCUE

If something goes wrong when you're cooking – be it for a family supper or a formal dinner – the essential rule is don't panic. Take a good look at the dish in question – taste it – and think what can be done to save it. If the flavour is wrong, it can often be saved (see our specific examples). If there's time, use it as the base for another dish altogether (if necessary, give your guests another drink to keep them happy).

If the result looks a disaster, but the flavour is fine, change its appearance – cover it up with sauce, for instance, or turn a collapsed cake into a delicious trifle. Whatever you do, don't serve something that looks a failure – it will make you feel bad and embarrass your guests. If you've under-calculated badly on quantities, serve an extra variety of vegetable – or try to serve another course (be inventive – see what you have in the store cupboard by way of canned soups, or hors d'oeuvre). Be sure you always have some cans of attractive vegetables available –

French beans, asparagus or artichoke hearts.

SWEETS

To eke out a scanty sweet course
Top each serving with a portion of bought ice cream.

If a chocolate cake turns out rather too moist
Call it a pudding and serve it hot with a fluffy sauce.

If homemade biscuits crumble badly
Use them to make a biscuit crumb flan case.

If the top of a fruit cake gets burnt
Cut if off and use a well-flavoured almond paste to disguise it.

If apples or pears stew unevenly
Some fluffy and some still hard? Put them in the blender and purée to make a fool.

If a jelly won't set
Put in a warm place to completely melt, then add more dissolved gelatine and place in the coldest part of the refrigerator. If you haven't time to wait any longer turn it into a jelly trifle, with sherry-soaked sponge on the bottom, fruit and cream.

If meringues break as you lift them from the baking sheet
Meringue shells can be served on top of fruit and cream if the pieces are large enough. A meringue gâteau can usually be stuck together and suitably disguised with large quantities of whipped cream and fruit or grated chocolate.

If your custard sauce curdles
Whip in 1–2 level teaspoons cornflower per pint; continue cooking

If a pastry flan case breaks
Put 4 tablespoons jam in a small pan, boil and brush well into the broken edges. Press together and brush over the join again with more jam. Allow to cool before filling.

If your sponge cake turns out a thin, flat, biscuity layer
Cut into fancy shapes with a biscuit cutter and sandwich together with jam and cream.

If your cake rises unevenly
Level the top, turn it over and ice the bottom.

If a cake breaks up as you take it out of the tin
It can often be disguised as a hot pudding, with custard sauce or fruit.

If a cake sinks in the middle
Cut out the centre and decorate with fruit, cream or butter cream. If it is a heavy fruit cake, cut out the centre and turn into a ring cake, decorating with almond paste and royal icing if you wish.

SAUCES

If a sweet sauce is too sickly
Add some lemon juice to give it zest. This is also a good ploy with puddings generally which are too bland.

If a sauce turns lumpy
Whisk with a rotary whisk, purée in a blender or press through a fine sieve.

If a savoury sauce lacks flavour but will not stand more salt and pepper
Add lemon juice (especially good with sauces for fish).

If French dressing tastes too oily
Add more salt and a splash of vinegar or lemon juice.

If mayonnaise curdles
Start again with a fresh egg yolk in a clean basin and add the curdled mixture slowly to it – the whole should then blend properly.

MEATS, POULTRY AND FISH

If a chicken is over-cooked (flesh falls apart, skin breaks)
Cut into pieces and mix with the vegetables instead of serving separately. Dish up on a bed of buttered noodles or rice.

If fish breaks up
Mix it with rice to make a kedgeree, or serve in piped potato nests, or allow it to cool, flake it and make up a fish salad.

If a curry sauce is too hot
Add yoghourt, soured cream, milk, lemon juice or potato, or a combination of these.

If a casserole is too spicy
Add a few tablespoons of cream or milk.

If a casserole has too much liquid
Work together butter and flour in the proportion 1 oz. butter to ½ oz. flour with a fork and stir into the hot liquid in small pieces until the sauce is the desired consistency. Continue to cook a little longer.

SOUPS

If a soup is too salty but not too thick
Add a small quantity of instant mashed potato.

VEGETABLES AND FRUIT

If your potatoes – or other vegetables – boil dry
Cut off the burnt part and remove whatever is salvageable to another pan. If necessary, add more boiling water, or toss in butter and season well.

If creamed potatoes are lumpy
Purée in a blender with plenty of butter, salt and pepper.

If rice is overcooked and soggy
Rinse in a colander with cold running water to stop it cooking any further. Cool any other vegetables similarly, drain and mix together as a rice salad, using French dressing to moisten.

If soft fruits are damaged
Cut off the damaged parts and purée the remainder for use as a fruit sauce with ice cream.

If jam won't set
Small quantities of runny jam can be used as fruit sauce for hot puddings or ice cream. ●

COOK'S TOOLS

It's difficult to be a successful cook without the right equipment. By that, we don't mean that you should go to your nearest big store and spend the month's housekeeping money in the kitchen gadget department! It simply means that if you *are* going to buy a piece of kitchen equipment, make sure it's something that is really useful—and that it's well made. It's far better to spend a little more and buy something that's going to last, rather than buy a cheaper version that will break the first time it has something tough to cope with. And if you're buying bakeware—cake tins and so on—do consider the easy clean type; they are well worth the extra money in time- and temper-saving. To give you an idea, we have assembled a variety of pieces that we consider essential basic equipment and photographed them all together.

1 Scales
2 Colander
3 Forcing bag and nozzles
   Pie plate
   Swiss roll pan
4 Rolling pin
5 Flour dredger
6 Loaf pan
7 Deep cake pan
   Sandwich pan
   Cooling tray
8 Tongs
9 Set of non-stick saucepans and frying pan
10 Measuring jug
11 Peppermill
12 Set of mixing bowls
13 Lemon squeezer
14 Kitchen scissors

15 Sieve
16 Mouli grater
17 4-sided grater
18 Set of kitchen knives
   Skewers
   5-hour timer
   Chopping board
19 Egg beater
20 Whisk
21 Hand-held electric beater
22 Set of measuring spoons
23 Garlic crusher
24 Corkscrew
25 Wall-fixed can opener
26 Egg and tomato slicer
27 Potato peeler
28 Corer
29 Rubber spatula

30 Set of wooden spoons
31 Pastry brush
   Yorkshire pudding tin
   Bun pan
In addition, you will probably find the following very useful to have in your kitchen:
Metal basting spoon and draining spoon
2- or 3-pronged kitchen fork
Palette knife
Butter spreader (a small palette knife)
Deep fat fryer (or a collapsible wire basket to fit your largest saucepan)
Omelette pan
Set of flan rings
Jelly moulds
Mincer
Spare baking sheets to fit your oven
Assortment of casserole dishes

Herbs and Spices

	Meat	Fish	Poultry, game	Soups	Vegetables
Basil *Use sparingly*	Lamb, pork, veal, beef casseroles	Shrimps, white fish		Many soups, especially tomato	Tomatoes, broad beans
Bay	Kebabs, marinades for beef, casseroles	Baked or casseroled fish	Marinades	As a background seasoning, remove before serving	
Chervil *Use generously*	Chervil butter for veal cutlets	Crab	Fricassees, rub into chicken before roasting/grilling	Herb soup	Chervil butter for peas, tomatoes, aubergines
Chives *According to taste*	Hamburgers, meat loaves, garnish for casseroles	Fish cakes, fish stuffings	With dishes containing tomatoes	Garnish for vegetable soups, especially vichyssoise	Garnish to potatoes, other vegetables
Dill *Use carefully*	Lamb and rich pork dishes, beef and chicken ragoût	All fish dishes, especially salmon, crab, mackerel	Creamed chicken, add a spray to roasting pan	Fish, pea, tomato and bean soups	With delicate vegetables
Garlic *Use judiciously*	Continental cookery, pasta, sauces, casseroles	Use sparingly in most fish dishes	Together with other robust flavours	Most soups	Ratatouille
Marjoram *Use judiciously*	Veal, lamb, pork, sausages, liver	Salt fish, shellfish	Stuffings, rub unstuffed chicken, duck before roasting	Onion, potato, lentil, pea soups	Tomatoes, peas, carrots, spinach, mushrooms
Oregano *Use judiciously*	Veal, lamb, pork, sausages, liver	Many fish dishes	Stuffings	Onion, potato, lentil, pea soups	Tomatoes, peas, carrots, courgettes, spinach, mushroom
Parsley *Use freely*	Stuffings, casseroles	Fish cakes, stuffings	Stuffings	Garnish for any soup	Parsley butter, new potatoes, celery
Rosemary *Use sparingly*	Roast lamb, tripe, kidneys, marinades	Marinades for salmon, eel, mackerel	Sprinkle lightly inside before roasting; stuffings	Minestrone	Sauté potatoes, beans (cassoulet), spinach, tomatoes
Sage *Use carefully*	Stuffing for pork		Stuffing for duck, goose, turkey	Robust chicken, turtle, mushroom soups; fish chowder	
Tarragon *Use carefully*	Marinades, steak, casseroles	Many fish dishes	Classic Tarragon Chicken, chicken liver pâté, hare		
Thyme *Use very carefully*	Stuffings, gravies, sausages	All types of fish	Stuffing for chicken, rabbit; jugged hare	Thick soups	Tomatoes, sauté vegetables
Allspice *ground* Spicy-sweet, mild	Pot roasts, meat balls, baked ham, beef stews	Boiled fish, oyster stews		Broths	Add a little to tomatoes, cream potatoes, carrots
Cayenne *ground* Hot, pungent	Use sparingly in meat dishes and gravies, mince	Shellfish	Chicken dishes	All soups	Baked beans, vegetable curries, aubergines
Celery seeds *whole* Slightly bitter	Casseroles	Most fish dishes		Meat soups	
Chillies *whole* Spicy, hot	Mexican dishes		Excellent in a chicken pie filling		Use sparingly (crushed) in tomato dishes
Cinnamon *stick or ground* Sweet, spicy	Ham glaze, pork				
Cloves *whole or ground* Strong and spicy	Ham, tongue		Poultry and game casseroles, marinades	Beef, tomato, bean, pea, beetroot soups	Pumpkin, spinach
Curry *powder* Strong and spicy	Casseroles, left-over meat dishes, meat loaves	Shellfish, devilled fish	Chicken	Mulligatawny, apple, tomato soups	Vegetable curries
Ginger *root or ground* Hot, rich, aromatic	Curries	Many fish dishes	Duck, rub into the flesh of chicken and brush with butter		
Mace *blade or ground* Sweet, softly spicy	Meat stuffings, mince dishes, veal, lamb chops, pâté	Potted shrimps, fish dishes with sauces	Chicken à la King	Cream of chicken soup	Mashed potato, creamed spinach
Mustard *seed or ground* Hot, pungent	Beef, ham, bacon, frankfurters, cold meats			Cream of celery, lentil, mushroom, chicken soups	
Nutmeg *whole or ground* Sweet, spicy	Veal, meat loaves	Fish cakes, croquettes	Chicken		Spinach, carrots, beans
Paprika *ground* Colourful, mild	Lamb, pork, veal, mince dishes, goulash	Shellfish	Chicken	Cream soups, chowders	Beans, potatoes, cauliflower
Pepper *whole or ground* Strong	Most meat dishes	Most fish dishes	Most poultry and game dishes		Most vegetable dishes
Saffron *powder* Mildly spicy, golden colour	Oriental cooking	Spanish cod dishes	Chicken, rabbit	Bouillabaise, chicken, turkey	Rice
Turmeric *powdered* Aromatic, slightly bitter	Curries	Fish kedgeree, fish stew			Rice dishes

Salads and salad dressings	Cheese	Eggs	Sauces	Preserves	Baked goods	Other uses
Green, tomato, rice salads		Fines herbes or tomato omelette	For pasta, rice			
			Infuse in milk for béchamel sauce			Rice pudding
Most salads, French dressing	Excellent with cream cheese	Fines herbes omelettes and soufflés	Most lightly seasoned sauces, béarnaise, green			
All salads and dressings	Cottage and cream cheeses	Scrambled eggs, soufflés, fondue	In savoury white and herb sauces, mayonnaise			
Most salads, soured cream dressing, avocado	Cream cheese and other dishes	Egg mayonnaise	Dill sauce with pike, eel	Pickled cucumber		In egg sandwiches, dill tea
French dressing	Pizza	Pickled eggs	Use sparingly in many sauces especially for pasta			
Green, chicken salads	Cottage and cream cheeses	Egg based quiches, omelettes	Cheese sauces			Pizza, tomato juice cocktail
Green and chicken salads	Cottage and cream cheeses	Egg based quiches, omelettes	Cheese sauces			Pizza
Most salads	Most cheese dishes	Fines herbes omelettes and other dishes	Sauces for ham, chicken, fish			
	Cottage and cream cheeses		Apple jelly, jams			Herb tea, fruit salads, wine/cider cups, vegetable cocktail
	Many cheese dishes					
Asparagus, chicken salads; soured cream dressing		Tarragon pickled eggs	Béarnaise, hollandaise, mousseline, tarragon			Tomato and fish cocktails, sandwich spread, aspic glaze
Many salads	Most cheese dishes, cheese herb bread	Many egg dishes				Lemon thyme in fruit salads, liqueurs
Fruit salads	Cottage cheese	Egg dishes with sauce	Tomato and barbecue sauces	Pickles, chutneys, relishes, mincemeat	Fruit cakes, rice puddings, apple pies, poached fruit	Ingredient in mixed spice
Cocktail sauce for prawns			Use sparingly in sauces for fish			Ingredient in curry powder
Salads and dressings, coleslaw	Cream cheese as a sandwich spread.			Pickles, chutneys	Bread	
			Tomato sauce for pasta, also meat sauces	Pickles	Cakes, pies	
		Egg nog		Pickles, mincemeat	Fruit cake, milk pudding, pumpkin pie, Christmas fare	Mulled wine (stick), cinnamon toast (ground)
			Bread, apple, cranberry sauces	Chutneys, mincemeat, bottled sauces	Fruit cake, apple and pear pies	Mulled wine
Mayonnaise		Curried eggs	For shellfish, chicken, eggs, meat	Chutneys, pickles		
				Fruit chutneys	Cakes, biscuits	With melon (ground), stewed fruit (root)
	Welsh rarebit or other cheese dishes		For fish and vegetables	Chutneys, pickles	Fruit cakes, pies, cherry pie, chocolate	Tomato juice
French dressing, mayonnaise	Strengthens the flavour of cooked cheese	Stuffed eggs	For meat, fish, barbecues	Pickles		Sandwiches
		Scrambled eggs	Cheese sauce		Cakes, pies, puddings, doughnuts	Milk, egg nog, puddings
Dressings, coleslaw	Cream cheese	Devilled eggs	Cream sauces			
Most dressings and salads	Many cheese dishes	Many egg dishes	Most sauces	Most preserves		
Rice salads, seafood, chicken	Cream cheese		Veal and fish sauces		Buns, cakes	Risotto, paella
		Devilled eggs, creamed eggs	Adds colour and flavour to white sauces	Pickles, relishes	For colouring cakes	Ingredient of curry powder

GLOSSARY OF COOKING TERMS

Aspic jelly Savoury jelly used for setting and garnishing savoury dishes.

Au gratin Food coated with a sauce, sprinkled with breadcrumbs (and sometimes grated cheese) and browned under the grill. Usually served in the dish in which it has been cooked.

Bain marie A flat, open vessel, half-filled with water, which is kept at a temperature just below boiling point; used to keep sauces, etc. hot without further cooking. Also a baking tin half-filled with water in which custards and other egg dishes stand whilst cooking to prevent over-heating.

Making a sauce in a bain marie

Baking Cooking in the oven by dry heat. The method used for most cakes, biscuits and pastries, and for many other dishes.

Baking blind Baking pastry shapes without a filling. Line the flan case or pie dish with pastry and trim. Line with greaseproof paper and fill with haricot beans, rice or stale crusts of bread. Or press kitchen foil into the pastry case and omit beans etc. When pastry has set, remove the grease-proof paper or foil and return to the oven to dry out.

Barding Covering the breast of poultry or game birds with pieces of fat bacon to prevent it drying out during roasting.

Basting Moistening meat, poultry or game during roasting by spooning over it the juices and melted fat from the tin, to prevent the food drying out.

Beating Agitating an ingredient or mixture by vigorously turning it over with an upward motion so as to introduce air; a spoon, fork, whisk or electric mixer may be used.

Béchamel A rich white sauce, one of the four basic types of sauce.

Binding Adding a liquid, egg or melted fat to a dry mixture to hold it together.

Blanching Treating food with boiling water in order to whiten it, preserve its natural colour, loosen the skin or remove a flavour which is too strong. Two methods are:–
1. To plunge the food into boiling water; used for skinning tomatoes or to prepare vegetables for freezing.
2. To bring it to the boil in the water; used to whiten veal and sweetbreads or to reduce the saltiness of kippers or pickled meat.

Blending Mixing flour, cornflour and similar ground cereals to a smooth cream with a cold liquid (milk, water or stock) before a boiling liquid is added, as in the preparation of soups, stews, or gravies.

Boiling Cooking in liquid at a temperature of 212°F. (100°C.). The chief foods that are boiled are vegetables, rice, pasta and suet puddings; syrups that need to be reduced are also boiled. Meat, fish and poultry should be simmered – fast boiling makes them shrink, lose flavour, and toughen.

Bouquet garni A small bunch of herbs tied together in muslin and used to give flavour to stews, etc. Usually consists of a sprig of parsley and thyme, a bay leaf, 2 cloves and a few peppercorns.

Braising A method of cooking either meat or vegetables which is a combination of roasting and stewing. A casserole or pan with a tightly fitting lid is used to prevent evaporation. The meat is placed on a bed of vegetables (a mirepoix), with just sufficient liquid to cover the vegetables and to keep the food moist.

Brining Immersing food (mainly meat or fish which is to be pickled and vegetables which are to be preserved) in a salt and water solution.

Browning 1. Giving a dish (usually already cooked) an appetising golden brown colour by placing it under the grill or in a hot oven for a short time.
2. Preparing a dish for stewing or casseroling, by frying to seal and colour.

Caramel A substance obtained by heating sugar syrup very slowly in a thick pan until it is a rich brown colour. Used for flavouring cakes and puddings and for lining pudding moulds.

Casserole A baking dish with a tightly fitting lid, used for cooking meat and vegetables in the oven. The food is usually served straight from the dish. May be 'ovenproof' (for oven use only) or 'flameproof' (suitable for use on top of the stove and in the oven).

Chaudfroid A jellied sauce with a béchamel base, used for masking cold fish, poultry and game.

Chining Severing the rib bones from the backbone by sawing through the ribs close to the spine. Used on joints such as loin or neck of lamb, mutton, veal or pork.

Use a special saw for chining

Chopping Dividing food into very small pieces. The ingredient is placed on a chopping board and a very sharp knife is used with a quick up-and-down action.

Clarifying Clearing or purifying fat from water, meat juices or salt.
1. Butter or margarine – Heat the fat gently until it melts, then continue to heat slowly without browning until all bubbling ceases (this shows the water has been driven off). Remove from the heat and allow to stand for a few minutes until the sediment has settled. Pour the fat off gently. It is not usually necessary to strain the fat through muslin.
2. Dripping – Melt the fat and strain into a large basin to remove any big particles. Then pour over it 2–3 times as much boiling water, stir well and leave to cool; the clean fat will rise to the top. When it has solidified, lift it off, dab the underside dry and scrape off any sediment.

Coating 1. Covering food which is to be fried with flour, egg and breadcrumbs, batter, etc.
2. Covering food which is cooked or ready to serve with a thin layer of mayonnaise, sauce, etc.

Coddling A method of soft-boiling eggs: they are put into a pan of boiling water, withdrawn from the heat and allowed to stand for 8–10 minutes.

Compôte Fruit stewed in a sugar syrup and served hot or cold.

Consistency The term used to describe the texture of a dough, batter, etc.

Creaming The beating together of fat and sugar to resemble whipped cream in colour and texture, i.e. until pale and fluffy. This method of mixing is used for cakes and puddings containing a high proportion of fat.

Crimping 1. To remove the skin in strips from cucumber and similar foods, to give the finished slices a ridged appearance.
2. To decorate the double edge of a pie or tart or the edge of a short-

Use thumbs and fore-fingers to crimp the edge of a pastry case

bread by pinching it at regular intervals, giving a fluted effect.

Croquettes A mixture of meat, fish, poultry or potatoes, bound together and formed into various shapes, then coated with egg and breadcrumbs and fried in deep fat.

Croûte A large round or finger of toasted or fried bread, about ¼ in. thick, on which game and some entrées and savouries are served.

Croûtons Small pieces of bread which are fried or toasted and served as an accompaniment or garnish to soup.

Curd 1. The solid part of soured milk or junket.
2. A creamy preserve made from fruit – usually lemons or oranges – sugar, eggs and butter.

Dariole A small, narrow mould with sloping sides, used for setting creams and jellies and for baking or steaming puddings, especially castle puddings. Also used to prepare English madeleines.

Devilled Food which has been grilled or fried with sharp, hot seasonings.

Dough A thick mixture of uncooked flour and liquid, often combined with other ingredients. As well as the usual yeast dough, it can also mean mixtures such as pastry, scones and biscuits.

Dredging The action of sprinkling food lightly and evenly with flour, sugar, etc. Fish and meat are often dredged with flour before frying, while pancakes, etc. may be dredged with fine sugar to improve their appearance. A pierced container of metal or plastic (known as a dredger) is usually used.

Dripping The fat obtained from roasted meat during cooking or from small pieces of new fat that have been rendered down.

Dropping consistency The term used to describe the texture of a cake or pudding mixture before cooking. To test, fill a spoon with the mixture and hold it on its side – the mixture should fall in 5 seconds, without jerking the spoon.

Egg-and-crumbing A method of coating fish, cutlets, rissoles, etc., before they are fried or baked. Have a beaten egg on a plate and some breadcrumbs on a piece of kitchen paper; dip the food in the egg and lift out, letting it drain for a second or two. Transfer it to the crumbs and tip the paper until the food is well covered. Press in the crumbs, then shake the food to remove any surplus.

Entrée A hot or cold dressed savoury dish consisting of meat, poultry, game, fish, eggs or vegetables, served complete with sauce and garnish.

Escalope A slice of meat (usually veal) cut from the top of the leg. Escalopes are generally egg-and-crumbed and fried.

Espagnole A rich brown sauce, one of the four basic sauces.

Farce, forcemeat Stuffing used for meat, fish or vegetables. A farce is based on meat, bacon, etc. while the basic forcemeat is made from breadcrumbs, suet, onion and herbs.

Fillet A term used for the under-cut of a loin of beef, veal, pork or game, for boned breasts of poultry and birds and for boned sides of fish.

Fines herbes A combination of finely chopped herbs. In practice, the mixture is usually parsley, chervil, tarragon and chives, and it is most commonly used in omelettes. When fresh herbs are used one can add enough to make the omelette look green, but when dried ones are used, ½ level teaspoon of the mixture is plenty for a 4-egg omelette. For other dishes, the blend is sometimes varied.

Flaking Breaking up cooked fish into flakes with a fork.

Folding in (Sometimes called cutting-and-folding). Combining a whisked or creamed mixture with other ingredients so that it retains its lightness. It is used for certain cake mixtures and for meringues and soufflés. A typical example is folding dry flour into a whisked sponge cake mixture. Important points to remember are that the mixture must be folded very lightly and that it must not be agitated more than absolutely necessary, because with every movement some of the air bubbles are broken down. Do not use an electric mixer.

Fricassee A white stew of chicken, veal or rabbit.

Frosting 1. A method of decorating the rim of a glass in which a cold drink is to be served. Coat the edge with whipped egg white, dip into caster sugar and allow to dry. **2.** An icing, especially of the American type.

Iced and creamy desserts look good in a frosted glass

Frying The process of cooking food in hot fat or oil. There are two main methods:

1. Shallow frying A small quantity of fat is used in a shallow pan. Used for steak, chops, sausages, fish steaks and white fish, which need only sufficient fat to prevent them sticking to the pan. Made-up dishes such as fish cakes can also be shallow-fried, but need enough fat to half-cover them. In most cases the food requires coating.

2. Deep frying The food is cooked in sufficient fat to cover it completely. Used for batter-coated fish, whitebait, chipped potatoes, doughnuts and made-up dishes such as croquettes and fritters. A deep pan and a wire basket are needed, with fat to come about ¾ up the pan; clarified beef fat, lard and cooking oil are suitable. The fat must be pure and free from moisture, to avoid spurting or boiling over, and it must be heated to the right temperature or the food will be either grease-sodden or burnt. If the fat is strained into a basin,

jug or wide-necked jar and covered, it may be stored in a cool place for further use. A frying thermometer should always be used with oil for deep fat frying.

Galantine White meat, such as poultry or veal, which has been cooked, rolled and pressed. Sometimes glazed or finished with toasted breadcrumbs.

Garnish An edible decoration, such as parsley, watercress, hard-boiled egg or lemon added to a savoury dish to improve the appearance and flavour.

Glaze Beaten egg, egg white, milk, etc. used to give a glossy surface to certain sweets and to savouries such as galantines. The meat glaze used for savouries is home-made meat stock reduced by rapid boiling. Stock made from a cube cannot be treated this way.

Grating Shaving foods such as cheese and vegetables into small shreds. Foods to be grated must be firm and cheese should be allowed to harden.

Grilling Cooking food by direct heat under a grill or over a hot fire. Good quality, tender meat (steak, chops), whole fish (herring, trout) and fish cutlets are the foods most generally cooked in this way. Some cooked dishes are put under the grill to give them a brown top surface or to heat them through before they are served.

Grinding The process of reducing hard foodstuffs, such as nuts and coffee beans, to small particles by means of a food mill, grinder or electric blender.

Hors d'oeuvre Small dishes served cold, usually before the soup, as an appetiser. Hors d'oeuvre are generally small and piquant.

Infusing Extracting flavour from spices, herbs, etc. by pouring on boiling liquid and then covering and allowing to stand in a warm place.

Jardinière A garnish of diced, mixed, spring vegetables, plus green peas, cauliflower sprigs, etc.

Julienne A garnish of fine strips of mixed vegetables.

Kneading Working a dough firmly, using the knuckles for bread-making, the fingertips in pastry-making. In both cases the outside of the dough is drawn into the centre.

Knocking up Preparing a pastry edge ready for crimping. Hold a round bladed knife parallel with the pastry and knock against the knife, to open up the pastry in ridges.

Larding Inserting small strips of fat bacon into the flesh of game birds, poultry and meat before cooking, to prevent it drying out when roasting. A special larding needle is used for the process.

Liaison A thickening agent, such as flour; cornflour or arrowroot, which is used for thickening or binding sauces and soups.

Lukewarm Moderately warm; approximately 100°F. (38°C.).

Macedoine A mixture of fruits or vegetables cut into evenly sized dice, generally used as a decoration or garnish. Alternatively, the fruits may be set in jelly.

Marinade A seasoned mixture of oil and vinegar, lemon juice or wine, in which food is left for a given time. This helps to soften the fibres of meat and fish and adds flavour to the food.

Masking 1. Covering or coating a cooked meat or similar dish with savoury jelly, glaze or sauce. **2.** Coating the inside of a mould with jelly.

Ice helps to set the thin layer of jelly quickly

Meringue Egg white whisked until stiff, mixed with caster sugar and dried in a cool oven till crisp.

Mincing Chopping or cutting into very small pieces with a knife or, more commonly, in a mincer.

Mixed herbs These most commonly consist of a blend of dried parsley, tarragon, chives, thyme and chervil, but other variations may occur in certain recipes.

Mirepoix A mixture of carrot, celery and onion, often including some ham or bacon, cut into large pieces, lightly fried in fat and used as a 'bed' on which to braise meat.

Noisettes Neatly trimmed round or oval shapes of lamb, mutton or beef, not less than ½ in. thick.

Panada A thick binding sauce (using 1 oz. fat and 1 oz. flour to ¼ pint liquid) made by the roux method and used for binding croquettes and similar mixtures.

Parboiling Part-boiling; the food is boiled for part of the normal cooking time, then finished by some other method.

Paring Peeling or trimming, especially vegetables or the rind of citrus fruits.

A potato peeler makes paring a lemon easy

Petits fours Very small fancy cakes, often iced, and almond biscuits, served at the end of a formal meal.

Piping Forcing cream, icing or butter out of a forcing bag through a nozzle, to decorate cakes etc. Also used for potatoes and meringues. The bag may be made of cotton, nylon or plastic.

Poaching Cooking in an open pan at simmering point with sufficient seasoned liquid to cover. Used in egg, fish and some meat dishes.

Pot-roasting Cooking meat in a saucepan with fat and a very small amount of liquid; it is particularly good for small and less tender cuts.

Pulses Dried beans, peas, split peas and lentils.

Purée Fruit, vegetable, meat or fish which has been pounded, sieved or pulverised in an electric blender (usually after cooking), to give a smooth pulp. A soup made by sieving vegetables with the liquor in which they were cooked is also called a purée.

Raspings Fine crumbs made from stale bread; used for coating fried foods and for au gratin dishes. The bread is first dried in a cool oven and then crushed.

Réchauffé Reheated leftover foods.

Reducing Boiling a liquid in an uncovered pan in order to evaporate it and give a more concentrated result. Used especially when making soups, sauces, or syrups.

Refreshing 1. After cooking vegetables, pouring cold water over them to preserve the colour; they are then reheated before serving. 2. Crisping up already-cooked pastry in the oven. 3. For home-freezing, plunging partly-cooked or blanched vegetables and meat into ice-cold water immediately after removing from the heat.

Rendering Extracting fat from meat trimmings by cutting them up small and heating in a cool oven (300°F., mark 1) until the fat has melted out, or boiling them in an uncovered pan with very little water until the water is driven off and the fat is melted; the fat is then strained into a basin.

Rennet An extract from calves' stomachs. It contains rennin and is used for curdling or coagulating milk for junket and for cheese-making.

Rissoles Small portions of minced meat enclosed in rounds of pastry and folded to form a semi-circle, then egg-and-crumbed and fried in deep fat. The term is now loosely applied to a round cake of a meat or fish mixture, egg-and-crumbed and fried.

Roasting In its true sense, roasting means cooking by direct heat in front of an open fire. Thus rôtisserie cooking is true roasting, but the modern method of cooking in a closed oven is really baking. Only good quality poultry, and the best cuts of meat, should be cooked in this way.

Roux A mixture of equal amounts of fat and plain flour cooked together to form the basis for a sauce and for thickening sauces and stews.

Rubbing in Incorporating fat into flour; used when making shortcrust pastry, plain cakes and biscuits, when a short texture is required. Put the fat in small pieces in the flour, then rub it into the flour with the fingertips.

Rusks Fingers or slices of bread dried in a slow oven.

Salmi A ragoût or stew, usually of game.

Sauté To cook in an open pan over a strong heat in fat or oil, shaking the pan to make whatever is in it 'sauter' or jump, to keep it from sticking. The pan used should be heavy, wide and shallow. This may be used as a complete cooking method or as the initial cooking before finishing in a sauce.

Scalding Pouring boiling water over food to clean it, to loosen hairs (as from a joint of pork) or to remove the skin (as on tomatoes or peaches). The food must not be left in the boiling water or it will begin to cook.

Scalloped dishes Food (often previously cooked) baked in a scallop shell or similar small container; it is usually combined with a creamy sauce, topped with breadcrumbs and surrounded with a border of piped potato.

Scalloping A means of decorating the double edge of the pastry covering of a pie. Make close horizontal cuts with a knife round the edge of the pie, giving a flaked effect (see **knocking up**) then, with the back of the knife, pull the edge up vertically at regular intervals to form scallops. Traditionally these should be close together for a sweet pie and wider apart for a savoury one.

Scoring To make shallow, parallel cuts in the surface of food in order to improve its flavour or appearance or to help it cook more quickly (e.g. fish).

Searing Browning meat quickly in a little fat before grilling or roasting.

Seasoned flour Used for dusting meat and fish before frying or stewing. Mix about 2 level tablespoons flour with about 1 level teaspoon salt and a good sprinkling of pepper. Either pat it onto the food or dip the pieces in the flour and shake them gently before cooking.

Shredding Slicing a food such as cheese or raw vegetables into very fine pieces. A sharp knife or coarse grater is generally used.

Sieving Rubbing or pressing food (e.g. cooked vegetables) through a sieve; a wooden spoon is used to force it through.

Sifting Shaking a dry ingredient through a sieve or flour sifter to remove lumps and aerate it.

Simmering Keeping a liquid just below boiling point (approximately 205°F. or 96°C.). First bring the liquid to the boil, then adjust the heat so that the surface of the liquid is kept just moving or 'shivering'; continuous bubbling indicates the temperature is too high.

Skimming To take fat off the surface of stock, gravy or stews, or scum from other foods (e.g. jams) while they are cooking. A piece of absorbent kitchen paper or a metal spoon may be used.

Steaming An economical method of cooking food in the steam from rapidly boiling water. There are several ways of steaming, according to the equipment available.

Steeping The process of pouring hot or cold water over food and leaving it to stand, either to soften it or to extract its flavour and colour.

Stewing A long, slow method of cooking in a liquid which is kept at simmering point; particularly suitable for coarse-fibred foods. The liquid is served with the food, so that flavour is not wasted.

Stock The liquid produced when meat, bones, poultry, fish or vegetables are simmered in water with herbs and flavourings for several hours, to extract their flavour. Stock forms the basis of soups, sauces and stews and many savoury dishes.

Sweating Cooking a food (usually a vegetable) very gently in a covered pan with melted fat until it exudes juices. The food should not colour.

Syrup A concentrated solution of sugar in water, prepared by boiling and used in making water ices, drinks and fruit desserts.
Golden syrup is a by-product of sugar refining.
Maple syrup is extracted from the North American sugar maple.

Tammy To strain soups, sauces, etc. through a fine woollen cloth.

Tepid Approximately at blood heat. Tepid water is obtained by adding 2 parts cold water to 1 part boiling.

Thickening Giving body to soups, sauces or gravies by the addition of flour, cornflour or arrowroot.

Trussing Tying or skewering a bird into a compact shape before cooking.

Vol-au-vent A round or oval case made of puff pastry and filled with diced meat, poultry, game or fish in a well-flavoured sauce.

Whipping or whisking To beat air rapidly into a mixture:
1. By hand, using an egg beater or whisk.
2. By rotary beater.
3. By electric beater.

Whisk eggs and sugar over gentle heat for best results

Zest The coloured part of orange or lemon peel containing the oil that gives the characteristic flavour. To obtain zest, remove the rind very thinly, with no pith, by grating, or use a zester. If it is required for a sweet dish, you can rub it off with a lump of sugar.

  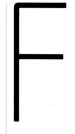 

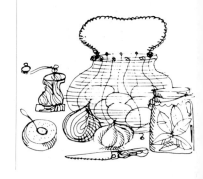

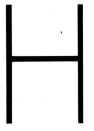

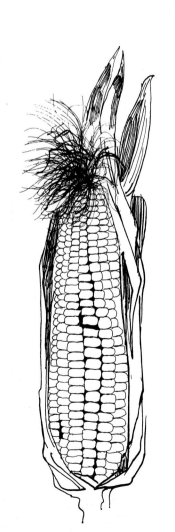

M N O P

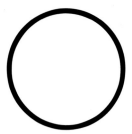

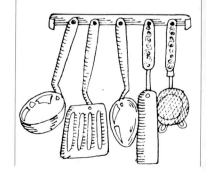

R S

T

U

V

W

Y

We wish to thank the following companies for the loan of accessories for photography:

Bosch, Casa Pupo, Civil Service Stores, Collets Chinese Art Gallery; Cona; Craftsmen Potters' Association; Cucina; Dartington; David Mellor; Denby; Design and Crafts, Farnham; Divertimenti; Domecq; Elizabeth David; Garrards; Grants of St James; Gratnel; Habitat; Heal's; Henry's; Hoover; John Lewis; Kenco; Kenwood; Langley London; Loon Fung Supermarket; Macdonald Imports and Exports, Exeter; Melita; Midwinter; Optima; Phillips; Presents, Farnham; Prestige; Robert Carrier Cookshop; Robert Jackson; Robinson and Cleaver; Rosenthal; Russell Hobbs; Selfridges; Shaplans; Staines Kitchen Supplies; Tiarco; Viners; Wedgwood; Wilson and Gill.

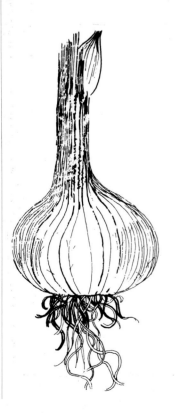

Notes

Notes

Notes

Notes